Essentials of
Computer Architecture

Essentials of Computer Architecture

Earl Bermann

WILLFORD PRESS
www.willfordpress.com

Published by Willford Press,
118-35 Queens Blvd., Suite 400,
Forest Hills, NY 11375, USA

ISBN: 978-1-68285-728-1

Cataloging-in-Publication Data

Essentials of computer architecture / Earl Bermann.
    p. cm.
Includes bibliographical references and index.
ISBN 978-1-68285-728-1
1. Computer architecture. 2. Computer engineering. I. Bermann, Earl.
QA76.9.A73 E87 2019
004.22--dc23

For information on all Willford Press publications
visit our website at www.willfordpress.com

Contents

Permissions

Index

Preface

Computer architecture is an important aspect of computer engineering. It refers to a set of rules and methods that reflects the functioning, organization and use of computer systems. The objective of computer architecture is to design a computer with optimum performance, power efficiency, low cost and maximum reliability. The primary subcategories of computer architecture are instruction set architecture, microarchitecture and system design. Some other types are macroarchitecture, pin architecture, programmer visible macroarchitecture, etc. This book elucidates the concepts and innovative models around prospective developments with respect to computer architecture. It picks up individual categories of computer architecture and explains their need and contribution in the modern scenario. This book is an essential guide for both academicians and those who wish to pursue this discipline further.

A detailed account of the significant topics covered in this book is provided below:

Chapter 1- Computer architecture is a framework of rules and techniques that is concerned with the organization, functionality and utilization of computer systems. It involves microarchitecture design, instruction set architecture design, logic design and implementation. This chapter has been carefully written to provide an overview of computer architecture and includes the fundamental topics of dataflow architecture, cellular architecture, Von Neumann architecture and Harvard architecture, besides others.

Chapter 2- An instruction set architecture (ISA) is an abstract computer model. An ISA serves as an interface between hardware and software, and allows multiple implementations varying in performance, monetary cost and physical size. The aim of this chapter is to explore the fundamental principles of instruction set architecture. Some of the varied topics covered in this chapter include complex instruction set computer and reduced instruction set computer, very long instruction word, one instruction set computer, etc.

Chapter 3- A central processing unit or the CPU is the electronic circuitry within a computer, which carries out basic logical, arithmetic, control and input/output operations. This chapter discusses in detail the different elements of a central processing unit, such as control unit, arithmetic logic unit, CPU modes, microprocessor, scalar processor, coprocessor, etc.

Chapter 4- Computer memory refers to the integrated circuits, which store information form instant use in a computer. There are two kinds of computer memory, volatile and non-volatile memory. Memory management is a type of resource management, which is applied to computer memory, for allocating memory to programs at request or free it for reuse. The topics elaborated in this chapter related to computer memory and memory management, such as random-access memory, read-only memory, virtual memory, memory segmentation, etc. will help in developing a better perspective of the field.

Chapter 5- Study of the principles of computer architecture is vital for an all-inclusive understanding of the subject. The following chapter elucidates the concepts of Amdahl's law, Gustafson's law, Sun-Ni law, Rent's rule, Moore's law, Grosch's law, etc. for an extensive understanding of computer architecture.

I would like to make a special mention of my publisher who considered me worthy of this opportunity and also supported me throughout the process. I would also like to thank the editing team at the back-end who extended their help whenever required.

Earl Bermann

Introduction to Computer Architecture

Computer architecture is a framework of rules and techniques that is concerned with the organization, functionality and utilization of computer systems. It involves microarchitecture design, instruction set architecture design, logic design and implementation. This chapter has been carefully written to provide an overview of computer architecture and includes the fundamental topics of dataflow architecture, cellular architecture, Von Neumann architecture and Harvard architecture, besides others.

Computer architecture is a specification detailing how a set of software and hardware technology standards interact to form a computer system or platform. In short, computer architecture refers to how a computer system is designed and what technologies it is compatible with.

As with other contexts and meanings of the word architecture, computer architecture is likened to the art of determining the needs of the user/system/technology, and creating a logical design and standards based on those requirements.

A very good example of computer architecture is von Neumann architecture, which is still used by most types of computers today. This was proposed by the mathematician John von Neumann in 1945. It describes the design of an electronic computer with its CPU, which includes the arithmetic logic unit, control unit, registers, memory for data and instructions, an input/output interface and external storage functions.

There are three categories of computer architecture:

- System Design: This includes all hardware components in the system, including data processors aside from the CPU, such as the graphics processing unit and direct memory access. It also includes memory controllers, data paths and miscellaneous things like multiprocessing and virtualization.

- Instruction Set Architecture (ISA): This is the embedded programming language of the central processing unit. It defines the CPU's functions and capabilities based on what programming it can perform or process. This includes the word size, processor register types, memory addressing modes, data formats and the instruction set that programmers use.

- Microarchitecture: Otherwise known as computer organization, this type of architecture defines the data paths, data processing and storage elements, as well as how they should be implemented in the ISA.

A general-purpose computer has these parts:

1. *Processor*: the "brain" that does arithmetic, responds to incoming information, and generates outgoing information.

2. *Primary storage (memory or RAM)*: the "scratchpad" that remembers information that can be used by the processor. It is connected to the processor by a *system bus* (wiring).

3. *System and expansion busses*: the transfer mechanisms (wiring plus connectors) that connect the processor to primary storage and input/output devices.

A computer usually comes with several input/output devices: For input: a keyboard, a mouse; For output, a display (monitor), a printer; For both input and output: an internal disk drive, memory key, CD reader/writer, etc., as well as connections to external networks.

For reasons of speed, primary storage is connected "more closely" to the processor than are the input/output devices. Most of the devices (e.g., internal disk, printer) are themselves primitive computers in the sense that they contain simple processors that help transfer information to/from the processor to/from the device.

Here is a simple picture that summarizes the above:

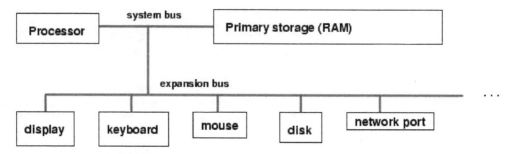

Information and Binary Coding

For humans, information can be pictures, symbols, words, sounds, movements, and more. A typical computer has a keyboard and mouse so that words and movements can be sent to the processor as information. The information must be converted into electrical off-on ("0 and 1") pulses that travel on the bus and arrive to the processor, which can save them in primary storage.

It is premature to study precisely how numbers and symbols can be represented as off-on (0-1) pulses, but here base-2 (*binary*) coding of numbers, which is the concept upon which computer information is based:

```
number          binary coding

0               0000

1               0001

2               0010

3               0011

4               0100

5               0101

6               0110

7               0111
```

```
8               1000

      . . .

14              1110

15              1111
```

and so on. It is possible to do arithmetic in base two, e.g. 3+5 is written:

```
 0011

+0101

-----

 1000
```

The addition works like normal (base-10) arithmetic, where 1 + 1 = 10 (0 with a carry of 1). Subtraction, multiplication, etc., work this way, too, and it is possible to wire an electrical circuit that mechancially does the addition of the 0s and 1s. Indeed, a processor uses such a wiring, which operates on binary numbers held in *registers*, where a register is a sequence of *bits* (electronic "flip-flops" each of which can remember a 0 or 1). Here is a picture of an 8-bit register that holds the number 9:

```
+--+--+--+--+--+--+--+--+

| 0| 0| 0| 0| 1| 0| 0| 1|

+--+--+--+--+--+--+--+--+
```

A processor has multiple such registers, and it can compute 3+5 by placing 3 (0000 0011) and 5 (0000 0101) into two registers and then using the wiring between the registers to compute the sum, which might be saved in a third register. A typical, modern register has 32 bits, called a *full-word*. Such a register can store a value in the approximate range of -2 billion to +2 billion.

When an answer, like 3+5 = 8, is computed, the processor might copy the answer to primary storage to save it for later use. Later, the processor can copy the number from storage back into a register and do more arithmetic with it.

Central Processing Unit

The processor is truly *the* computer --- it is wired to compute arithmetic and related operations on numbers that it can hold in its data registers. A processor is also called a *Central Processing Unit (CPU)*.

Here is a simplistic picture of the parts of a processor:

- The data registers hold numbers for computation.

- There is a simple *clock* - a pulse generator - that helps the Control Unit do instructions in proper time steps.

- The *arithmetic-logic unit (ALU)* holds the wiring for doing arithmetic on the numbers held in the *data registers*.

- The *control unit* holds wiring that triggers the arithmetic operations in the ALU. How does the control unit know to request an addition or a subtraction? The answer is: it obtains instructions, one at a time that have been stored in primary storage.

- The *instruction counter* is a register that tells the control unit where to find the instruction that it must do.

- The *instruction register* is where the instruction can be copied and held for study by the control unit.

- The *address buffer* and *data buffer* are two registers that are a "drop-off" point when the processor wishes to copy information from a register to primary storage (or read information from primary storage to a register).

- The *interrupt register* is studied much later.

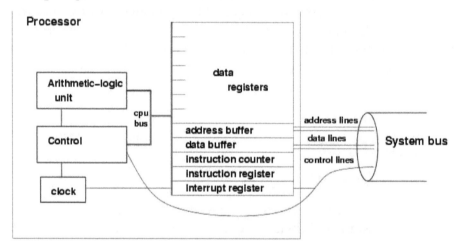

A processor's speed is measured in Hertz (a kind of vibration speed) and is literally the speed of the computer's internal clock; the larger the Hertz number, the faster the processor.

Primary Storage

Primary storage (also called *random-access memory - RAM*) is literally a long sequence of full words, also called *cells*, where numbers can be saved for later use by the processor. (Recall that a full word is 32 bits). Here is a simplistic picture:

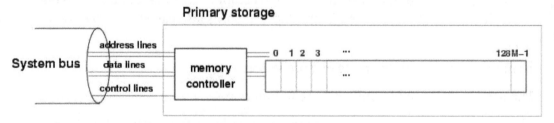

The figure shows that each fullword (cell) is numbered by a unique *address* (analogous to street addresses for houses), so that information transferred from the processor can be saved at a specific cell's address and can be later retrieved by referring to that same address.

The figure shows an additional component, the *memory controller*, which is itself a primitive processor that can quickly find addresses and copy information stored in the addresses to/from the system bus. This works faster than if the processor did the work of reaching into storage to extract information.

When a number is copied from the processor into storage, we say it is *written*; when it is copied from storage into the processor, we say it is *read*.

As the figure suggests, the *address lines* in the system bus are wires that transfer the bits that form the address of the cell in storage that must be read or written; the *data lines* are wires that transfer the information between the processor's data buffer and the cell in storage; and the control lines transmit whether the operation is a read or write to primary storage.

The tradition is to measure size of storage in *bytes*, where 8 bits equal one byte, and 4 bytes equal one full word. The larger the number, the larger the storage.

Stored Programs

In the 1950's, John von Neumann realized that primary storage could hold not only numbers, but patterns of bits that represented *instructions* that could tell the processor (actually, tell the processor's control unit) what to do. A sequence of instructions was called a *program*, and this was the beginning of *stored-program, general purpose computers*, where each time a computer was started, it could receive a new program in storage, which told the processor what computations to do.

Here is a simplistic example of a stored program that tells the processor to compute the sum of three numbers held in primary storage at addresses, 64, 65, and 66 and place the result into the cell at address 67:

```
LOAD (read) the number at storage address 64 into data register 1

LOAD the number at storage address 65 into data register 2

ADD register 1 to register 2 and leave the sum in register 2

LOAD the number at address 66 to register 1

ADD register 1 to register 2 and leave the sum in register 2

STORE (write) the value in register 2 to storage address 67
```

instructions like LOAD, ADD, and STORE can be represented as bit patterns that are copied into the processor's instruction register.

Here is a simple coding of the six-instruction program, which is situated at addresses 1-6 of primary storage (and the numbers are at 64-66). The instructions are coded in bit patterns, and we assume that LOAD is 1001, ADD is 1010, and STORE is 1011. Registers 1 and 2 are 0001 and 0010. Storage addresses 64 -- 67 are of course 0100 0000 to 0100 0011.

The format of each instruction is: IIII RRRR DDDD DDDD, where IIII is the coding that states the operation required, RRRR is the coding of which data register to use, and DDDD DDDD is the data, which is either a storage address or another register number.

```
PRIMARY STORAGE

address: contents

------- --------

0: ...

1: 1001 0001 0100 0000

2: 1001 0010 0100 0001

3: 1010 0010 0000 0001

4: 1001 0001 0100 0010

5: 1010 0010 0000 0001

6: 1011 0010 0100 0011

7: ...

...

64: 0000 0000 0000 0100

65: 0000 0000 0000 0011

66: 0000 0000 0000 0001

67: ...

...
```

The example is a contrived, but it should convince you that it is indeed possible to write instructions in terms of binary codings that a control unit can decode, disassemble, and execute.

It is painful for humans to read and write such codings, which are called *machine language*, and there are abbreviations, called *assembly language*, that use text forms. Here is a sample assembly-language version of the addition program:

```
LOAD  R1 64

LOAD  R2 65

ADD  R2  R1

LOAD  R1 66

ADD  R2  R1

STORE R2 67
```

Instruction Cycle

The *instructor cycle* are the actions taken by the processor to execute one instruction. Each time the processor's clock pulses (ticks) the control unit does these steps: (actually, modern processors do multiple instruction cycles for each clock pulse).

1. Uses the number in the instruction counter to *fetch* an instruction from primary storage and copy it into the instruction register.

2. Reads the pattern of bits in the instruction register and *decodes* the instruction

3. Based on the decoding, tells the ALU to *execute* the instruction, which means that the ALU manipulates the registers accordingly.

4. There is a fourth step in the instruction cycle, an *interrupt check*.

Of course, the control unit is not alive, and it does not "read" or "tell" anything to anyone, but there is wiring between electrical components that propagate electrical 0-1 signals- a kind of falling domino game- that gives the appearance of conscious execution.

Here is a small example. Say that the clock has "ticked" (pulsed), and the instruction register holds 3. Say that address 3 in primary storage holds the coding of the instruction, ADD R2 R1. The instruction cycle might go like this:

1. Fetch: Consult the instruction counter; see it holds 0000 0011, that is, 3. Signal the memory controller to copy the contents of the cell at address 0000 0010 into the data buffer.

   When the instruction arrives, copy it from the data buffer into the instruction register.

   Increment the instruction counter to 4 (that is, 0000 0100).

2. Decode: Read the first (leading or high-order) bits and see that they indicate an ADD. Extract the bits that state the two registers to be added, here, R2 and R1.

3. Execute: Signal the ALU to add the values in registers 1 and 2 and place the result in register 2.

The previous description reads a bit tediously. This is ok, because the processor is incredibly fast. Nonetheless, modern processors can be made even faster, because while the ALU is doing the execution step, the controller can start the fetch-and-decode steps of the *next* instruction cycle. This form of speedup is called *pipelining* and is a topic intensively studied in computer architecture.

The forms of instruction that the processor can execute are called the *instruction set*.

There are these forms of instructions found in an instruction set:

1. Data transfer between storage and registers (LOAD and STORE).

2. Arithmetic and logic (ADD, SUBTRACT, ...).

3. Control (test and branch) (the ALU perhaps resets the instruction counter).

4. Input and output (the ALU sends a request on the system bus to an input/output device to read or write new information into storage).

Even small examples are painful to write in assembly language, and people quickly developed simpler notations that could be mechanically converted to assembly (which could itself be mechanically converted into base-2 codings).

FORTRAN (formula translator language) is a famous example, developed in the 1950's by John Backus. When a human writes a program using FORTRAN, she writes a set of mathematical equations that the computer executes. Instead of using specific numerical storage addresses, names from algebra ("variable names"), like x and y, can be used instead.

Here is an example, coded in FORTRAN, that places a value in a storage cell, named x, and then divides it by 2, saving the result again in the same cell:

$$x = 3.14159$$

$$x = x / 2$$

And here is an example that divides x by y, saving the answer in x's cell, *provided that y has a non-zero value*:

$$If (y .NEQ. 0) x = x / y$$

(Read this as "if y not-equal-to 0, then compute x = x / y")

With some work, one can write a program that mechanically translates FORTRAN programs into (long) sequences of machine code; such a program is called a *compiler*. There is another "translation program," called an *interpreter*, which does not convert a program to machine code, but instead reads a program one line at a time and tells the processor to execute "pre-fabricated" sequences of instructions that match the program's lines.

Languages like FORTRAN (and COBOL and LISP and C and Java and ...) are called *high-level programming languages*.

Secondary Storage: Disks

There is a limited amount of primary storage, and it is used to hold the program that the computer executes now. Programs and information that are saved for later use can be copied to *secondary storage*, such as the internal disk that is common to almost all computers.

Although it looks and operates differently than primary storage, it is perfectly fine to think of disk storage (and other forms of secondary storage, like a memory key or a CD), as a variant of primary storage, connected to the processor by means of the system bus, using its own controller to help read and write information. The main distinction is that secondary storage is *cheaper* (to buy) than primary storage, but it is *slower* to read and write information to and from it.

A typical computer uses disk secondary storage to hold a wide variety of programs that can be copied into primary storage for execution, as requested by the user. Secondary storage is also used to archive data files.

Secondary-storage devices are activated when the processor executes a READ or WRITE instruction. These instructions are not as simple to do as the LOAD and STORE instructions, because the secondary-storage devices are so slow, and the processor should not waste time, doing nothing, waiting for the device to finish its work.

The solution is: *The processor makes the request for a read or write and then proceeds to do other work.*

Consider how a processor might execute a WRITE instruction to the disk; here is how the instruction cycle might go:

1. Fetch: The control unit obtains the instruction from primary storage and places it in the instruction register, as usual.

2. Decode: The control unit reads the instruction and determines that it is a WRITE. It extracts that name of the device to be read (the disk), it extracts the address on the device where the information should be written, and it extracts the name of the register than holds the information to be written.

3. Execute: The control unit writes the address and data to the disk's *address buffer* and *data buffer*, which are two full words in primary storage. When these writes are finished, the controller signals the disk along the control lines of the system bus that there is information waiting for it in primary storage.

Now that the processor has initiated the disk-write, it proceeds to the next instruction to execute, and at the same time, the disk starts to spin, its own controller does a read of primary storage for the address and data information saved there, and finally, the data is written from primary storage to the disk.

Each secondary-storage device has its own "buffers" reserved for it in primary storage- this is simpler than wiring the processor for buffers for each possible storage device.

An important "secondary storage" device (actually, it is an output device!) is the computer's display. A typical display is a huge grid of pixels (colored dots), each of which is defined by a trio of red-green-blue numerical values. The display has a huge buffer in primary storage, where there is one (or more) cell that describes the color of each pixel. A write instruction executed by the processor causes the display's buffer to be altered at the appropriate cells, and the display's controller (called the "video controller") reads the information in the buffer and copies its contents to the display, thus repainting the display.

To summarize, here is a picture of a computer with buffers reserved for input/output devices in primary storage:

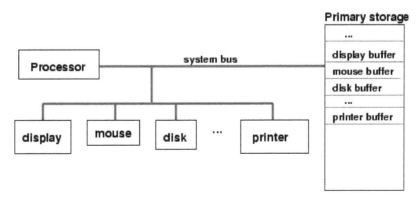

It is important to see in the picture that (the controllers in) the various storage devices can use the system bus to read/write from primary storage *without bothering the processor*. So, input and output can proceed at the same time that the processor executes instructions.

When a computer is connected to an outside network, the network can also be considered a kind of secondary-storage device that responds to read and write instructions, but the format of the reads and writes is far more complex they must include the address of the destination computer, the kind of data transmitted, the stage of interaction that is being done, etc. So, there are standardized patterns of bits, called *protocols*, that must be transmitted as "reads" and "writes" from the processor to the system bus to the port to the network. To accomplish a complete read or write, there might well be multiple transmissions from processor to bus to port to network. The design of protocols is a crucial issue to computer networks.

Interrupts

A processor should not wait for a secondary-storage device to complete a write operation. But what if the processor asks the device to perform a read operation, how will the processor know when the information has been successfully read and deposited into the device's buffer in storage?

Here is a second, similar situation: A human presses the mouse's button, demanding attention from the processor (perhaps to start or stop a program or to provide input to the program that the processor is executing). How is the processor signalled about the mouse click?

To handle these situations, all processors are wired for interruption of their normal executions. Such an interruption is called an *interrupt*.

Recall the standard execution cycle:

1. Fetch
2. Decode
3. Execute
4. Check for interrupts.

And recall the extra register, the *interrupt register*, that is embedded in the processor:

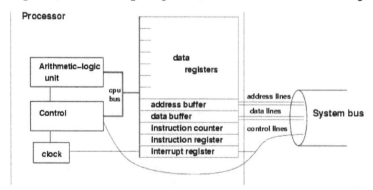

The interrupt register is connected to the the system bus, so that when a secondary storage device has completed an action, it signals the control unit by setting to 1 one of the bits in the interrupt register.

Now, we can explain the final step of the execution cycle, the check for interrupts: After the execution step, the control unit examines the contents of the interrupt register, checking to see if any bit in the register is set to 1. If all bits are 0, then no device has completed an action, so the processor can start a new instruction.

But if a bit is set to 1, then there is an *interrupt* the processor must pause its execution and do whatever instructions are needed.

For example, perhaps the user has pressed the mouse button. The device controller for the mouse sends a signal on the system bus to set to 1 the bit for a "mouse interrupt" in the interrupt register. When the control unit examines the interrupt register at the end of its current execution cycle, it sees that the bit for the mouse is set to 1. So, it resets the bit to 0 and *resets the instruction counter to the address of the program that must be executed whenever the mouse button is pressed.* Once the mouse-button program finishes, the processor can resume the work it was doing.

The mouse-button program is called an *interrupt handler.*

Where does the processor find the interrupt-handler program for the mouse? What happens to the information resting in the registers if we must pause execution and start a new program, namely, the interrupt handler? What if more than one interrupt bit is set? What if a new interrupt bit gets set while the processor is executing the mouse-button program?

Some of the answers are a bit complex. Based on this picture, we can provide simplistic answers:

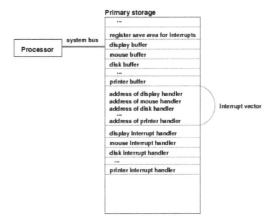

Cells in primary storage hold the addresses of the starting instructions for each of the interrupt handlers for the devices. The sequence of addresses is called an *interrupt vector.* The processor finds the address of the needed interrupt handler from the interrupt vector.

Before the processor starts executing an interrupt handler, it must copy the current values in all its registers to a *register-save area* in primary storage. When the interrupt handler is finished, the values in the register-save area are copied back into the registers in the processor, so that the processor can resume what it was doing before the interrupt.

The case of multiple interrupts is not covered here, but the basic idea is that an executing interrupt handler can itself be interrupted and its own registers can be saved.

The Operating System

The computer's operation is getting complicated there are special storage areas, special programs, etc. It is useful to have a start-up program that creates these special items and manages everything.

The start-up and manager-program is the *operating system*. When the computer is first started, the operating system is the program that executes first. As noted, it initializes the computer's storage as well as the controllers for the various devices. The interrupt handlers just discussed as considered parts of the operating system.

In addition, the operating system helps the processor execute multiple programs "simultaneously" by executing each program a bit at a time. This technique, is crucial so that a human user can start and use, say, a web browser and a text editor, at the same time.

The operating system is especially helpful at managing one particular output device --- the computer's display. The operating system includes a program called the *window manager*, which when executed, paints and repaints as needed the pixels in the display. The window manager must be executing "all the time," even while the human user starts programs like a web browser, text editor, etc.

The operating system lets the window manager repaint the display in stages: when the window-manager program repaints the display, it must execute a sequence of WRITE instructions. When the processor executes one of the WRITE instructions, this triggers the display's controller to paint part of the display. When the display controller finishes painting the part, it sets a bit in the interrupt register so that the interrupt handler for the display can execute and tell the processor to restart the window manager and continue repainting the display. In this way, the window manager is executing "all the time," in starts and stops.

Here is a revised picture of the computer's storage, which shows the inclusion of the operating system ("OS") and the division of the remaining storage for the multiple user programs that are executing:

Dataflow Architecture

In data flow architecture, the whole software system is seen as a series of transformations on consecutive pieces or set of input data, where data and operations are independent of each other. In this approach, the data enters into the system and then flows through the modules one at a time until they are assigned to some final destination (output or a data store).

The connections between the components or modules may be implemented as I/O stream, I/O buffers, piped, or other types of connections. The data can be flown in the graph topology with cycles, in a linear structure without cycles, or in a tree type structure.

The main objective of this approach is to achieve the qualities of reuse and modifiability. It is suitable for applications that involve a well-defined series of independent data transformations or computations on orderly defined input and output such as compilers and business data processing applications. There are three types of execution sequences between modules:

- Batch sequential
- Pipe and filter or non-sequential pipeline mode
- Process control.

Batch Sequential

Batch sequential is a classical data processing model, in which a data transformation subsystem can initiate its process only after its previous subsystem is completely through:

- The flow of data carries a batch of data as a whole from one subsystem to another.
- The communications between the modules are conducted through temporary intermediate files which can be removed by successive subsystems.
- It is applicable for those applications where data is batched, and each subsystem reads related input files and writes output files.
- Typical application of this architecture includes business data processing such as banking and utility billing.

Advantages

Normally, Batch Sequential provides simpler divisions on subsystems. Each subsystem can be an independent program working on input data and producing output data.

Disadvantages

Does not provide concurrency and interactive interface rather it provides high latency and low throughput. Further, external control is required for the implementation.

Pipe and Filter Architecture

This approach lays emphasis on the incremental transformation of data by successive component. In this approach, the flow of data is driven by data and the whole system is decomposed into components of data source, filters, pipes, and data sinks.

The connections between modules are data stream which is first-in/first-out buffer that can be stream of bytes, characters, or any other type of such kind. The main feature of this architecture is its concurrent and incremented execution.

Filter

A filter is an independent data stream transformer or stream transducers. It transforms the data of the input data stream, processes it, and writes the transformed data stream over a pipe for the next filter to process. It works in an incremental mode, in which it starts working as soon as data arrives through connected pipe. There are two types of filters – active filter/ and passive filter.

Active Filter

Active filter lets connected pipes to pull data in and push out the transformed data. It operates with passive pipe, which provides read/write mechanisms for pulling and pushing. This mode is used in UNIX pipe and filter mechanism.

Passive Filter

Passive filter lets connected pipes to push data in and pull data out. It operates with active pipe, which pulls data from a filter and pushes data into the next filter. It must provide read/write mechanism.

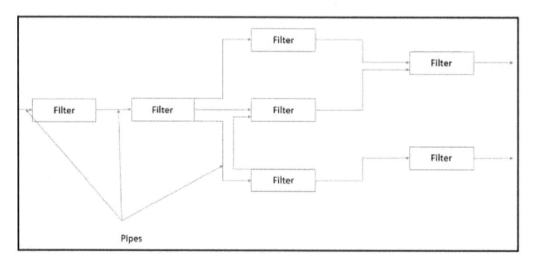

Advantages

It has following advantages:

- Provides concurrency and high throughput for excessive data processing.

- Provides reusability and simplifies system maintenance.
- Provides modifiability and low coupling between filters.
- Provides simplicity by offering clear divisions between any two filters connected by pipe.
- Provides flexibility by supporting both sequential and parallel execution.

Disadvantages

It has some of the following disadvantages:

- Not suitable for dynamic interactions.
- A low common denominator is needed for transmission of data in ASCII formats.
- Overhead of data transformation between filters.
- Does not provide a way for filters to cooperatively interact to solve a problem.
- Difficult to configure this architecture dynamically.

Pipe

Pipes are stateless and they carry binary or character stream which exist between two filters. It can move a data stream from one filter to another. Pipes use a little contextual information and retain no state information between instantiations.

Process Control Architecture

It is a type of data flow architecture where data is neither batched sequential nor pipelined stream. The flow of data comes from a set of variables, which controls the execution of process. It decomposes the entire system into subsystems or modules and connects them.

Types of Subsystems

Process control architecture would have a processing unit for changing the process control variables and a controller unit for calculating the amount of changes.

A controller unit must have the following elements:

- Controlled Variable: Controlled Variable provides values for the underlying system and should be measured by sensors. For example, speed in cruise control system.
- Input Variable: Measures an input to the process. For example, temperature of return air in temperature controls system.
- Manipulated Variable: Manipulated Variable value is adjusted or changed by the controller.
- Process Definition: It includes mechanisms for manipulating some process variables.

- Sensor: Obtains values of process variables pertinent to control and can be used as a feedback reference to recalculate manipulated variables.

- Set Point: It is the desired value for a controlled variable.

- Control Algorithm: It is used for deciding how to manipulate process variables.

Application Areas

Process control architecture is suitable in the following domains:

- Embedded system software design, where the system is manipulated by process control variable data.

- Applications, which aim is to maintain specified properties of the outputs of the process at given reference values.

- Applicable for car-cruise control and building temperature control systems.

- Real-time system software to control automobile anti-lock brakes, nuclear power plants, etc.

Cellular Architecture

A consequence of Service Oriented Architectures is the burning need to provide services at scale. The architecture that has evolved to satisfy these requirements is a little known technique called the cell architecture.

A cell architecture is based on the idea that massive scale requires parallelization and parallelization requires components be isolated from each other. These islands of isolation are called cells. A cell is a self-contained installation that can satisfy all the operations for a shard. A shard is a subset of a much larger dataset, typically a range of users, for example.

Cell architectures have several advantages:

- Cells provide a unit of parallelization that can be adjusted to any size as the user base grows.

- Cell are added in an incremental fashion as more capacity is required.

- Cells isolate failures. One cell failure does not impact other cells.

- Cells provide isolation as the storage and application horsepower to process requests is independent of other cells.

- Cells enable nice capabilities like the ability to test upgrades, implement rolling upgrades, and test different versions of software.

- Cells can fail, be upgraded, and distributed across datacentres independent of other cells.

A number of startups make use of cell architectures:

- Tumblr: Users are mapped into cells and many cells exist per data centre. Each cell has an HBase cluster, service cluster, and Redis caching cluster. Users are homed to a cell and all cells consume all posts via firehose updates. Background tasks consume from the firehose to populate tables and process requests. Each cell stores a single copy of all posts.

- Flickr: Uses a federated approach where all a user's data is stored on a shard which is a cluster of different services.

- Facebook: The Messages service has as the basic building block of their system a cluster of machines and services called a cell. A cell consists of ZooKeeper controllers, an application server cluster, and a metadata store.

- Salesforce: Salesforce is architected in terms of pods. Pods are self-contained sets of functionality consisting of 50 nodes, Oracle RAC servers, and Java application servers. Each pod supports many thousands of customers. If a pod fails only the users on that pod are impacted.

The key to the cell is you are creating a scalable and robust MTBF friendly service. A service than can be used as a bedrock component in a system of other services coordinated by a programmable orchestration layer. It works just as well in a data center as in a cloud. If you are looking for a higher level organization pattern, the Cell Architecture is a solid choice.

Von Neumann Architecture

Von Neumann Architecture also known as the *Von Neumann model*, the computer consisted of a CPU, memory and I/O devices. The program is stored in the memory. The CPU fetches an instruction from the memory at a time and executes it.

Thus, the instructions are executed sequentially which is a slow process. Neumann m/c are called control flow computer because instruction are executed sequentially as controlled by a program counter. To increase the speed, parallel processing of computer have been developed in which serial CPU's are connected in parallel to solve a problem. Even in parallel computers, the basic building blocks are Neumann processors.

The von Neumann architecture is a design model for a stored-program digital computer that uses a processing unit and a single separate storage structure to hold both instructions and data. It is named after mathematician and early computer scientist John von Neumann. Such a computer implements a universal Turing machine, and the common "referential model" of specifying sequential architectures, in contrast with parallel architectures.

One shared memory for instructions (program) and data with one data bus and one address bus between processor and memory. Instructions and data have to be fetched in sequential order (known as the Von Neuman Bottleneck), limiting the operation bandwidth. Its design is simpler than that of the Harvard architecture. It is mostly used to interface to external memory.

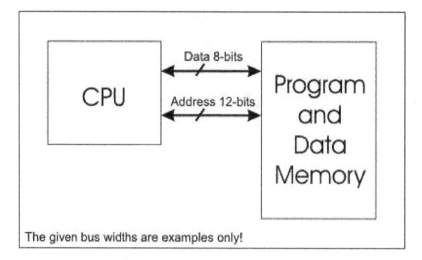

The given bus widths are examples only!

A von Neumann-based computer is a computer that:

- Uses a single processor.

- Uses one memory for both instructions and data. A von Neumann computer cannot distinguish between data and instructions in a memory location! It 'knows' only because of the *location* of a particular bit pattern in RAM.

- Executes programs by doing one instruction after the next in a serial manner using a fetch-decode-execute cycle.

The von Neuman architecture consists of some important features.

- Memory: We all know that the von Neuman is nothing but a computer having the feature of data storage. In the architecture of the von Neuman the memory plays a vital role and it is considered as one of the important feature. Mainly this is responsible for both holding and starting of data and programming data. In modern days this has been replaced by the RAM and now we are using RAM for this purpose.

- Control Unit: This unit is mainly responsible for the controlling aspect. All the data stored in the memory and during the processing of data the control unit plays the role and it manages the data flow. In fact, to be more typically it is "One At A Time". The control unit follows the principle of the One At A Time and accordingly it process all the data.

- Input output: Like all electronics devices the von Neuman architecture also has an input/output architecture. It is the basic function is same and nothing specially has been designed for the input and output architecture. With the Input and output device on a person can communicate with the device.

- ALU: ALU or the Arithmetic Logic Unit has a great importance in the von Neuman architecture. Any sort of addition, subtraction, multiplication and division of the data will be carried out by this ALU. In addition to that any other kind of algorithmic function and activities will be carried out by the ALU. These are the basic aspect of the Von Neuman architecture which you must aware of.

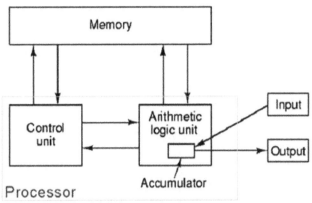

Features of the von Neuman Architecture

Capabilities

On a large scale, the ability to treat instructions as data is what makes assemblers, compilers, linkers, loaders, and other automated programming tools possible. It makes "programs that write programs" possible. This has made a sophisticated self-hosting computing ecosystem flourish around von Neumann architecture machines.

Some high level languages such as LISP leverage the von Neumann architecture by providing an abstract, machine-independent way to manipulate executable code at runtime, or by using runtime information to tune just-in-time compilation (e.g. in the case of languages hosted on the Java virtual machine, or languages embedded in web browsers).

On a smaller scale, some repetitive operations such as BITBLT or pixel and vertex shaders can be accelerated on general purpose processors with just-in-time compilation techniques. This is one use of self-modifying code that has remained popular.

Von Neumann Bottleneck

The shared bus between the program memory and data memory leads to the *von Neumann bottleneck*, the limited throughput (data transfer rate) between the central processing unit (CPU) and memory compared to the amount of memory. Because the single bus can only access one of the two classes of memory at a time, throughput is lower than the rate at which the CPU can work. This seriously limits the effective processing speed when the CPU is required to perform minimal processing on large amounts of data. The CPU is continually forced to wait for needed data to move to or from memory. Since CPU speed and memory size have increased much faster than the throughput between them, the bottleneck has become more of a problem, a problem whose severity increases with every new generation of CPU.

The von Neumann bottleneck was described by John Backus in his 1977 ACM Turing Award lecture. According to Backus:

> "Surely there must be a less primitive way of making big changes in the store than by pushing vast numbers of words back and forth through the von Neumann bottleneck. Not only is this tube a literal bottleneck for the data traffic of a problem, but, more importantly, it is an intellectual bottleneck that has kept us tied to word-at-a-time thinking instead of

encouraging us to think in terms of the larger conceptual units of the task at hand. Thus programming is basically planning and detailing the enormous traffic of words through the von Neumann bottleneck, and much of that traffic concerns not significant data itself, but where to find it."

Mitigations

There are several known methods for mitigating the Von Neumann performance bottleneck. For example, the following all can improve performance:

- Providing a cache between the CPU and the main memory;

- providing separate caches or separate access paths for data and instructions (the so-called Modified Harvard architecture);

- Using branch predictor algorithms and logic;

- Providing a limited CPU stack or other on-chip scratchpad memory to reduce memory access.

The problem can also be sidestepped somewhat by using parallel computing, using for example the non-uniform memory access (NUMA) architecture—this approach is commonly employed by supercomputers. It is less clear whether the *intellectual bottleneck* that Backus criticized has changed much since 1977. Backus's proposed solution has not had a major influence. Modern functional programming and object-oriented programming are much less geared towards "pushing vast numbers of words back and forth" than earlier languages like FORTRAN were, but internally, that is still what computers spend much of their time doing, even highly parallel supercomputers.

As of 1996, a database benchmark study found that three out of four CPU cycles were spent waiting for memory. Researchers expect that increasing the number of simultaneous instruction streams with multithreading or single-chip multiprocessing will make this bottleneck even worse.

Self-modifying Code

Aside from the von Neumann bottleneck, program modifications can be quite harmful, either by accident or design. In some simple stored-program computer designs, a malfunctioning program can damage itself, other programs, or the operating system, possibly leading to a computer crash. Memory protection and other forms of access control can usually protect against both accidental and malicious program modification.

Von Neumann Architecture	
Advantages	Disadvantages
• Less physical space is required than Harvard	• Shared memory - a defective program can overwrite another in memory, causing it to crash
• Handling just one memory block is simpler and easier to achieve	• Memory leaks - some defective programs fail to release memory when they are finished with it, which could cause the computer to crash due to insufficient memory

• Cheaper to use than Harvard	• Data bus speed - the CPU is much faster than the data bus, meaning it often sits idle (Von Neumann bottleneck) • Fetch rate - data and instructions share the same data bus, even though the rate at which each needs to be fetched is often very different
Evaluation	
Von Neumann is used over Harvard much of the time as it is cheaper to implement - Harvard is used only when speed advantages outweigh the cost.	

Harvard Architecture

The Harvard architecture is nothing but a kind of storage of data. When it comes to the physical storage of the data the Harvard architecture always stood first. Though the concept is a not a new one still the Harvard architecture has got huge appreciation form all. The Harvard Mark I relay-based computer is the term from where the concept of the Harvard architecture first arises and then onwards there has been a significant development with this architecture. The main function of this architecture is to separate and physical storage of the data and giving the signal pathways for instruction and data.

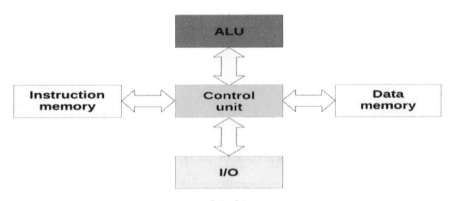

Harvard Architecture

Application and Features of the Harvard Architecture

It has got an extensive application in the audio and video processing products and with every audio and video processing instrument you will notice the presence of Havard architecture. A Blackfin processor by Analog Devices, Inc. is the particular device where it has got a premier use. In other electronic chip based product the Havard architecture is also widely used.

Memory Status

In the previous architecture, we have witnessed the presence of two memories. However, in case of the Harvard architecture you will not find two memories and there will be one memory. The existing memory will be able to perform all the functions. Yes, there will be only read only memory and this memory will be used for the purpose of reading, coding, decoding and storing of data.

The Speed Aspect

A lot has been discussed about the Harvard architecture, but without the speed any architecture can't be accepted. But in case of the Havard architecture the manufacturers have designed the architecture in such a way that it will be able to process the data with a much higher speed. Yes, all care has been taken so that the architecture can process data with a high speed.

By implementing the same formula the modern days CPU are being manufactured so that the new CPU can run with a much faster sped and can also process the data effectively. The concept of the CPU cache is also being implemented while designing the Harvard architecture.

Reason for Harvard Architecture being Effective

After coming across all, the fact definitely one question will strike to your mind that why Harvard architecture is so effective. The answer is quite clear and simple that the architecture is able to read an instruction and it can also perform data memory access simultaneously at a fast speed. Hence the Harvard architecture is being widely accepted.

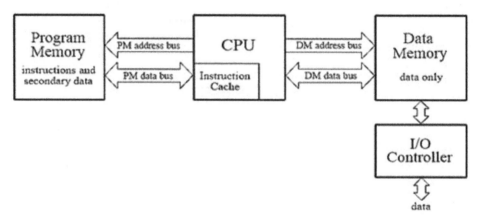

Features of the Harvard Architecture

Von Neuman vs. Harvard Architecture

The features and the specifications of both the architectures are discussed and the basic function of both architectures is to design the computer architecture. However, in certain aspects, both the architectures differ from one another and here we will elaborate the basic difference between the von Neuman and Harvard Architecture.

Whenever you are watching a video it is synchronized between the audio and the video. If the audio microphone or chip goes out of control you can't enjoy the video and vice versa, and the same concept is applicable here also.

The von Neuman is a kind of architecture which is more prominently seen in the case of the conventional processor and in today also the same principle is being implemented. PCs and Servers, and embedded systems are coming under the conventional and the traditional processors which run only with control function and here you will notice the Van Neuman architecture.

On the contrast the Havard architecture is seen in the case of the modern and the latest processors like DSPs and other processors. In addition to the above Mobile communication systems, audio, speech and image processing systems are the place where you will find the application of the Havard architecture.

In von Neuman both the data and the programs are ignored in same memory, but in the later case separate memory is used for the above purpose. Hence, in the storing the data aspect both differs from each other.

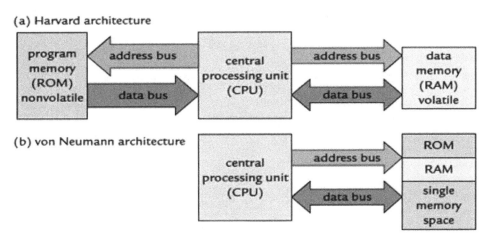

Von Neuman and Harvard Architectures for Memory

Coding also differ in both the architecture. The von Neuman is a kind of architecture where you will find that the codes are executed serially and takes more clock cycles, whereas in case of the later the same does not happen. The Havard architecture follows a parallel level of coding.

You will not find excessive number of multiplier in the case of the von Neuman architecture, but in case of the Havard architecture you will find a large number of the multiplier. In addition to that, both architectures differ from each other in various aspects like presence of barrel shifter, optimization of programming, processing speed and lot more.

Modified Harvard Architecture

The "modified" Harvard architecture merges instruction and data address spaces, allowing instructions to be read as data.

There is one type of modified Harvard Architecture, on which there is an addition pathway between CPU and the Instruction memory. It allows words in instruction memory be treated as "read-only data", so that const data (e.g. text string) can be read into Instruction memory instead of Data memory. This method preserves more data memory for read/write variables. The picture below shows how Modified Harvard Architecture works, when there is constant data in data memory.

Modified Harvard architecture allows the contents of the Instruction memory to be treated as if it was data, but the high-level programming language standard C doesn't support this architecture, so that need to add In-line assembly and non-standard extended C library.

The principal historical advantage of the Harvard architecture (simultaneous access to more than one memory system) has been nullified by modern cache systems, allowing the more flexible Von Neumann machine equal performance in most cases. The modified Harvard architecture has thus been relegated to niche applications where the ease-of-programming/complexity/performance trade-off favours it.

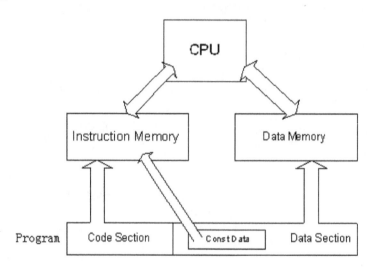

Since the C Language was not designed for Harvard architectures, it was designed for Von Neumann architectures where code and data exist in the same address space, so that any compiler for a Harvard architecture processor, like the AVR, has to use other methods to operate with separate address spaces. Some compilers use non-standard C language keywords, or they extend the standard syntax in ways that are nonstandard. The AVR toolset takes a different approach.

Accordingly, some pure Harvard machines are specialty products. Most modern computers instead implement a *modified* Harvard architecture. Those modifications are various ways to loosen the strict separation between code and data, while still supporting the higher performance concurrent data and instruction access of the Harvard architecture.

Split-cache (or Almost-von-Neumann) Architecture

The most common modification builds a memory hierarchy with a CPU cache separating instructions and data. This unifies all except small portions of the data and instruction address spaces, providing the von Neumann model. Most programmers never need to be aware of the fact that the processor core implements a (modified) Harvard architecture, although they benefit from its speed advantages. Only programmers who write instructions into data memory need to be aware of issues such as cache coherency.

Instruction-memory-as-data Architecture

Another change preserves the "separate address space" nature of a Harvard machine, but provides special machine operations to access the contents of the instruction memory as data. Because data is not directly executable as instructions, such machines are not always viewed as "modified" Harvard architecture:

- Read access: initial data values can be copied from the instruction memory into the data memory when the program starts. Or, if the data is not to be modified (it might be a constant value, such as pi, or a text string), it can be accessed by the running program directly from instruction memory without taking up space in data memory (which is often at a premium).

- Write access: a capability for reprogramming is generally required; few computers are purely ROM-based. For example, a microcontroller usually has operations to write to the flash memory used to hold its instructions. This capability may be used for purposes including software updates and EEPROM replacement.

Data-memory-as-instruction Architecture

A few Harvard architecture processors, such as the MAXQ, can execute instructions fetched from any memory segment – unlike the original Harvard processor, which can only execute instructions fetched from the program memory segment. Such processors, like other Harvard architecture processors – and unlike pure von Neumann architecture – can read an instruction and read a data value simultaneously, if they're in separate memory segments, since the processor has (at least) two separate memory segments with independent data buses. The most obvious programmer-visible difference between this kind of modified Harvard architecture and a pure von Neumann architecture is that – when executing an instruction from one memory segment – the same memory segment cannot be simultaneously accessed as data.

Comparisons

Three characteristics may be used to distinguish modified Harvard machines from pure Harvard and von Neumann machines:

- Instruction and data memories occupy different address spaces

  For pure Harvard machines, there is an address "zero" in instruction space that refers to an instruction storage location and a separate address "zero" in data space that refers to a distinct data storage location. By contrast, von Neumann and split-cache modified Harvard machines store both instructions and data in a single address space, so address "zero" refers to only one location and whether the binary pattern in that location is interpreted as an instruction or data is defined by how the program is written. However, just like pure Harvard machines, instruction-memory-as-data modified Harvard machines have separate address spaces, so have separate addresses "zero" for instruction and data space, therefore this does not distinguish this type of modified Harvard machines from pure Harvard machines.

- Instruction and data memories have separate hardware pathways to the central processing unit (CPU)

This is the point of pure or modified Harvard machines, and why they co-exist with the more flexible and general von Neumann architecture: separate memory pathways to the CPU allow instructions to be fetched and data to be accessed at the same time, improving throughput. The pure Harvard machines have separate pathways with separate address spaces. Split-cache modified Harvard machines have such separate access paths for CPU caches or other tightly coupled memories, but a unified address space covers the rest of the memory hierarchy. A von Neumann processor has only that unified address space. From a programmer's point of view, a modified Harvard processor in which instruction and data memories share an address space is usually treated as a von Neumann machine until cache coherency becomes an issue, as with self-modifying code and program loading. This can be confusing, but such issues are usually visible only to systems programmers a nd integrators. Other modified Harvard machines are like pure Harvard machines in this regard.

- Instruction and data memories may be accessed in different ways

The original Harvard machine, the Mark I, stored instructions on a punched paper tape and data in electro-mechanical counters. This, however, was entirely due to the limitations of technology available at the time. Today a Harvard machine such as the PIC microcontroller might use 12-bit wide flash memory for instructions, and 8-bit wide SRAM for data. In contrast, a von Neumann microcontroller such as an ARM7TDMI, or a modified Harvard ARM9 core, necessarily provides uniform access to flash memory and SRAM (as 8 bit bytes, in those cases).

Modern uses of the Modified Harvard Architecture

Outside of applications where a cache less DSP or microcontroller is required, most modern processors have a CPU cache which partitions instruction and data.

There are also processors which are Harvard machines by the most rigorous definition (that program and data memory occupy different address spaces), and are only *modified* in the weak sense that there are operations to read and/or write program memory as data. For example, LPM (Load Program Memory) and SPM (Store Program Memory) instructions in the Atmel AVR implement such a modification. Similar solutions are found in other microcontrollers such as the PIC and Z8Encore!, many families of digital signal processors such as the TI C55x cores, and more. Because instruction execution is still restricted to the program address space, these processors are very unlike von Neumann machines.

Having separate address spaces creates certain difficulties in programming with high-level languages that do not directly support the notion that tables of read-only data might be in a different address space from normal writable data (and thus need to be read using different instructions). The C programming language can support multiple address spaces either through non-standard extensions or through the now standardized extensions to support embedded processors.

References

- Lukoff, Herman (1979). From Dits to Bits: A personal history of the electronic computer. Portland, Oregon, USA: Robotics Press. ISBN 0-89661-002-0. LCCN 79-90567

- Computer-architecture-26757: techopedia.com, Retrieved 15 June 2018

- Campbell-Kelly, Martin (April 1982). "The Development of Computer Programming in Britain (1945 to 1955)". IEEE Annals of the History of Computing. 4 (2): 121–139. doi:10.1109/MAHC.1982.10016

- Data-flow-architecturem, software-architecture-design: tutorialspoint.com, Retrieved 11 July 2018

- Johnson, Roger (April 2008). "School of Computer Science & Information Systems: A Short History" (PDF). Birkbeck College. University of London. Retrieved 2017-07-23

- Explain-about-the-von-neumann-architectures, introduction-to-computer: ecomputernotes.com, Retrieved 09 July 2018

- Grosch, Herbert R. J. (1991), Computer: Bit Slices From a Life, Third Millennium Books, ISBN 0-88733-085-1

- Difference-between-von-neumann-and-harvard-architecture: edgefxkits.com, Retrieved 19 May 2018

- Backus, John W. "Can Programming Be Liberated from the von Neumann Style? A Functional Style and Its Algebra of Programs". doi:10.1145/359576.359579.

- Von-neumann-architecture: getrevising.co.uk, Retrieved 28 April 2018

- Dijkstra, Edsger W. "E. W. Dijkstra Archive: A review of the 1977 Turing Award Lecture". Retrieved 2008-07-11

Instruction Set Architecture

An instruction set architecture (ISA) is an abstract computer model. An ISA serves as an interface between hardware and software, and allows multiple implementations varying in performance, monetary cost and physical size. The aim of this chapter is to explore the fundamental principles of instruction set architecture. Some of the varied topics covered in this chapter include complex instruction set computer and reduced instruction set computer, very long instruction word, one instruction set computer, etc.

The Instruction Set Architecture (ISA) is the part of the processor that is visible to the programmer or compiler writer. The ISA serves as the boundary between software and hardware.

The ISA of a processor can be described using 5 categories:

- Operand Storage in the CPU

  Where are the operands kept other than in memory?

- Number of explicit named operands

  How many operands are named in a typical instruction?

- Operand location

  Can any ALU instruction operand be located in memory? Or must all operands be kept internaly in the CPU?

- Operations

  What operations are provided in the ISA.

- Type and size of operands

  What is the type and size of each operand and how is it specified?

Of all the above the most distinguishing factor is the first.

The 3 most common types of ISAs are:

1. *Stack* - The operands are implicitly on top of the stack.

2. *Accumulator* - One operand is implicitly the accumulator.

3. *General Purpose Register (GPR)* - All operands are explicitly mentioned, they are either registers or memory locations.

Let's look at the assembly code of

    C = A + B;

in all 3 architectures:

Stack	Accumulator	GPR
PUSH A	LOAD A	LOAD R1,A
PUSH B	ADD B	ADD R1,B
ADD	STORE C	STORE R1,C
POP C	-	-

Not all processors can be neatly tagged into one of the above categories. The i8086 has many instructions that use implicit operands although it has a general register set. The i8051 is another example, it has 4 banks of GPRs but most instructions must have the A register as one of its operands. What are the advantages and disadvantages of each of these approaches?

Stack

Advantages: Simple Model of expression evaluation (reverse polish). Short instructions.
Disadvantages: A stack can't be randomly accessed this makes it hard to generate efficient code. The stack itself is accessed every operation and becomes a bottleneck.

Accumulator

Advantages: Short instructions.
Disadvantages: The accumulator is only temporary storage so memory traffic is the highest for this approach.

GPR

Advantages: Makes code generation easy. Data can be stored for long periods in registers.
Disadvantages: All operands must be named leading to longer instructions.

Classification of ISAs

An ISA may be classified in a number of different ways. A common classification is by architectural *complexity*. A complex instruction set computer (CISC) has many specialized instructions, some of which may only be rarely used in practical programs. A reduced instruction set computer (RISC) simplifies the processor by efficiently implementing only the instructions that are frequently used in programs, while the less common operations are implemented as subroutines, having their resulting additional processor execution time offset by infrequent use.

Other types include very long instruction word (VLIW) architectures, and the closely related *long instruction word* (LIW) and *explicitly parallel instruction computing* (EPIC) architectures. These architectures seek to exploit instruction-level parallelism with less hardware than RISC and CISC by making the compilerresponsible for instruction issue and scheduling.

Architectures with even less complexity have been studied, such as the minimal instruction set computer (MISC) and one instruction set computer (OISC). These are theoretically important types, but have not been commercialized.

Instructions

Machine language is built up from discrete *statements* or *instructions*. On the processing architecture, a given instruction may specify:

- Particular registers for arithmetic, addressing, or control functions
- Particular memory locations or offsets
- Particular addressing modes used to interpret the operands.

More complex operations are built up by combining these simple instructions, which are executed sequentially, or as otherwise directed by control flow instructions.

Instruction Types

Examples of operations common to many instruction sets include the following.

Data Handling and Memory Operations

- *Set* a register to a fixed constant value.
- *Copy* data from a memory location to a register, or vice versa (a machine instruction is often called *move*; however, the term is misleading). Used to store the contents of a register, result of a computation, or to retrieve stored data to perform a computation on it later. Often called load and store operations.
- *Read* and *write* data from hardware devices.

Arithmetic and Logic Operations

- *Add*, *subtract*, *multiply*, or *divide* the values of two registers, placing the result in a register, possibly setting one or more condition codes in a status register.
- *Increment*, *decrement* in some ISAs, saving operand fetch in trivial cases.
- Perform bitwise operations, e.g., taking the *conjunction* and *disjunction* of corresponding bits in a pair of registers, taking the *negation* of each bit in a register.
- *Compare* two values in registers (for example, to see if one is less, or if they are equal).
- *Floating-point instructions* for arithmetic on floating-point numbers.

Control Flow Operations

- *Branch* to another location in the program and execute instructions there.
- *Conditionally branch* to another location if a certain condition holds.

- *Indirectly branch* to another location.

- *Call* another block of code, while saving the location of the next instruction as a point to return to.

Coprocessor Instructions

- Load/store data to and from a coprocessor, or exchanging with CPU registers.

- Perform coprocessor operations.

Complex instructions

Processors may include "complex" instructions in their instruction set. A single "complex" instruction does something that may take many instructions on other computers. Such instructions are typified by instructions that take multiple steps, control multiple functional units, or otherwise appear on a larger scale than the bulk of simple instructions implemented by the given processor. Some examples of "complex» instructions include:

- Transferring multiple registers to or from memory (especially the stack) at once

- Moving large blocks of memory (e.g. string copy or DMA transfer)

- Complicated integer and floating-point arithmetic (e.g. square root, or transcendental functions such as logarithm, sine, cosine, etc.)

- *SIMD instructions*, a single instruction performing an operation on many homogeneous values in parallel, possibly in dedicated SIMD registers

- Performing an atomic test-and-set instruction or other read-modify-write atomic instruction

- Instructions that perform ALU operations with an operand from memory rather than a register.

Complex instructions are more common in CISC instruction sets than in RISC instruction sets, but RISC instruction sets may include them as well. RISC instruction sets generally do not include ALU operations with memory operands, or instructions to move large blocks of memory, but most RISC instruction sets include SIMD or vector instructions that perform the same arithmetic operation on multiple pieces of data at the same time. SIMD instructions have the ability of manipulating large vectors and matrices in minimal time. SIMD instructions allow easy parallelization of algorithms commonly involved in sound, image, and video processing. Various SIMD implementations have been brought to market under trade names such as MMX, 3DNow!, and AltiVec.

Parts of an Instruction

On traditional architectures, an instruction includes an opcode that specifies the operation to perform, such as *add contents of memory to register*—and zero or more operand specifiers, which may specify registers, memory locations, or literal data. The operand specifiers may have addressing modes determining their meaning or may be in fixed fields. In very long instruction word (VLIW) architectures, which include many microcode architectures, multiple simultaneous opcodes and operands are specified in a single instruction.

MIPS32 Add Immediate Instruction

001000	00001	00010	0000000101011110
OP Code	Addr 1	Addr 2	Immediate value

Equivalent mnemonic: addi $r1, $r2,

One instruction may have several fields, which identify the logical operation, and may also include source and destination addresses and constant values. This is the MIPS "Add Immediate" instruction, which allows selection of source and destination registers and inclusion of a small constant

Some exotic instruction sets do not have an opcode field, such as transport triggered architectures (TTA), only operand(s).

The Forth virtual machine and other "0-operand" instruction sets lack any operand specifier fields, such as some stack machines including NOSC.

Conditional instructions often have a predicate field—a few bits that encode the specific condition to cause the operation to be performed rather than not performed. For example, a conditional branch instruction will be executed, and the branch taken, if the condition is true, so that execution proceeds to a different part of the program, and not executed, and the branch not taken, if the condition is false, so that execution continues sequentially. Some instruction sets also have conditional moves, so that the move will be executed, and the data stored in the target location, if the condition is true, and not executed, and the target location not modified, if the condition is false. Similarly, IBM z/Architecture has a conditional store instruction. A few instruction sets include a predicate field in every instruction; this is called branch predication.

Number of Operands

Instruction sets may be categorized by the maximum number of operands *explicitly* specified in instructions.

(In the examples that follow, *a*, *b*, and *c* are (direct or calculated) addresses referring to memory cells, while *reg1* and so on refer to machine registers.)

C = A+B

- 0-operand (*zero-address machines*), so called stack machines: All arithmetic operations take place using the top one or two positions on the stack: push a, push b, *add*, pop c.

    o   C = A+B needs *four instructions*. For stack machines, the terms "0-operand" and "zero-address" apply to arithmetic instructions, but not to all instructions, as 1-operand push and pop instructions are used to access memory.

- 1-operand (*one-address machines*), so called accumulator machines, include early computers and many small microcontrollers: most instructions specify a single right operand (that is, constant, a register, or a memory location), with the implicit accumulator as the left operand (and the destination if there is one): load a, add b, store c.

- o C = A+B needs *three instructions.*

- 2-operand — many CISC and RISC machines fall under this category:

- o CISC — move A to *C*; then add B to *C.*

  - ◇ C = A+B needs *two instructions.* This effectively 'stores' the result without an explicit *store* instruction.

- o CISC — Often machines are limited to one memory operand per instruction: load a,reg1; add b,reg1; store reg1,c; This requires a load/store pair for any memory movement regardless of whether the *add* result is an augmentation stored to a different place, as in C = A+B, or the same memory location: A = A+B.

  - ◇ C = A+B needs *three instructions.*

- o RISC — Requiring explicit memory loads, the instructions would be: load a,reg1; load b,reg2; add reg1,reg2; store reg2,c.

  - ◇ C = A+B needs *four instructions.*

- 3-operand, allowing better reuse of data:

- o CISC — It becomes either a single instruction: add a,b,c

  - ◇ C = A+B needs *one instruction.*

- o CISC — Or, on machines limited to two memory operands per instruction, move a,reg1; add reg1,b,c;

- o C = A+B needs *two instructions.*

- o RISC — arithmetic instructions use registers only, so explicit 2-operand load/store instructions are needed: load a,reg1; load b,reg2; add reg1+reg2->reg3; store reg3,c;

  - ◇ C = A+B needs *four instructions.*

- o Unlike 2-operand or 1-operand, this leaves all three values a, b, and c in registers available for further reuse.

- o More operands—some CISC machines permit a variety of addressing modes that allow more than 3 operands (registers or memory accesses), such as the VAX "POLY» polynomial evaluation instruction.

Due to the large number of bits needed to encode the three registers of a 3-operand instruction, RISC architectures that have 16-bit instructions are invariably 2-operand designs, such as the Atmel AVR, TI MSP430, and some versions of ARM Thumb. RISC architectures that have 32-bit instructions are usually 3-operand designs, such as the ARM, AVR32, MIPS, Power ISA, and SPARC architectures.

Each instruction specifies some number of operands (registers, memory locations, or immediate values) *explicitly*. Some instructions give one or both operands implicitly, such as by being stored on top of the stack or in an implicit register. If some of the operands are given implicitly, fewer operands need be specified in the instruction. When a "destination operand» explicitly specifies the destination, an additional operand must be supplied. Consequently, the number of operands encoded in an instruction may differ from the mathematically necessary number of arguments for a logical or arithmetic operation (the arity). Operands are either encoded in the "opcode" representation of the instruction, or else are given as values or addresses following the instruction.

Register Pressure

Register pressure measures the availability of free registers at any point in time during the program execution. Register pressure is high when a large number of the available registers are in use; thus, the higher the register pressure, the more often the register contents must be spilled into memory. Increasing the number of registers in an architecture decreases register pressure but increases the cost.

While embedded instruction sets such as Thumb suffer from extremely high register pressure because they have small register sets, general-purpose RISC ISAs like MIPS and Alpha enjoy low register pressure. CISC ISAs like x86-64 offer low register pressure despite having smaller register sets. This is due to the many addressing modes and optimizations (such as sub-register addressing, memory operands in ALU instructions, absolute addressing, PC-relative addressing, and register-to-register spills) that CISC ISAs offer.

Instruction Length

The size or length of an instruction varies widely, from as little as four bits in some microcontrollers to many hundreds of bits in some VLIW systems. Processors used in personal computers, mainframes, and supercomputers have instruction sizes between 8 and 64 bits. The longest possible instruction on x86 is 15 bytes (120 bits). Within an instruction set, different instructions may have different lengths. In some architectures, notably most reduced instruction set computers(RISC), instructions are a fixed length, typically corresponding with that architecture's word size. In other architectures, instructions have variable length, typically integral multiples of a byte or a halfword. Some, such as the ARM with *Thumb-extension* have *mixed* variable encoding, that is two fixed, usually 32-bit and 16-bit encodings, where instructions can not be mixed freely but must be switched between on a branch (or exception boundary in ARMv8).

A RISC instruction set normally has a fixed instruction length (often 4 bytes = 32 bits), whereas a typical CISC instruction set may have instructions of widely varying length (1 to 15 bytes for x86). Fixed-length instructions are less complicated to handle than variable-length instructions for several reasons (not having to check whether an instruction straddles a cache line or virtual memory page boundary for instance), and are therefore somewhat easier to optimize for speed.

Code Density

In early computers, memory was expensive, so minimizing the size of a program to make sure it would fit in the limited memory was often central. Thus the combined size of all the instructions needed to perform a particular task, the *code density*, was an important characteristic of any instruction set. Computers with high code density often have complex instructions for procedure entry, parameterized returns, loops, etc. (therefore retroactively named *Complex Instruction Set Computers*, CISC). However, more typical, or frequent, "CISC" instructions merely combine a basic ALU operation, such as "add", with the access of one or more operands in memory (using addressing modes such as direct, indirect, indexed, etc.). Certain architectures may allow two or three operands (including the result) directly in memory or may be able to perform functions such as automatic pointer increment, etc. Software-implemented instruction sets may have even more complex and powerful instructions.

Reduced instruction-set computers, RISC, were first widely implemented during a period of rapidly growing memory subsystems. They sacrifice code density to simplify implementation circuitry, and try to increase performance via higher clock frequencies and more registers. A single RISC instruction typically performs only a single operation, such as an "add" of registers or a "load" from a memory location into a register. A RISC instruction set normally has a fixed instruction length, whereas a typical CISC instruction set has instructions of widely varying length. However, as RISC computers normally require more and often longer instructions to implement a given task, they inherently make less optimal use of bus bandwidth and cache memories.

Certain embedded RISC ISAs like Thumb and AVR32 typically exhibit very high density owing to a technique called code compression. This technique packs two 16-bit instructions into one 32-bit instruction, which is then unpacked at the decode stage and executed as two instructions.

Minimal instruction set computers (MISC) are a form of stack machine, where there are few separate instructions (16-64), so that multiple instructions can be fit into a single machine word. These type of cores often take little silicon to implement, so they can be easily realized in an FPGA or in a multi-core form. The code density of MISC is similar to the code density of RISC; the increased instruction density is offset by requiring more of the primitive instructions to do a task.

There has been research into executable compression as a mechanism for improving code density. The mathematics of Kolmogorov complexity describes the challenges and limits of this.

Representation

The instructions constituting a program are rarely specified using their internal, numeric form (machine code); they may be specified by programmers using an assembly language or, more commonly, may be generated from programming languages by compilers.

Design

The design of instruction sets is a complex issue. There were two stages in history for the microprocessor. The first was the CISC (Complex Instruction Set Computer), which had many different instructions. In the 1970s, however, places like IBM did research and found that many instructions in the set could be eliminated. The result was the RISC (Reduced Instruction Set Computer), an architecture that uses a smaller set of instructions. A simpler instruction set may offer the potential for higher speeds, reduced processor size, and reduced power consumption. However, a more complex set may optimize common operations, improve memory and cache efficiency, or simplify programming.

Some instruction set designers reserve one or more opcodes for some kind of system call or software interrupt. For example, MOS Technology 6502 uses 00_H, Zilog Z80 uses the eight codes C7,CF,D7,DF,E7,EF,F7,FF$_H$ while Motorola 68000 use codes in the range A000..AFFF$_H$.

Fast virtual machines are much easier to implement if an instruction set meets the Popek and Goldberg virtualization requirements.

The NOP slide used in immunity-aware programming is much easier to implement if the "unprogrammed" state of the memory is interpreted as a NOP.

On systems with multiple processors, non-blocking synchronization algorithms are much easier to implement if the instruction set includes support for something such as "fetch-and-add", "load-link/store-conditional" (LL/SC), or "atomic compare-and-swap".

Instruction Set Implementation

Any given instruction set can be implemented in a variety of ways. All ways of implementing a particular instruction set provide the same programming model, and all implementations of that instruction set are able to run the same executables. The various ways of implementing an instruction set give different tradeoffs between cost, performance, power consumption, size, etc.

When designing the microarchitecture of a processor, engineers use blocks of "hard-wired» electronic circuitry (often designed separately) such as adders, multiplexers, counters, registers, ALUs, etc. Some kind of register transfer language is then often used to describe the decoding and sequencing of each instruction of an ISA using this physical microarchitecture. There are two basic ways to build a control unit to implement this description (although many designs use middle ways or compromises):

1. Some computer designs "hardwire" the complete instruction set decoding and sequencing (just like the rest of the microarchitecture).

2. Other designs employ microcode routines or tables (or both) to do this—typically as on-chip ROMs or PLAs or both (although separate RAMs and ROMshave been used historically). The Western Digital MCP-1600 is an older example, using a dedicated, separate ROM for microcode.

Some designs use a combination of hardwired design and microcode for the control unit.

Some CPU designs use a writable control store—they compile the instruction set to a writable RAM or flash inside the CPU (such as the Rekursiv processor and the Imsys Cjip), or an FPGA (reconfigurable computing).

An ISA can also be emulated in software by an interpreter. Naturally, due to the interpretation overhead, this is slower than directly running programs on the emulated hardware, unless the hardware running the emulator is an order of magnitude faster. Today, it is common practice for vendors of new ISAs or microarchitectures to make software emulators available to software developers before the hardware implementation is ready.

Often the details of the implementation have a strong influence on the particular instructions selected for the instruction set. For example, many implementations of the instruction pipeline only allow a single memory load or memory store per instruction, leading to a load-store architecture (RISC). For another example, some early ways of implementing the instruction pipeline led to a delay slot.

The demands of high-speed digital signal processing have pushed in the opposite direction—forcing instructions to be implemented in a particular way. For example, to perform digital filters fast enough, the MAC instruction in a typical digital signal processor (DSP) must use a kind of Harvard architecture that can fetch an instruction and two data words simultaneously, and it requires a single-cycle multiply–accumulate multiplier.

Addressing Mode

The term *addressing modes* refers to the way in which the operand of an instruction is specified. Information contained in the instruction code is the value of the operand or the address of the result/operand. Following are the main addressing modes that are used on various platforms and architectures.

Immediate Mode

The operand is an immediate value is stored explicitly in the instruction:

Example: SPIM (opcode dest, source)

li $11, 3 // loads the immediate value of 3 into register $11

li $9, 8 // loads the immediate value of 8 into register $9

Example: (textbook uses instructions type like, opcode source, dest)

move #200, R0; // move immediate value 200 in register R0

Index Mode

The address of the operand is obtained by adding to the contents of the general register (called index register) a constant value. The number of the index register and the constant value are included in the instruction code. Index Mode is used to access an array whose elements are in successive memory locations. The content of the instruction code, represents the starting address of the array and the value of the index register, and the index value of the current element. By incrementing or decrementing index register different element of the array can be accessed.

Example: SPIM/SAL - accessing arrays,

.data

array1: .byte 1,2,3,4,5,6

.text

___start:

```
move $3, $0              #$3 initialize index register with 0

add $3, $3,4             # compute the index value of the fifth element

sb $0, array1($3)        # array1[4]=0

                         # store byte 0 in the fifth element of the array

                         # index addressing mode
```

done

Indirect Mode

The effective address of the operand is the contents of a register or main memory location, location whose address appears in the instruction. Indirection is noted by placing the name of the register or the memory address given in the instruction in parentheses. The register or memory location that contains the address of the operand is a pointer. When an execution takes place in such mode, instruction may be told to go to a specific address. Once it's there, instead of finding an operand, it finds an address where the operand is located.

Two memory accesses are required in order to obtain the value of the operand (fetch operand address and fetch operand value).

Example: (textbook) ADD (A), R0

(address A is embedded in the instruction code and (A) is the operand address = pointer variable)

Example: SPIM - simulating pointers and indirect register addressing,

The following "C" code:

int *alpha=0x00002004, q=5;

*alpha = q;

could be translated into the following assembly code:

alpha: .word 0x00002004 # alpha is and address variable # address value is 0x00002004

q: .word 5

....

```
lw $10,q  # load word value from address q in into $10

              # $10 is 5

lw $11,alpha    # $11 gets the value 0x0002004

                # this is similar with a load immediate address value

sw$10,($11)     # store value from register $10 at memory location
```

whose address is given by the contents of register $11

(store 5 at address 0x00002004)

Example: SPIM/SAL - array pointers and indirect register addressing,

.data

array1: .byte 1,2,3,4,5,6

.text

___start:

la $3, array1   # array1 is direct addressing mode

add $3, $3,4   # compute the address of the fifth element

sb $0, ($3)   # array1=0 , byte accessing

                # indirect addressing mode

done

Absolute Direct Mode

The address of the operand is embedded in the instruction code.

Example: (SPIM),

beta: .word 2000

lw $11, beta   # load word (32 -bit quantity) at address beta into register $11

                # address of the word is embedded in the instruction code

                # (register $11 will receive value 2000)

Register Mode

The name (the number) of the CPU register is embedded in the instruction. The register contains the value of the operand. The number of bits used to specify the register depends on the total number of registers from the processor set.

Example (SPIM),

add$14, $14, $13 # add contents of register $13 plus contents of

                # register $14 and save the result in register $14

No memory access is required for the operand specified in register mode.

Displacement Mode

Similar to index mode, except instead of a index register a base register will be used. Base register contains a pointer to a memory location. An integer (constant) is also referred to as a displacement. The address of the operand is obtained by adding the contents of the base register plus the constant. The difference between index mode and displacement mode is in the number of bits used to represent the constant. When the constant is represented a number of bits to access the memory, then we have index mode. Index mode is more appropriate for array accessing; displacement mode is more appropriate for structure (records) accessing.

Example: SPIM/SAL - accessing fields in structures,

.data

student: .word 10000 #field code

.ascii "Smith" #field name

.byte # field test

.byte 80,80,90,100 # fields hw1,hw2,hw3,hw4

.text

___start:

```
la $3, student      # load address of the structure in $3

                    # $3 base register

add $17, $0,90      # value 90 in register $17

                    # displacement of field "test" is 9 bytes

                    #

sb $17, 9($3)       # store contents of register $17 in field "test"

                    # displacement addressing mode
```

done

Auto Increment/Auto Decrement Mode

A special case of indirect register mode. The register, whose number is included in the instruction code, contains the address of the operand. Auto increment Mode = after operand addressing, the contents of the register is incremented. Decrement Mode = before operand addressing, the contents of the register is decrement.

Example: SPIM/SAL - simulating auto increment/auto decrement addressing mode,

(MIPS has no auto increment/auto decrement mode)

lw $3, array1($17) #load in reg. $3 word at address array1($17)

addi $17, $17,4   #increment address (32-bit words) after accessing

                                   #operand this can be re-written in a "auto increment like mode":

lw+ $3,array1($17)   # lw+ is not a real MIPS instruction

subi $17, $17,4   # decrement address before accessing the operand

lw $3,array1($17)

Complex Instruction Set Computer and Reduced Instruction Set Computer

Central Processing Unit Architecture operates the capacity to work from "Instruction Set Architecture" to where it was designed. The architectural designs of CPU are RISC (Reduced instruction set computing) and CISC (Complex instruction set computing). CISC has the ability to execute addressing modes or multi-step operations within one instruction set. It is the design of the CPU where one instruction performs many low-level operations. For example, memory storage, an arithmetic operation and loading from memory. RISC is a CPU design strategy based on the insight that simplified instruction set gives higher performance when combined with a microprocessor architecture which has the ability to execute the instructions by using some microprocessor cycles per instruction.

RISC and CISC Architectures

Hardware designers invent numerous technologies & tools to implement the desired architecture in order to fulfill these needs. Hardware architecture may be implemented to be either hardware specific or software specific, but according to the application both are used in the required quantity. As far as the processor hardware is concerned, there are 2 types of concepts to implement the processor hardware architecture. First one is RISC and other is CISC.

CISC Architecture

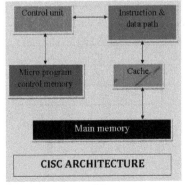

CISC Architecture

The CISC approach attempts to minimize the number of instructions per program, sacrificing the number of cycles per instruction. Computers based on the CISC architecture are designed to decrease the memory cost. Because, the large programs need more storage, thus increasing the memory cost and large memory becomes more expensive. To solve these problems, the number of instructions per program can be reduced by embedding the number of operations in a single instruction, thereby making the instructions more complex.

- MUL loads two values from the memory into separate registers in CISC.

- CISC uses minimum possible instructions by implementing hardware and executes operations.

- Instruction Set Architecture is a medium to permit communication between the programmer and the hardware. Data execution part, copying of data, deleting or editing is the user commands used in the microprocessor and with this microprocessor the Instruction set architecture is operated.

The main keywords used in the above instruction set architecture are as below:

- Instruction Set: Group of instructions given to execute the program and they direct the computer by manipulating the data. Instructions are in the form – Opcode (operational code) and Operand. Where, opcode is the instruction applied to load and store data, etc. The operand is a memory register where instruction applied.

- Addressing Modes: Addressing modes are the manner in the data is accessed. Depending upon the type of instruction applied, addressing modes are of various types such as direct mode where straight data is accessed or indirect mode where the location of the data is accessed. Processors having identical ISA may be very different in organization. Processors with identical ISA and nearly identical organization are still not nearly identical.

CPU performance is given by the fundamental law:

$$CPU\ Time = \frac{sec\,onds}{program} = \frac{Instructions}{Program}\ X\ \frac{Cycles}{Instructions}\ X\ \frac{sec\,onds}{Cycles}$$

Thus, CPU performance is dependent upon Instruction Count, CPI (Cycles per instruction) and Clock cycle time. And all three are affected by the instruction set architecture.

	Instruction Count	CPI	Clock
Program	X		
Compiler	X	X	
Instruction Set Architecture	X	X	X
Microarchitecture		X	X
Physica Design			X

Instruction Count of the CPU

This underlines the importance of the instruction set architecture. There are two prevalent instruction set architectures.

Examples of CISC Processors

IBM 370/168 – It was introduced in the year 1970. CISC design is a 32 bit processor and four 64-bit floating point registers.

VAX 11/780 – CISC design is a 32-bit processor and it supports many numbers of addressing modes and machine instructions which is from Digital Equipment Corporation.

Intel 80486 – It was launched in the year 1989 and it is a CISC processor, which has instructions varying lengths from 1 to 11 and it will have 235 instructions.

Characteristics of CISC Architecture

- Instruction-decoding logic will be Complex.

- One instruction is required to support multiple addressing modes.

- Less chip space is enough for general purpose registers for the instructions that are ooperated directly on memory.

- Various CISC designs are set up two special registers for the stack pointer, handling interrupts, etc.

- MUL is referred to as a "complex instruction" and requires the programmer for storing functions.

RISC Architecture

RISC (Reduced Instruction Set Computer) is used in portable devices due to its power efficiency. For Example, Apple iPod and Nintendo DS. RISC is a type of microprocessor architecture that uses highly-optimized set of instructions. RISC does the opposite, reducing the cycles per instruction at the cost of the number of instructions per program Pipelining is one of the unique feature of RISC. It is performed by overlapping the execution of several instructions in a pipeline fashion. It has a high performance advantage over CISC.

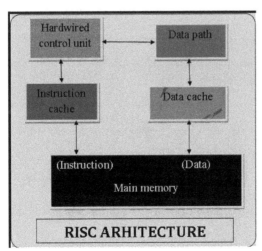

RISC processors take simple instructions and are executed within a clock cycle.

RISC Architecture Characteristics

- Simple Instructions are used in RISC architecture.

- RISC helps and supports few simple data types and synthesizes complex data types.

- RISC utilizes simple addressing modes and fixed length instructions for pipelining.

- RISC permits any register to use in any context.

- One Cycle Execution Time.

- The amount of work that a computer can perform is reduced by separating "LOAD" and "STORE" instructions.

- RISC contains Large Number of Registers in order to prevent various numbers of interactions with memory.

- In RISC, Pipelining is easy as the execution of all instructions will be done in a uniform interval of time i.e. one click.

- In RISC, more RAM is required to store assembly level instructions.

- Reduced instructions need a less number of transistors in RISC.

- RISC uses Harvard memory model means it is Harvard Architecture.

- A compiler is used to perform the conversion operation means to convert a high-level language statement into the code of its form.

RISC and CISC Comparison

CISC	RISC
It is Prominent on Hardware	It is Prominent on the software
It has high cycles per second	It has low cycles per second
It has transistors used for storing Instruction which are complex	More transistors used for storing memory
LOAD and STORE memory-to-memory is induced in instructions	LOAD and STORE register-register are independent
It has multi-clock	It has a single - clock

MUL instruction is divided into three instructions:

- "LOAD" – moves data from the memory bank to a register;

- "PROD" – finds product of two operands located within the registers;

- "STORE" – moves data from a register to the memory banks.

The main difference between RISC and CISC is the number of instructions and its complexity.

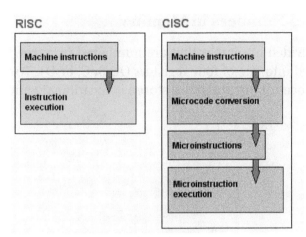

RISC vs CISC

Semantic Gap

Both RISC and CISC architectures have been developed as an attempt to cover the semantic gap.

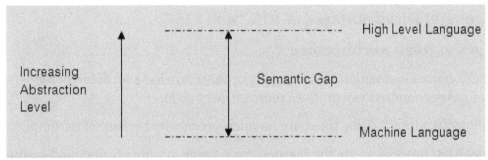

Semantic Gap

With an objective of improving efficiency of software development, several powerful programming languages have come up, viz., Ada, C, C++, Java, etc. They provide a high level of abstraction, conciseness and power. By this evolution the semantic gap grows. To enable efficient compilation of high level language programs, CISC and RISC designs are the two options.

CISC designs involve very complex architectures, including a large number of instructions and addressing modes, whereas RISC designs involve simplified instruction set and adapt it to the real requirements of user programs.

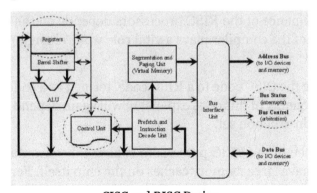

CISC and RISC Design

Multiplication of Two Numbers in Memory

If the main memory is divided into areas that are numbered from row1: column 1 to row 5 :column 4. The data is loaded into one of four registers (A, B, C, or D). To find multiplication of two numbers- One stored in location 1:3 and other stored in location 4:2 and store back result in 1:3.

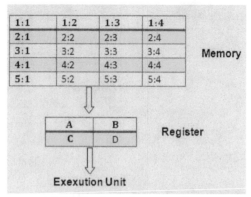

Multiplication of Two Numbers

Advantages and Disadvantages of RISC and CISC

Advantages of RISC Architecture

- RISC(Reduced instruction set computing)architecture has a set of instructions, so high-level language compilers can produce more efficient code.

- It allows freedom of using the space on microprocessors because of its simplicity.

- Many RISC processors use the registers for passing arguments and holding the local variables.

- RISC functions use only a few parameters, and the RISC processors cannot use the call instructions, and therefore, use a fixed length instruction which is easy to pipeline.

- The speed of the operation can be maximized and the execution time can be minimized. Very less number of instructional formats, a few numbers of instructions and a few addressing modes are needed.

Disadvantages of RISC Architecture

- Mostly, the performance of the RISC processors depends on the programmer or compiler as the knowledge of the compiler plays a vital role while changing the CISC code to a RISC code.

- While rearranging the CISC code to a RISC code, termed as a code expansion, will increase the size. And, the quality of this code expansion will again depend on the compiler, and also on the machine's instruction set.

- The first level cache of the RISC processors is also a disadvantage of the RISC, in which these processors have large memory caches on the chip itself. For feeding the instructions, they require very fast memory systems.

Advantages of CISC Architecture

- Microprogramming is easy assembly language to implement, and less expensive than hard wiring a control unit.

- The ease of micro coding new instructions allowed designers to make CISC machines upwardly compatible.

- As each instruction became more accomplished, fewer instructions could be used to implement a given task.

Disadvantages of CISC Architecture

- The performance of the machine slows down due to the amount of clock time taken by different instructions will be dissimilar.

- Only 20% of the existing instructions are used in a typical programming event, even though there are various specialized instructions in reality which are not even used frequently.

- The conditional codes are set by the CISC instructions as a side effect of each instruction which takes time for this setting – and, as the subsequent instruction changes the condition code bits – so, the compiler has to examine the condition code bits before this happens.

Very Long Instruction Word

Very long instruction word (VLIW) describes a computer processing architecture in which a language compiler or pre-processor breaks program instruction down into basic operations that can be performed by the processor in parallel (that is, at the same time). These operations are put into a very long instruction word which the processor can then take apart without further analysis, handing each operation to an appropriate functional unit.

VLIW is sometimes viewed as the next step beyond the reduced instruction set computing (RISC) architecture, which also works with a limited set of relatively basic instructions and can usually execute more than one instruction at a time (a characteristic referred to as superscalar). The main advantage of VLIW processors is that complexity is moved from the hardware to the software, which means that the hardware can be smaller, cheaper, and require less power to operate. The challenge is to design a compiler or pre-processor that is intelligent enough to decide how to build the very long instruction words. If dynamic pre-processing is done as the program is run, performance may be a concern.

The Crusoe family of processors from Transmeta uses very long instruction words that are assembled by a pre-processor that is located in a flash memory chip. Because the processor does not need to have the ability to discover and schedule parallel operations, the processor contains only about a fourth of the transistor s of a regular processor. The lower power requirement enables computers based on Crusoe technology to be operated by battery almost all day without a recharge. The Crusoe processors emulate Intel's x86 processor instruction set. Theoretically, pre-processors could be designed to emulate other processor architectures.

VLIW

The key to higher performance in microprocessors for a broad range of applications is the ability to exploit fine-grain, instruction-level parallelism. Some methods for exploiting fine-grain parallelism include:

- Pipelining

- Multiple processors

- Superscalar implementation

- Specifying multiple independent operations per instruction.

Pipelining is now universally implemented in high-performance processors. Little more can be gained by improving the implementation of a single pipeline.

Using multiple processors improves performance for only a restricted set of applications.

Superscalar implementations can improve performance for all types of applications. Superscalar (super: beyond; scalar: one dimensional) means the ability to fetch, issue to execution units, and complete more than one instruction at a time. Superscalar implementations are required when architectural compatibility must be preserved, and they will be used for entrenched architectures with legacy software, such as the x86 architecture that dominates the desktop computer market.

Specifying multiple operations per instruction creates a very-long instruction word architecture or VLIW. A VLIW implementation has capabilities very similar to those of a superscalar processor—issuing and completing more than one operation at a time—with one important exception: the VLIW hardware is not responsible for discovering opportunities to execute multiple operations concurrently. For the VLIW implementation, the long instruction word already encodes the concurrent operations. This explicit encoding leads to dramatically reduced hardware complexity compared to a high-degree superscalar implementation of a RISC or CISC.

The big advantage of VLIW, then, is that a highly concurrent (parallel) implementation is much simpler and cheaper to build than equivalently concurrent RISC or CISC chips. VLIW is a simpler way to build a superscalar microprocessor.

Design

In superscalar designs, the number of execution units is invisible to the instruction set. Each instruction encodes one operation only. For most superscalar designs, the instruction width is 32 bits or fewer.

In contrast, one VLIW instruction encodes multiple operations, at least one operation for each execution unit of a device. For example, if a VLIW device has five execution units, then a VLIW instruction for the device has five operation fields, each field specifying what operation should be done on that corresponding execution unit. To accommodate these operation fields, VLIW instructions are usually at least 64 bits wide and far wider on some architectures.

For example, the following is an instruction for the Super Harvard Architecture Single-Chip Computer (SHARC). In one cycle, it does a floating-point multiply, a floating-point add, and two autoincrement loads. All of this fits in one 48-bit instruction:

f12 = f0 * f4, f8 = f8 + f12, f0 = dm(i0, m3), f4 = pm(i8, m9);

Since the earliest days of computer architecture, some CPUs have added several arithmetic logic units (ALUs) to run in parallel. Superscalar CPUs use hardware to decide which operations can run in parallel at runtime, while VLIW CPUs use software (the compiler) to decide which operations can run in parallel in advance. Because the complexity of instruction scheduling is moved into the compiler, complexity of hardware can be reduced substantially.

A similar problem occurs when the result of a parallelisable instruction is used as input for a branch. Most modern CPUs *guess* which branch will be taken even before the calculation is complete, so that they can load the instructions for the branch, or (in some architectures) even start to compute them speculatively. If the CPU guesses wrong, all of these instructions and their context need to be *flushed* and the correct ones loaded, which takes time.

This has led to increasingly complex instruction-dispatch logic that attempts to guess correctly, and the simplicity of the original reduced instruction set computing(RISC) designs has been eroded. VLIW lacks this logic, and thus lacks its energy use, possible design defects, and other negative aspects.

In a VLIW, the compiler uses heuristics or profile information to guess the direction of a branch. This allows it to move and preschedule operations speculatively before the branch is taken, favoring the most likely path it expects through the branch. If the branch takes an unexpected way, the compiler has already generated compensating code to discard speculative results to preserve program semantics.

Implementations

Cydrome was a company producing VLIW numeric processors using emitter-coupled logic (ECL) integrated circuits in the same timeframe (late 1980s). This company, like Multiflow, failed after a few years.

One of the licensees of the Multiflow technology is Hewlett-Packard, which Josh Fisher joined after Multiflow's demise. Bob Rau, founder of Cydrome, also joined HP after Cydrome failed. These two would lead computer architecture research at Hewlett-Packard during the 1990s.

Along with the above systems, during the same time (1989–1990), Intel implemented VLIW in the Intel i860, their first 64-bit microprocessor, and the first processor to implement VLIW on one chip. This processor could operate in both simple RISC mode and VLIW mode:

> "In the early 1990s, Intel introduced the i860 RISC microprocessor. This simple chip had two modes of operation: a scalar mode and a VLIW mode. In the VLIW mode, the processor always fetched two instructions and assumed that one was an integer instruction and the other floating-point."

The i860's VLIW mode was used extensively in embedded digital signal processor (DSP) applications since the application execution and datasets were simple, well ordered and predictable, allowing designers to fully exploit the parallel execution advantages enabled by VLIW. In VLIW mode, the i860 could maintain floating-point performance in the range of 20-40 double-precision MFLOPS; a very high value for its time and for a processor running at 25-50Mhz.

In the 1990s, Hewlett-Packard researched this problem as a side effect of ongoing work on their PA-RISC processor family. They found that the CPU could be greatly simplified by removing the complex dispatch logic from the CPU and placing it in the compiler. Compilers of the day were far more complex than those of the 1980s, so the added complexity in the compiler was considered to be a small cost.

VLIW CPUs are usually made of multiple RISC-like execution units that operate independently. Contemporary VLIWs usually have four to eight main execution units. Compilers generate initial instruction sequences for the VLIW CPU in roughly the same manner as for traditional CPUs, generating a sequence of RISC-like instructions. The compiler analyzes this code for dependence relationships and resource requirements. It then schedules the instructions according to those constraints. In this process, independent instructions can be scheduled in parallel. Because VLIWs typically represent instructions scheduled in parallel with a longer instruction word that incorporates the individual instructions, this results in a much longer opcode (termed *very long*) to specify what executes on a given cycle.

Examples of contemporary VLIW CPUs include the TriMedia media processors by NXP (formerly Philips Semiconductors), the Super Harvard Architecture Single-Chip Computer (SHARC) DSP by Analog Devices, the C6000 digital signal processor (DSP) family by Texas Instruments, the ST200 family by STMicroelectronics based on the Lx architecture (designed in Josh Fisher's HP lab by Paolo Faraboschi), and the MPPA Manycore family by Kalray. These contemporary VLIW CPUs are mainly successful as embedded media processors for consumer electronic devices.

VLIW features have also been added to configurable processor cores for system-on-a-chip (SoC) designs. For example, Tensilica's Xtensa LX2 processor incorporates a technology named Flexible Length Instruction eXtensions (FLIX) that allows multi-operation instructions. The Xtensa C/C++ compiler can freely intermix 32- or 64-bit FLIX instructions with the Xtensa processor's one-operation RISC instructions, which are 16 or 24 bits wide. By packing multiple operations into a wide 32- or 64-bit instruction word and allowing these multi-operation instructions to intermix with shorter RISC instructions, FLIX allows SoC designers to realize VLIW's performance advantages while eliminating the code bloat of early VLIW architectures. The Infineon Carmel DSP is another VLIW processor core intended for SoC. It uses a similar code density improvement method called *configurable long instruction word* (CLIW).

Outside embedded processing markets, Intel's Itanium IA-64 explicitly parallel instruction computing (EPIC) and Elbrus 2000 appear as the only examples of a widely used VLIW CPU architecture. However, EPIC architecture is sometimes distinguished from a pure VLIW architecture, since EPIC advocates full instruction predication, rotating register files, and a very long instruction word that can encode non-parallel instruction groups. VLIWs also gained significant consumer penetration in the graphics processing unit (GPU) market, though both Nvidia and AMD have since moved to RISC architectures to improve performance on non-graphics workloads.

ATI Technologies' (ATI) and Advanced Micro Devices' (AMD) TeraScale microarchitecture for graphics processing units (GPUs) is a VLIW microarchitecture.

Architecture Comparison: CISC, RISC and VLIW

From the larger perspective, RISC, CISC, and VLIW architectures have more similarities than differences. The differences that exist, however, have profound effects on the implementations of these architectures.

Obviously these architectures all use the traditional state-machine model of computation: Each instruction effects an incremental change in the state (memory, registers) of the computer, and the hardware fetches and executes instructions sequentially until a branch instruction causes the flow of control to change.

ARCHITECTURE CHARACTERISTIC	CISC	RISC	VLIW
INSTRUCTION SIZE	Varies	One size, usually 32 bits	One size
INSTRUCTION FO RMAT	Field placement varies	Regular, consistent placement of fields	Regular, consistent placement of fields
INSTRUCTION SEMANTICS	Varies from simple to complex; possibly many dependent operations per instruction	Almost always one simple operation	Many simple, independent operations
REGISTERS	Few, sometimes special	Many, general-purpose	Many, general-purpose
MEMORY REFE RENCES	Bundled with operations in many different types of instructions	Not bundled with operations, i.e., load/store architecture	Not bundled with operations, i.e., load/store architecture
HARDWARE DESIGN FOCUS	Exploit microcoded implementations	Exploit implementations with one pipeline and & no microcode	Exploit implementations with multiple pipelines, no microcode & no complex dispatch logic
PICTURE OF FIVE TYPICAL INSTRU CTIONS ▢ = I BYTE			

The differences between RISC, CISC, and VLIW are in the formats and semantics of the instructions. Table above compares architecture characteristics.

CISC instructions vary in size, often specify a sequence of operations, and can require serial (slow) decoding algorithms. CISCs tend to have few registers, and the registers may be special-purpose, which restricts the ways in which they can be used. Memory references are typically combined with other operations (such as add memory to register). CISC instruction sets are designed to take advantage of microcode.

RISC instructions specify simple operations, are fixed in size, and are easy (quick) to decode. RISC architectures have a relatively large number of general-purpose registers. Instructions can reference main memory only through simple load-register-from-memory and store-register-to-memory operations. RISC instruction sets do not need microcode and are designed to simplify pipelining.

VLIW instructions are like RISC instructions except that they are longer to allow them to specify multiple, independent simple operations. A VLIW instruction can be thought of as several RISC instructions joined together. VLIW architectures tend to be RISC-like in most attributes.

Above figure shows a C-language code fragment containing small function definition. This function adds a local variable to a parameter passed from the caller of the function.

The implementation of this function in CISC, RISC, and VLIW code is also shown. This example is extremely unfair to the RISC and VLIW machines, but it illustrates the differences between the architectures.

The CISC code consists of one instruction because the CISC architecture has an add instruction that can encode a memory address for the destination. So, the CISC instruction adds the local variable in register r2 to the memory-based parameter. The encoding of this CISC instruction might take four bytes on some hypothetical machine.

The RISC code is artificially inefficient. Normally, a good compiler would pass the parameter in a register, which would make the RISC code consist of only a single register-to-register add instruction. For the sake of illustration, however, the code will consist of three instructions as shown. These three instructions load the parameter to a register, add it to the local variable already in a register, and then store the result back to memory. Each RISC instruction requires four bytes.

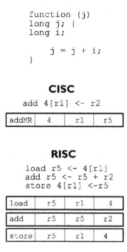

```
function (j)
long j; {
long i;

    j = j + i;
}
```

CISC

```
add 4[r1] <- r2
```

| addMR | 4 | r1 | r5 |

RISC

```
load r5 <- 4[r1]
add r5 <- r5 + r2
store 4[r1] <-r5
```

load	r5	r1	4
add	r5	r5	r2
store	r5	r1	4

VLIW

```
load r5 <- 4[r1]
add r5 <- r5 + r2
store 4[r1] <-r5
```

–	–	–	–	–	–	–	–	load	r5	r1	4
–	–	–	–	add	r5	r5	r2	–	–	–	–
–	–	–	–	–	–	–	–	store	r5	r1	4

The VLIW code is similarly hampered by poor register allocation. The example VLIW architecture shown has the ability to simultaneously issue three operations. The first slot (group of four bytes) is for branch instructions, the middle slot is for ALU instructions, and the last slot is for the load/store unit. Since the three RISC operations needed to implement the code fragment are dependent, it is not possible to pack the load and add in the same VLIW instruction. Thus, three separate VLIW instructions are necessary.

With the code fragment as shown, the VLIW instruction is depressingly inefficient from the point of view of code destiny. In a real program situation, the compiler for the VLIW would use several program optimization techniques to fill all three slots in all three instructions. It is instructive to contemplate the performance each machine might achieve for this code. We need to assume that each machine has an efficient, pipelined implementation.

A CISC machine such as the 486 or Pentium would be able to execute the code fragment in three cycles.

A RISC machine would be able to execute the fragment in three cycles as well, but the cycles would likely be faster than on the CISC.

The VLIW machine, assuming three fully-packed instructions, would effectively execute the code for this fragment in one cycle. To see this, observe that the fragment requires three out of nine slots, for one-third use of resources. One-third of three cycles is one cycle.

To be even more accurate, we can assume good register allocation as shown in figure above . This example may actually be giving the CISC machine a slight unfair advantage since it will not be possible to allocate parameters to registers on the CISC as often as is possible for the RISC and VLIW.

The CISC and RISC machines with good register allocation would take one cycle for one register-to-register instruction, but notice that the RISC code size is now much more in line with that of the CISC. Again assuming fully packed instructions, the VLIW execution time would also gain a factor of three benefits from good register allocation, yielding an effective execution time for the fragment of one-third of a cycle.

Note that these comparisons have been between scalar (one-instruction per cycle maximum) RISC and CISC implementations and a relatively narrow VLIW. While it would be more realistic to compare superscalar RISCs and CISCs against a wider VLIW, such a comparison is more complicated. Suffice it to say that the conclusions would be roughly the same.

```
function (j)
long j; {
long i;

    j = j + i;
}
```

CISC

add r3 <- r2

addRR	r1	r5

RISC

add r3 <- r3 + r2

add	r3	r3	r2

VLIW

add r3 <- r3 + r2

-	-	-	-	add	r3	r3	r2	-	-	-	-

One Instruction Set Computer

The single or one instruction set computer (OISC, pronounced, "whisk") is the penultimate reduced instruction set computer (RISC)[1]. In OISC, the instruction set consists of one instruction, and then by the orthogonality of the instruction along with composition, a complete set of operations is synthesized. This approach is completely opposed to a complex instruction set computer (CISC), which incorporates many complex instructions as micro programs within the processor.

A processor that is implemented with one instruction may appear to be lacking the necessary functionality to be seriously considered. Yet there are some interesting benefits in employing a one instruction computer. For example, hardware level functionality is simplified when implemented around a single instruction. This greatly simplifies the underlying implementation, as the same functional element is repeatedly used to form the processor core. Another advantage is that since all the instructions are the same, the instruction decoder circuitry and complexity can be eliminated.

A one instruction computer architecture is also the most flexible, as instructions can be synthesized from the fundamental one, allowing for a customizable view of the processor instruction set. This allows for creating an instruction set that is well suited to a specific problem domain.

Finally, because a one instruction computer uses such simplified hardware it does not require a high degree of tailoring to a specific implementation. This leads to the possibility of hardware implementation using alternate materials to silicon.

Even with the aforementioned benefits, it is unlikely that anyone would be motivated to build a working OISC. Indeed, OISC might be viewed as "just" a very specialized form of instruction set, one that is so rare that it is unlikely to be of interest. So, why study OISC? One possible answer is that although CISC and RISC are the preeminent instruction set schemes, OISC represents the "worse-case" and therefore is worthy of study as a curiosity.

There are also other reasons. For example, OISC is also very simple, so by examining its properties and features, greater insight can be found in the CISC and RISC architectures. In more complex and varied instruction sets, such features can be hidden.

OISC can also be used as a basis for comparing and contrasting existing instruction sets. Synthesizing the more complex instructions of a particular computer architecture or system is a way to evaluate the instruction set without reference to the architecture. Using OISC then, a more objective and independent metric for examining instruction sets is obtained.

Reconfigurable or "programmable" complete architecture is a new technological trend. Part or all of the architecture can be reconfigured to organize the hardware resources more efficiently for the type of problem being solved. Here OISC allows for one instruction to work consistently with the underlying hardware, which changes for each problem. A more specific instruction set would limit how programmable a reconfigurable architecture could be, reducing the advantage of a reconfigurable computer.

Machine Architecture

In a Turing-complete model, each memory location can store an arbitrary integer, and – depending on the model – there may be arbitrarily many locations. The instructions themselves reside in memory as a sequence of such integers.

There exists a class of universal computers with a single instruction based on bit manipulation such as bit copying or bit inversion. Since their memory model is finite, as is the memory structure used in real computers, those bit manipulation machines are equivalent to real computers rather than to Turing machines.

Currently known OISCs can be roughly separated into three broad categories:

- Bit-manipulating machines

- Transport triggered architecture machines

- Arithmetic-based Turing-complete machines.

Bit-manipulating Machines

Bit-manipulating machines are the simplest class.

BitBitJump

A bit copying machine, called BitBitJump, copies one bit in memory and passes the execution unconditionally to the address specified by one of the operands of the instruction. This process turns out to be capable of universal computation (i.e. being able to execute any algorithm and to interpret any other universal machine) because copying bits can conditionally modify the code that will be subsequently executed.

Toga Computer

Another machine, called the Toga computer, inverts a bit and passes the execution conditionally depending on the result of inversion.

Multi-bit Copying Machine

Yet another bit operating machine, similar to BitBitJump, copies several bits at the same time. The problem of computational universality is solved in this case by keeping predefined jump tables in the memory.

Transport Triggered Architecture

Transport triggered architecture (TTA) is a design in which computation is a side effect of data transport. Usually, some memory registers (triggering ports) within common address space perform an assigned operation when the instruction references them. For example, in an OISC using a single memory-to-memory copy instruction, this is done by triggering ports that perform arithmetic and instruction pointer jumps when written to.

Arithmetic-based Turing-complete Machines

Arithmetic-based Turing-complete machines use an arithmetic operation and a conditional jump. Like the two previous universal computers, this class is also Turing-complete. The instruction operates on integers which may also be addresses in memory.

Currently there are several known OISCs of this class, based on different arithmetic operations:

- Addition (addleq, add and branch if less than or equal to zero)

- Decrement (DJN, decrement and branch (jump) if nonzero)

- Increment (P1eq, plus 1 and branch if equal to another value)

- Subtraction (subleq, subtract and branch if less than or equal)

- Subtraction when possible (Arithmetic machine).

Instruction Types

Common choices for the single instruction are:

- Subtract and branch if less than or equal to zero

- Subtract and branch if negative

- Reverse subtract and skip if borrow

- Move (used as part of a transport triggered architecture)

- Subtract and branch if non zero (SBNZ a, b, c, destination)

- Cryptoleq (heterogeneous encrypted and unencrypted computation).

Only *one* of these instructions is used in a given implementation. Hence, there is no need for an opcode to identify which instruction to execute; the choice of instruction is inherent in the design of the machine, and an OISC is typically named after the instruction it uses (e.g., an SBN OISC, the SUBLEQ language, etc.). Each of the above instructions can be used to construct Turing-complete OISC.

It is possible to construct Turing complete machines using an instruction based on other arithmetic operations, e.g., addition. For example, one variation known as DLN (Decrement and jump if not zero) has only two operands and uses decrement as the base operation.

Subtract and Branch if not Equal to Zero

The SBNZ a, b, c, d instruction (*"subtract and branch if not equal to zero"*) subtracts the contents at address *a* from the contents at address *b*, stores the result at address *c*, and then, *if the result is not 0*, transfers control to address *d* (if the result is equal to zero, execution proceeds to the next instruction in sequence).

Subtract and Branch if Less than or Equal to Zero

The subleq instruction ("*subtract and branch if less than or equal to zero*") subtracts the contents at address a from the contents at address b, stores the result at address b, and then, *if the result is not positive*, transfers control to address c (if the result is positive, execution proceeds to the next instruction in sequence).

Pseudocode:

```
subleq a, b, c    ; Mem[b] = Mem[b] - Mem[a]

                  ; if (Mem[b] ≤ 0) goto c
```

Conditional branching can be suppressed by setting the third operand equal to the address of the next instruction in sequence. If the third operand is not written, this suppression is implied.

A variant is also possible with two operands and an internal accumulator, where the accumulator is subtracted from the memory location specified by the first operand. The result is stored in both the accumulator and the memory location, and the second operand specifies the branch address:

```
subleq2 a, b      ; Mem[a] = Mem[a] - ACCUM

                  ; ACCUM = Mem[a]

                  ; if (Mem[a] ≤ 0) goto b
```

Although this uses only two (instead of three) operands per instruction, correspondingly more instructions are then needed to effect various logical operations.

Synthesized Instructions

It is possible to synthesize many types of higher-order instructions using only the subleq instruction.

Unconditional branch:

```
JMP c

          subleq Z, Z, c
```

Addition can be performed by repeated subtraction, with no conditional branching; e.g., the following instructions result in the content at location a being added to the content at location b:

```
ADD a, b

          subleq a, Z

          subleq Z, b

          subleq Z, Z
```

The first instruction subtracts the content at location a from the content at location Z (which is 0) and stores the result (which is the negative of the content at a) in location Z. The second instruction subtracts this result from b, storing in b this difference (which is now the sum of the contents originally at a and b); the third instruction restores the value 0 to Z.

A copy instruction can be implemented similarly; e.g., the following instructions result in the content at location b getting replaced by the content at location a, again assuming the content at location Z is maintained as 0:

```
MOV a, b
            subleq b, b

            subleq a, Z

            subleq Z, b

            subleq Z, Z
```

Any desired arithmetic test can be built. For example, a branch-if-zero condition can be assembled from the following instructions:

```
BEQ b, c
            subleq b, Z, L1

            subleq Z, Z, OUT

    L1:     subleq Z, Z

            subleq Z, b, c

    OUT:    ...
```

Subleq2 can also be used to synthesize higher-order instructions, although it generally requires more operations for a given task. For example, no fewer than 10 subleq2 instructions are required to flip all the bits in a given byte:

```
NOT a
            subleq2 tmp ; tmp = 0 (tmp = temporary register)

            subleq2 tmp

            subleq2 minus_one ; acc = -1

            subleq2 a ; a' = a + 1

            subleq2 Z ; Z = - a - 1

            subleq2 tmp ; tmp = a + 1

            subleq2 a ; a' = 0

            subleq2 tmp ; load tmp into acc
```

```
subleq2 a ; a' = - a - 1 ( = ~a )

subleq2 Z ; set Z back to 0
```

Emulation

The following program (written in pseudocode) emulates the execution of a subleq-based OISC:

```
int memory[], program_counter, a, b, c

program_counter = 0

while (program_counter >= 0):

    a = memory[program_counter]

    b = memory[program_counter+1]

    c = memory[program_counter+2]

    if (a < 0 or b < 0):

        program_counter = -1

    else:

        memory[b] = memory[b] - memory[a]

    if (memory[b] > 0):

        program_counter += 3

else:

        program_counter = c
```

This program assumes that memory is indexed by *nonnegative* integers. Consequently, for a subleq instruction (a, b, c), the program interprets a < 0, b < 0, or an executed branch to c < 0 as a halting condition. Similar interpreters written in a subleq-based language (i.e., self-interpreters, which may use self-modifying code as allowed by the nature of the subleq instruction) can be found.

Compilation

There is a compiler called Higher Subleq written by Oleg Mazonka that compiles a simplified C program into subleq code.

Subtract and Branch if Negative

The subneg instruction ("*subtract and branch if negative*"), also called SBN, is defined similarly to subleq:

```
subneg a, b, c    ; Mem[b] = Mem[b] - Mem[a]

                  ; if (Mem[b] < 0) goto c
```

Conditional branching can be suppressed by setting the third operand equal to the address of the next instruction in sequence. If the third operand is not written, this suppression is implied.

Synthesized Instructions

It is possible to synthesize many types of higher-order instructions using only the subneg instruction. For simplicity, only one synthesized instruction is shown here to illustrate the difference between subleq and subneg.

Unconditional branch:

```
JMP c

          subneg POS, Z, c

          . . .

      c: subneg Z, Z
```

where Z and POS are locations previously set to contain 0 and a positive integer, respectively.

Unconditional branching is assured only if Z initially contains 0 (or a value less than the integer stored in POS). A follow-up instruction is required to clear Z after the branching, assuming that the content of Z must be maintained as 0.

A variant is also possible with four operands – subneg4. The reversal of minuend and subtrahend eases implementation in hardware. The non-destructive result simplifies the synthetic instructions.

```
subneg4 s, m, r, j       ; subtrahend, minuend, result and jump addresses

                         ; Mem[r] = Mem[m] - Mem[s]

                         ; if (Mem[r] < 0) goto j
```

Arithmetic Machine

In an attempt to make Turing machine more intuitive, Z. A. Melzac consider the task of computing with positive numbers. The machine has an infinite abacus, an infinite number of counters (pebbles, tally sticks) initially at a special location S. The machine is able to do one operation:

```
 Take from location X as many counters as there are in location Y and transfer them
to location Z and proceed to next instruction.

 If this operation is not possible because there is not enough counter in Y, then
leave the abacus as it is an proceed to instruction T.
```

This essentially a subneg where the test is done before rather than after the subtraction, in order to keep all number positive and mimic a human operator computing on a real world abacus.

Pseudocode:

```
 command X, Y, Z, T       ; if (Mem[Y] < Mem[X]) goto T

                         ; Mem[Z] = Mem[Y] - Mem[X]
```

After giving a few programs: multiplication, gcd, computing the nth prime number, representation in base b of an arbitrary number, sorting in order of magnitude, Melzac shows explicitly how to simulate an arbitrary Turing machine on his Arithmetic Machine.

He mentions that it can easily be shown using the elements of recursive functions that every number calculable on the Arithmetic Machine is computable. A proof of which was given by Lambek on a equivalent two instruction machine : X+ (increment X) and X- else T (decrement X if it not empty, else jump to T).

Reverse Subtract and Skip if Borrow

In a *reverse subtract and skip if borrow* (RSSB) instruction, the accumulator is subtracted from the memory location and the next instruction is skipped if there was a borrow (memory location was smaller than the accumulator). The result is stored in both the accumulator and the memory location. The program counter is mapped to memory location 0. The accumulator is mapped to memory location 1.

Example

To set x to the value of y minus z:

```
# First, move z to the destination location x.

RSSB temp # Three instructions required to clear acc, temp

RSSB temp

RSSB temp

RSSB x # Two instructions clear acc, x, since acc is already clear

RSSB x

RSSB y # Load y into acc: no borrow

RSSB temp # Store -y into acc, temp: always borrow and skip

RSSB temp # Skipped

RSSB x # Store y into x, acc

   # Second, perform the operation.

RSSB temp # Three instructions required to clear acc, temp

RSSB temp

RSSB temp

RSSB z # Load z

RSSB x # x = y - z
```

If the value stored at "temp" is initially a negative value and the instruction that executed right before the first "RSSB temp" in this routine borrowed, then four "RSSB temp" instructions will be required for the routine to work.

If the value stored at "z" is initially a negative value then the final "RSSB x" will be skipped and thus the routine will not work.

Transport Triggered Architecture

Transport triggered architecture uses only the move instruction, hence it was originally called a "move machine». This instruction moves the contents of one memory location to another memory location combining with the current content of the new location:

```
move a to b ; Mem[b] := Mem[a] (+, -, *, /, ...) Mem[b]
```

sometimes written as:

```
a -> b ; Mem[b] := Mem[a] (+, -, *, /, ...) Mem[b]
```

The operation performed is defined by the destination memory cell. Some cells are specialized in addition, some other in multiplication, etc. So memory cells are not simple store but coupled with an arithmetic logic unit (ALU) setup to perform only one sort of operation with the current value of the cell. Some of the cells are control flow instructions to alter the program execution with jumps, conditional execution, subroutines, if-then-else, for-loop, etc..

A commercial transport triggered architecture microcontroller has been produced called MAXQ, which hides the apparent inconvenience of an OISC by using a "transfer map" that represents all possible destinations for the move instructions.

Cryptoleq

Cryptoleq processor

Cryptoleq is a language consisting of one, the eponymous, instruction, is capable of performing general-purpose computation on encrypted programs and is a close relative to Subleq. Cryptoleq works on continuous cells of memory using direct and indirect addressing, and performs two operations O_1 and O_2 on three values A, B, and C:

```
Cryptoleq a, b, c        [b] = O₁([a],[b]) ;
```

```
IP = c, if O₂[b] ≤ 0

IP = IP + 3, otherwise
```

where a, b and c are addressed by the instruction pointer, IP, with the value of IP addressing a, IP + 1 point to b and IP + 2 to c.

In Cryptoleq operations O_1 and O_2 are defined as follows:

$$O_1(x,y) = x_{N^2}^{-1} y \bmod N^2$$

$$O_2(x) = \left\lfloor \frac{x-1}{N} \right\rfloor$$

The main difference with Subleq is that in Subleq, $O_1(x,y)$ simply subtracts y from x and $O_2(x)$ equals to x. Cryptoleq is also homomorphic to Subleq, modular inversion and multiplication is homomorphic to subtraction and the operation of O_2 corresponds the Subleq test if the values were unencrypted. A program written in Subleq can run on a Cryptoleq machine, meaning backwards compatibility. Cryptoleq though, implements fully homomorphic calculations and since the model is be able to do multiplications. Multiplication on an encrypted domain is assisted by a unique function G that is assumed to be difficult to reverse engineer and allows re-encryption of a value based on the O_2 operation:

$$G(x,y) = \begin{cases} \tilde{0}, & \text{if } O_2(\overline{x}) \le 0 \\ \tilde{y}, & \text{otherwise} \end{cases}$$

where $\tilde{y}$ is the re-encrypted value of y and $\tilde{0}$ is encrypted zero. x is the encrypted value of a variable, let it be m, and $\overline{x}$ equals $Nm+1$.

The multiplication algorithm is based on addition and subtraction, uses the function G and does not have conditional jumps nor branches. Cryptoleq encryption is based on Paillier cryptosystem.

Zero Instruction Set Computer

ZISC is a general purpose computer architecture unique for its lack of a cpu or instruction set. Computation is distributed to address mapped functional units which pair off and share data under the direction of a simple sequencer. Customary traits of other general purpose architectures; branching, interrupt handling (and multitasking), are present. In addition, ZISC features on the fly configurability to the task at hand.

There is no single ZISC configuration. A requisite minimal set of functional units provide for branching, interrupt handling, etc., but the remainder can be chosen as desired. This means that adders, multipliers, transcendental functions, etc., can be added when an important application needs more performance.

The problem of designing a computer without an instruction set seemed interesting. We took the concept to one possible conclusion and found that there are benefits to a processor without an instruction set.

Motivation

A typical cpu design incorporates the register storage and functional Units necessary to implement the instruction set. Control hardware Oversees instruction fetch, decode and execution. External to the Processor is memory and I/O devices, possibly addressed by a single Address bus and sharing data with the processor via a data bus.

Each instruction is processed in stages: Fetch, Decode, Operand Fetch, Execute and Operand Write back. If the operands are not in registers already, they have to be loaded, either explicitly or implicitly, depending on the architecture. Consider for illustration the process of summing of two integers which are register resident:

- ADD RA,RB,RC

- Fetch instruction

- Decode instruction

- Get register A and register B

- Perform an addition

- Write result back to register C.

With respect to ZISC, a whole instruction cycle has been wasted. Had A and B been pre-associated with the adder, the addition could have been implicit. This would have reduced the process to 4 cycles.

- Fetch instruction

- Decode instruction

- Get register A and register B

- Write the result back to register C.

Furthermore, if operations can be made implicit as a function of the registers chosen, then you can eliminate a large portion of the instruction set. All operations can be accomplished by choosing the correct registers as the destinations of data moves. And if all functional units, registers and data memory can be mapped into the machine address space, then you can simplify the model further, and make all operations implicit, based upon location. This would have the effect of eliminating the instruction set altogether.

Imagine what happens if every component of the computer is memory-mapped. Moving data from memory to registers or from memory to functional units, etc., requires two addresses be generated: one for the source and one for the destination. If you were restricted to a single address bus, it would take two address cycles to move a value from one place to another. But since both the source and destination are known, there isn't a compelling reason to wait two cycles. The source and destination addresses can be accessed simultaneously using two address busses. The net result is a processor of increased efficiency and performance.

```
   left address space                          right address space
        ---
       mem
        ---
       mem
        ---
       ...          /_____\          FU
        ---        <          data bus        >         ---
       FU           \                        /          FU
        ---                                              ---
       FU FU
    _____                        _____
      / \                                    / \
     | | left address bus                   | | right addr bus
     | |_____              _____| |
     |_____    |          |   _____ |
                  | |              | |
            ------------------------------
            left addr | right addr
            =========================== program memory
                  ... | ...            (address pairs)
```

This diagram illustrates the fundamental structure of the ZISC architecture.

It consist of two address busses and a data bus. Every cycle, an "address pair" is presented to the "Left" and "Right" address busses and the chosen functional units are mated. All functions are address-mapped, including pedestrian units like adders, multipliers, etc., and also hardware associated with the operation of the machine itself, like program counters, and the Program Status Word, etc.

Each functional unit occupies a number of addresses dictated by the complement of operands taken in and results returned. For example, consider an integer adder, requiring four addresses.

```
          _____
         | operand 1 | operand 2 |    sum    |   carry   |
         |_____|_____|_____|_____|
  addr: A             A+1         A+2         A+3
```

Addition is performed by mating the adder with its operands. One bit of the address pair has been borrowed in order to designate the direction of the transfer. Here, represented for ZISC, is the addition discussed in the examples above.

```
     ins ~        left address bus      right address bus    dir
   _____|_____|_____|_____
      1          mem addr of operand1    A (operand1)         ->
```

```
2            mem addr of operand1      A+1 (operand2)        ->
3            address for result        A+2 (sum)             <-
```

Functional units may reside on one or both of the two address busses. Multiportedness is not implied, since there still is a single data bus. However, two sets of address decode logic may service each grouping of functional units.

The sequencer or program memory system, presents fixed length address pairs at regular intervals to the two address busses. It operates continuously, at full bandwidth, and is completely independent of the data memory. A multibank scheme allows for zero delay branching. That is, there is no pause in processing when a branch occurs.

Address pairs are fetched from the program memory under direction of of several program counters, one of which will be active, depending on the machine state. A pipelined fetch scheme and address scheme could be used for greater performance.

Several multibanked, non-cached data memory systems have been considered. A data cache is very attractive because of easy applicability and is currently the memory interface of choice.

The ZISC design is multitasking and general purpose.

Functional Units

The layout and use of a ZISC integer adder was detailed above. Several more functional units will considered from a virtually unlimited set of possibilities. Those which are used in direct computation of results have been loosely termed "external" functional units. Those whose operations direct the computer (i.e. the program counter) are called "internal".

The input operands for all external functional units are readable in as well as writable. This is necessary in order to be able to preserve state in case of a context switch. It yields an interesting side effect in that the more functional units a given ZISC configuration contains, the more expensive a context switch becomes.

External Functional Units

Registers

There actually few registers since operations can be cache-to-functional unit and back again. Registers must be readable and writable in order that context may be saved. Since all functional unit input operands share that property, they can be borrowed for temporary storage as well.

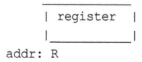

```
        | register  |
        |_____|
addr: R
```

Index Registers

Index registers have a number of possibilities in this architecture, including numerical use. Like any other functional unit, there may be an arbitrary number of them.

```
 _____
| i-registr | increment |
|_____|_____|
addr:  I            I+1
```

A value is written into address "i-registr" and a constant increment (can be negative) can be written to "increment". Each time "i-register" is read the value is bumped:

```
i-registr := i-register + increment.
```

If "increment" is 0 this becomes a general purpose register. The most obvious use is a memory reference index register. Other uses include multiplication of short integers by small numbers.

Logical Operations

```
logical:
 _____
| operand 1 | operand 2 | op1 && op2 | op1 || op2 | op1 >> 1   ....
|_____|_____|_____|_____|_____|__
addr: L       L+1         L+2          L+3          L+4
```

Misc Operations

```
ebcdic -> ascii (for example)

logical:
 _____
| ebcdic in | ascii out |
|_____|_____|
addr:  E           E+1
```

Comparators

These functional units serve both as "select" units and for generating targets for branches.

```
relop: (>,=, etc)

 _____
| operand 1 | operand 2 | target1 in | target2 in | target out | ...
|_____|_____|_____|_____|_____|__
addr: C       C+1         C+2          C+3          C+4
```

Comparators can be used for selecting one of two target values based on the result of <op1 -relop- op2>. If the test is true, "target1 in" will appear at "target out", otherwise "target2 in" will appear.

The functional unit is also employed for generating branch targets, in which case values in "target1" and "target2" will be program addresses. The address presented in "target out" is imposed on the program counter by a subsequent instruction.

Floating Point Functions

To date, our prototypes have not employed any floating point hardware. Generally, such operations will take a number of cycles to complete and will be pipelined. ZISC need not wait for completion of a single floating point calculation, but may focus activity elsewhere and return when the result is ready.

Where considerable parallelism exists, these functions are bandwidth limited.

Internal Functional Units

There is a minimal fixed set of internal functional units that must be present:

- Program Counters (2)
- Program Counter "Stuffs" (2)
- Indirect Memory Address "Stuff"
- Data and Instruction base registers
- PSW

Program Counters

```
Mem Bk #1 <=======++                    ++=======> Mem Bk #2
                  ||                  ___||___
                  ||                 | latch  |
                  ++============>    |_____|
                  ||          _____
                  ++===| PC system  |<----- enable       _____
                  ||   |_____|<=============| PC stuff |<=++==data
 |_____|<====++=addr
                  ++===| PC normal  |<----- enable          || ||
                  |   |_____|<=++                      || ||
          _____        ___||___                           || ||
         | Base |====>|  adder |    _____              || ||
         |_reg__|      |___+___|<=======| PC stuff |<=++ ||
                                   |_____|<====++
```

The program memory for the prototype is made of two banks. While one bank is driving the address busses, the other is being accessed.

Branching occurs without a processing delay. Since the address pair being presented lags the program counter by one cycle, there exists a one instruc-tion window after branch initiation in which to do something which may be of benefit to either of the two possible branch targets, depending on which way the branch is likely to go at runtime.

The program memory always operates at full bandwidth. Our first design includes fast static RAM. A full scale design would require some thoughts about an instruction memory cache backed by a larger, slower memory store.

In use, the program counter appears to be held steady as each of the two banks are presented, in turn, on the address busses. This organization requires that the instructions travel in pairs, and that branches be initiated to the first instruction of a pair, or "first half". For some operations, the two-bank instruction memory scheme necessitates that the two-halves of the instruction be non-symmetric.

Example: Program Counter Stuff functional unit,

In order to branch, the PC must be writable (there are in fact two PCs, one for "system" mode and one for "normal" mode), and in order to save context it must be readable.

To jump, the "PC stuff" is paired with a functional unit or memory containing the target address. The "PC stuff" will ignore negative addresses, and branch to positive ones. This feature facilitates use of the comparator detailed above as a source for branch targets by easing the number of values that need to be supplied. An negative value presented to the "PC stuff" by the comparator will result in a fall through without change of program counter.

The "PC stuff" has a soft restriction in that a target can only be stuffed during the first half of the instruction cycle. The branch target will not take effect until the beginning of the next whole cycle (the clock tick after next). This means that after the jump is initiated, there is a place for an instruction who's result may be available for either the fall through or the branch, depending on whether the branch was taken.

Reading from the PC stuff returns the current value of the Program Counter.

Example: Indirect Stuff,

Consider data memory access. On the Left address bus might appear the memory address of the data item, and on the right, the address of the functional unit where it is to be utilized.

```
ins ~        left address bus       right address bus    dir
_____|_____|_____|_____
  1          memory addr of value     address of FU        ->
```

Assume now that the item loaded from memory was not the desired data, but rather a pointer to the data. How on Earth could this design dereference a pointer? This is a problem since the program and data memories are separate, and the contents of the program memory are being shelled out at full bandwidth all the time, i.e. there is no bandwidth available with which the program memory can modify what it is going to present to the address busses in the future. (Actually, it is possible, though expensive, through I/O). What is needed is a method for forcing a value of the pointer onto one of the address busses at some fixed, predictable time later on.

This functional unit is called the "Indirect Stuff". It overrides the Left Address bus one cycle in the future. It operates a pipeline two deep. The last value stuffed and the state of the pipeline are readable and writable in order to be able to save context

During the first instruction of use, the "Indirect Stuff" receives the value of the pointer. In the second, the data at the address <ptr> is retrieved.

```
ins ~        left address bus       right address bus   dir
_____|_____|_____|_____
   1         addr of indirect stuff address of FU w/ptr    <-
   2              <ptr>                 address of dest. FU    ->
```

Example: Base registers,

Part of a process' context is two base registers, one for data memory addressing and one for program memory addressing. When in "normal" mode, the values in these base registers are added to memory references and branch targets automatically. This allows for programs which are compiled for absolute addresses to run concurrently.

Example: PSW,

The prototype has a primitive interrupt mechanism. Three lines are available, INT1, INT2 and SWI. Activation of any of the above places the machine in "system" mode immediately following the completion of the second half of the current instruction cycle, provided the interrupt occurred before the first half completed. In addition there is a SLEEP line for halting the processor internally or externally and an external WAKE line.

Reading the PSW in "system" mode returns information needed to determine the which line caused the interrupt (there are no vectors). Writing resets lines. Any access to the PSW in "normal" mode causes an SWI. This is the mechanism by which system calls are made.

There are a number of improvements which could be made in the handling of interrupts. The fastest response would be obtained with a set of prioritorized program counters (in lieu of vectors), the highest overriding all the lesser.

I/O System

I/O is all performed via a simple channel protocol involving trading of interrupts and setting reserved status registers. The I/O processor is intended to be a microcomputer with a set of peripherals already attached, such as a PC or clone.

It may seem ironic that an I/O channel protocol has been implemented in machine where all cpu functions are memory-mapped. We have a couple of reasons: First, PCs have a rich set of peripherals and controllers already available. Secondly, some DMA-like protocol was required since the program memory was not designed with the spare bandwidth needed to supervise its own downloading.

To initiate I/O, the processor sets the status registers, and toggles the interrupt line (for the PC) and puts itself to sleep. The PC grabs the status information and wakes the processor back up. When the I/O is complete the PC toggles the processors interrupt line, the processor finds a convenient spot and goes to sleep, and the PC completes the transfer.

Performance

Absolute performance is a function of more than architectural efficiency. However, talking about instruction latency as the number of clock ticks required for completion normalizes the speed of two processors so that they can be compared. Certainly, with semiconductor features approaching the sub-micron range, an external bus oriented architecture will not be able to compete in terms of raw speed with a complete single chip processor. However, the next few years should see a number of optical backplane designs, capable of withstanding nearly unlimited loading, and maintaining a very high bandwidth.

The RISC/CISC argument has been made repeatedly, so it makes sense to describe the ZISC's relative performance in terms of a RISC architecture. Since the arrangement of a given ZISC implementation is arbitrary, and since this paper advocates ZISC, we'll choose to make comparisons employing the optimal selection of functional units.

Some examples:

Here are several narrated examples of code fragments mapped onto a ZISC configuration. For comparison, each is also optimally coded for a SPARC machine, following the SPARC architecture.

Example - null loop body.

In C:
```
for (i=0; i<1000; i++);
```

In SPARC assembler code:
```
mov 0x0,%o0
    L1:
                cmp %o0,0x3e7
                blt L1
                add %o0,0x1,%o0
    L2:
    ...
```

Register oo is zeroed for use as a loop index. When the limit is reached, control is passed to the instruction at L2.

A SPARC machine will execute the instruction immediately following a branch instruction regardless of which way the branch goes (like ZISC). It is for that reason that the add instruction appears following the branch, making optimal use of the cycles.

On a ZISC configuration employing:

a) An index register

```
         _____
        | i-registr | increment |
        |_____|_____|
    addr: I            I+1
```

b) A comparator which tests for >=

```
    relop: >=
```

```
              | operand 1 | operand 2 | target1 in | target2 in | target out |  ...
              |_____|_____|_____|_____|_____|__
       addr: C           C+1         C+2          C+3          C+4
              ins ~        left address bus          right address bus      dir
              _____|_____|_____|_____
                      1      mem addr const.0x3e7    I (i-registr)           ->
                      2      mem addr const. -1      I+1 (increment)         ->
                      3      mem addr const. 0       C (comparator op1)      ->
                      4      mem addr const. -1      C+2 (target 1)          ->
                      5      mem addr const (ins 7)  C+3 (target 2)          ->
                      6      I (i-registr)           C+1 (comparator op2)    ->
                      7      C+4 (target out)        P (prog. ctr)           ->
                      8      I (i-registr)           C+1 (comparator op2)    ->
                      9      .....
```

First the index register is loaded with the loop limit and an increment of -1. Recall that each time the value at 'I' is read, the increment is added to the register value. This will cause the index register to count down from 999 to 0.

Next the comparator is set up so that when 'operand 1' is >= 'operand 2' the address of instruction 7 will appear at 'target out'.

When the test is no longer true, the -1 loaded into 'target 1' will appear at 'target out', causing a fall through to instruction 9.

Recall that the PC Stuff will accept positive addresses and ignore negative ones.

Note that there is a considerable amount of set-up before the loop can be executed. It may be argued that all the steps detailed may not be needed every time, but for sake of argument they will be counted here.

How many cycles will it take for each architecture to complete 1000 iterations of an empty loop (including startup)? SPARC requires 1 + 3000 = 3001 cycles. ZISC requires 6 + 2000 = 2006 cycles.

Example - simple integer arithmetic through pointers,

In C:
```
foo (a,b,c)
int *a, *b, *c;
{
        int x;
        x = *a + *b;
        if (x > *c)
                *c = x;
}
```

In SPARC assembler:
```
                    ...
            ld          [%fp+0x0],%o0
```

```
        ld      [%o0],%o1
        ld      [%fp+0x4],%o0
        ld      [%o0],%o2
        add     %o3,%o2,%o1
        ld      [%fp+0x8],%o0
        ld      [%o0],%o4
        cmp     %o3,%o4
        bgt     L1
        nop
        b       L2
L1:     st      [%o0],%o3
        ...
```

The argument pointer is assumed to point an argument list consisting of the addresses *a, *b and *c. Each load/store operation requires 2 cycles to complete.

On a ZISC configuration employing:

a) An index register

```
        |  i-registr  |  increment  |
        |_____|_____|
addr:  I                  I+1
```

b) A comparator which tests for >=

```
  relop: >=
```

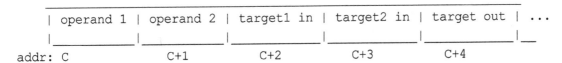

```
        | operand 1 | operand 2 | target1 in | target2 in | target out |  ...
        |_____|_____|_____|_____|_____|__
addr:  C              C+1          C+2          C+3          C+4
```

c) One adder

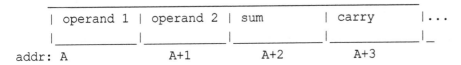

```
        | operand 1 | operand 2 | sum        | carry      |  ...
        |_____|_____|_____|_____|_
addr:  A              A+1          A+2          A+3
```

d) Two g.p. registers

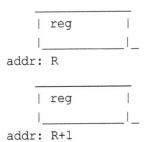

```
        | reg         |
        |_____|_
addr:  R

        | reg         |
        |_____|_
addr:  R+1
```

e) indirect stuff (standard in any configuration)

```
ins ~ left address bus        right address bus    dir
_____|_____|_____|_____
    1      mem addr const 0x4   I+1 (i-reg incr)      ->
    2      fp                   I (i-register)        ->
    3      I (i-register)       indirect stuff        ->
    4      [indirect stuff *(*a)] indirect stuff      ->
    5      [indirect stuff (*a)] A (adder1, op1)      ->
    6      I (i-register)       indirect stuff        ->
    7      [indirect stuff *(*b)]  indirect stuff     ->
    8      [indirect stuff (*b)]  A+1 (adder1, op2)   ->
    9      A+3 (adder1, sum)    C+2 (target 1)        ->
   10      I (i-register)       indirect stuff        ->
   11      [indirect stuff *(*c)] R (g.p. reg1)       ->
   12      R (g.p. reg1)        indirect stuff        ->
   13      [indirect stuff (*c)] C+3 (target 2)       ->
   14      C+3 (target 2)       R+1 (g.p. reg2)       ->
   15      R+1 (g.p. reg2)      C (comparator op1)    ->
   16      A+2 (adder sum)      C+1 (comparator op2)  ->
           17 R (g.p. reg1)     indirect stuff        ->
   18      [indirect stuff (*c)] target out           <-
```

The designation "fp" in the above example is made for clarity in comparison with the SPARC code fragment. It is assumed to be a general purpose register whose use is designated as a frame pointer. The index register is employed to step through the argument list. The increment is loaded with the value "4", the presumption being that each address is separated by 4 bytes. Recall that each time the index register is read its value is bumped. The value of *c is temporarily squirreled away into reg1 so that it will be available later should the value for 'c' need to be modified.

Notice the use of the "indirect stuff". The index register first supplies the address of the address of the desired variable, which is turned around through the indirect stuff to obtain the address of the variable, and finally the value of the variable itself.

No branch is made in this example, rather the comparator is used to 'select' either the value of 'x' or the value of 'c' for return to storage.

Each architecture, ZISC and SPARC, requires 18 cycles to complete the operation and return the result to memory.

Example:

Here is a code fragment where ZISC's configurability allows oneconfiguration to drastically outperform a standard processordesign:

Compute a^2 + 2ab + b^2, where a,b are halfword integers on a ZISC configuration employing 3 multipliers and two adders. Assume that the integer multipliers are not pipelined and require 6 cycles toproduce a product. The configuration contains:

a) Two adders

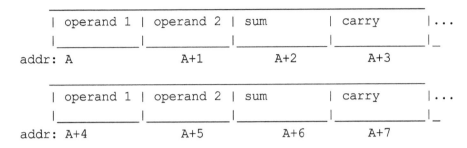

```
         _____
        | operand 1 | operand 2 | sum      | carry      |...
        |_____|_____|_____|_____|_
  addr: A           A+1         A+2         A+3

         _____
        | operand 1 | operand 2 | sum      | carry      |...
        |_____|_____|_____|_____|_
  addr: A+4         A+5         A+6         A+7
```

b) Three halfword multipliers

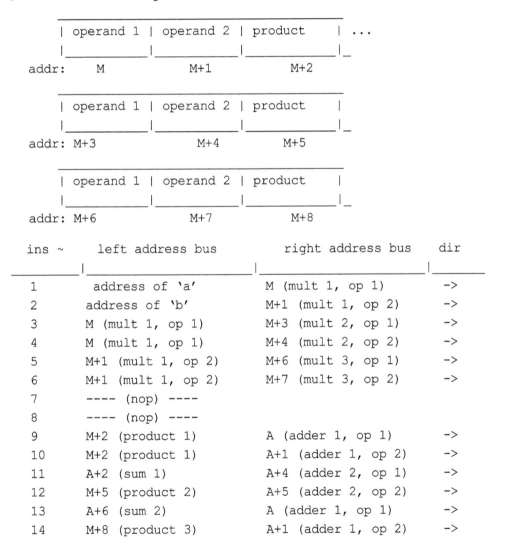

```
         _____
        | operand 1 | operand 2 | product  | ...
        |_____|_____|_____|_
  addr:    M           M+1         M+2

         _____
        | operand 1 | operand 2 | product  |
        |_____|_____|_____|_
  addr: M+3          M+4         M+5

         _____
        | operand 1 | operand 2 | product  |
        |_____|_____|_____|_
  addr: M+6          M+7         M+8
```

ins ~	left address bus	right address bus	dir
1	address of 'a'	M (mult 1, op 1)	->
2	address of 'b'	M+1 (mult 1, op 2)	->
3	M (mult 1, op 1)	M+3 (mult 2, op 1)	->
4	M (mult 1, op 1)	M+4 (mult 2, op 2)	->
5	M+1 (mult 1, op 2)	M+6 (mult 3, op 1)	->
6	M+1 (mult 1, op 2)	M+7 (mult 3, op 2)	->
7	---- (nop) ----		
8	---- (nop) ----		
9	M+2 (product 1)	A (adder 1, op 1)	->
10	M+2 (product 1)	A+1 (adder 1, op 2)	->
11	A+2 (sum 1)	A+4 (adder 2, op 1)	->
12	M+5 (product 2)	A+5 (adder 2, op 2)	->
13	A+6 (sum 2)	A (adder 1, op 1)	->
14	M+8 (product 3)	A+1 (adder 1, op 2)	->

The total time to complete the operation is 14 cycles.

References

- Page, Daniel (2009). "11. Compilers". A Practical Introduction to Computer Architecture. Springer. p. 464. ISBN 978-1-84882-255-9

- What-is-risc-and-cisc-architecture: edgefxkits.com, Retrieved 20 June 2018

- "EEMBC Publishes Benchmark Scores for Infineon Technologies' Carmel® DSP Core and TriCore® TC11IB Microcontroller". eembc.org. Retrieved 2016-07-28

- Oleg Mazonka, "Bit Copying: The Ultimate Computational Simplicity", Complex Systems Journal 2011, Vol 19, N3, pp. 263–285

- VLIW-very-long-instruction-word: techtarget.com, Retrieved 15 April 2018

- Catsoulis, John (2005), Designing embedded hardware (2 ed.), O'Reilly Media, pp. 327–333, ISBN 978-0-596-00755-3

- Crystal Chen; Greg Novick; Kirk Shimano (December 16, 2006). "RISC Architecture: RISC vs. CISC". cs.stanford.edu. Retrieved February 21, 2015

Central Processing Unit

A central processing unit or the CPU is the electronic circuitry within a computer, which carries out basic logical, arithmetic, control and input/output operations. This chapter discusses in detail the different elements of a central processing unit, such as control unit, arithmetic logic unit, CPU modes, microprocessor, scalar processor, coprocessor, etc.

Central processing unit (CPU) is the central component of the computer system. Sometimes it is called as microprocessor or processor. It is the brain that runs the show inside the computer. All functions and processes that is done on a computer is performed directly or indirectly by the processor. Obviously, computer processor is one of the most important elements of the computer system. CPU is consist of transistors, that receives inputs and produces output. Transistors perform logical operations which is called processing. It is also, scientifically, not only one of the most amazing parts of the PC, but one of the most amazing devices in the world of technology.

In terms of computing power, the *computer processor* is the most important element of a computer system. It add and compare its data in CPU chip.

CPU speed of executing an instruction depends on its clock frequency which is measured in MHz (megahertz) or GHz (gigahertz), more the clock frequency, more is the speed of computer's instruction execution.

Actual Working

Now let's try to understand the working of the CPU. Whenever a data or some instruction or program is requested by the user, the CPU draws it from the RAM (Random Access Memory) and might some other hardware for the purpose.

Now before sending the information back to the RAM, the CPU reads the information associated with the task given to it. After reading the information, the CPU starts its calculation and transporting the data.

Before the data is further executed, it has to travel through the System BUS. A bus in the computer is a communication system that is used to transfer the data among all the components of the computer.

The duty of the CPU is to make sure that the data is processed and is on the system bus. The CPU manages data to make it in a correct order while arranging the data on the system bus. Thus, the action requested by the user is done and the user gets the processed and calculated information. Now when the data is processed, the CPU is required to store it in the system's memory.

So, this is how actually a CPU works.

Components of CPU

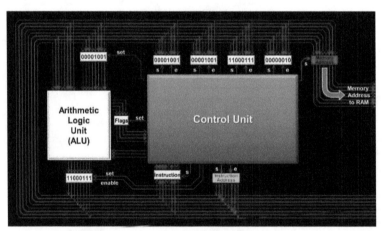

A Typical CPU Consists Of 2 Parts:

- Control Unit
- Logic Unit

Control Unit: This part of CPU is used to manage the operation of the CPU. It commands the various computer components to react according to the program's instruction. The computer programs are stored in the storage devices (hard disks and SSDs) and when a user run those programs, they load directly into the primary memory (RAM) for their execution. No program can be able to run without loading into primary memory. The control unit of the CPU is used to direct the whole computer system to process program's instruction using electrical signals. The control unit of a CPU communicates with ALU and memory to carry out the process instructions. Actually the control unit does not carry out the instruction of the program, instead, it commands the other part of the process. Without the control unit, the respective components will not be able to execute the program as they don't know what to do and when to do.

Logic Unit: Logic unit is also referred as Arithmetic Logic Unit (ALU). The ALU is a digital electronic circuit placed inside the CPU. Logic Unit is the basic building block of the CPU. The function of the ALU is to perform integer calculation and bitwise logic operations. Calculation of ALU includes addition, subtraction, shifting operations and Boolean comparisons (like AND, OR, XOR and NOT operations). The ALUs of different processor models may differ in design and functioning. In some simple computer, the processor may contain only one ALU while in the complex computer; the processor may have more than one ALU which work simultaneously to perform all the calculations. But we should remember that the main job of ALU is to calculate integer operations.

More Basic Elements of CPU

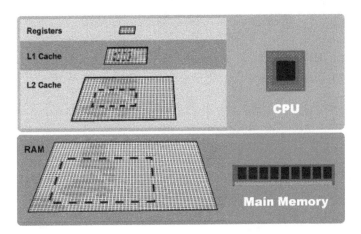

Register: A register is a very small place which is used to hold data of the processor. A register is used to store information such as instruction, storage address and any kind of data like bit sequence or any characters etc. A processor's register should be large enough to store all the given information. A 64-bit processor should have at least 64-bit registers and 32-bit register for a 32-bit processor. The register is the fastest of all the memory devices.

L1 and L2 Cache Memory: Cache Memory is a type of memory which is placed in the processor's chip or may be placed separately connected by a bus. The use of Cache Memory is to store program instructions which are again and again used by software for an operation. When the CPU processes data, the data is first looked into the cache memory. If the data is found, then it uses the data accordingly and if not, then the processor start to look in the larger memory, which is actually time-consuming. Cache memory is costly but it's really lightning fast.

There are levels of cache memory, they are as follows:

- L1 cache: L1 cache is extraordinary fast but it is very small. It is mainly placed on the CPU chip.

- L2 cache: L2 cache has more data holding capacity than L1 cache. It is situated in CPU chip or in the separate chip but connected to CPU with the high-speed alternative data bus.

Something about Multi-core CPUs

Nowadays computer comes with a multi-core processor. The multi-core processor means that more than one processor is embedded in the CPU Chip. Those multi-core processors work simultaneously and the main advantages of using the multi-core CPU is that it quickly achieved the high performance, consuming less energy power and the multi-tasking or parallel processing is really efficient. Since all the processor is plugged into the same plug so the connection between them is also actually fast.

Different Multi Core Processor Difference

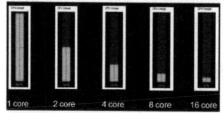

Dual Core Processor: In this, Dual or 2 processors are embedded in the chip and they work simultaneously. Multi-tasking is more than the single core processor.

Quad Core Processor: In this, Quad or 4 processors are embedded in the chip and work simultaneously. They are faster than dual core processor. Multi-tasking is more than the dual core processor.

Hexa Core Processor: In this, Hexa or 6 processors are embedded in the chip and work simultaneously. They are faster than quad core processor. Multi-tasking is more than the quad core processor.

Octa Core Processor: In this, Octa or 8 processors are embedded in the chip and they work simultaneously. They are faster than the hexacore processor.

Control Unit

A control unit (CU) handles all processor control signals. It directs all input and output flow, fetches code for instructions from micro programs and directs other units and models by providing control and timing signals. A CU component is considered the processor brain because it issues orders to just about everything and ensures correct instruction execution.

CU functions are as follows:

- Controls sequential instruction execution
- Interprets instructions
- Guides data flow through different computer areas
- Regulates and controls processor timing

- Sends and receives control signals from other computer devices

- Handles multiple tasks, such as fetching, decoding, execution handling and storing results.

Design of Control Unit

Control unit generates timing and control signals for the operations of the computer. The control unit communicates with ALU and main memory. It also controls the transmission between processor, memory and the various peripherals. It also instructs the ALU which operation has to be performed on data.

Control unit can be designed by two methods which are given below.

Hardwired Control Unit

It is implemented with the help of gates, flip flops, decoders etc. in the hardware. The inputs to control unit are the instruction register, flags, timing signals etc. This organization can be very complicated if we have to make the control unit large.

If the design has to be modified or changed, all the combinational circuits have to be modified which is a very difficult task.

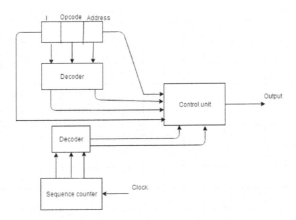

Microprogrammed Control Unit

It is implemented by using programming approach. A sequence of micro operations is carried out by executing a program consisting of micro-instructions. In this organization any modifications or changes can be done by updating the micro program in the control memory by the programmer.

Difference between Hardwired Control and Microprogrammed Control

Hardwired Control	Microprogrammed Control
Technology is circuit based.	Technology is software based.
It is implemented through flip-flops, gates, decoders etc.	Microinstructions generate signals to control the execution of instructions.

Fixed instruction format.	Variable instruction format (16-64 bits per instruction).
Instructions are register based.	Instructions are not register based.
ROM is not used.	ROM is used.
It is used in RISC.	It is used in CISC.
Faster decoding.	Slower decoding.
Difficult to modify.	Easily modified.
Chip area is less.	Chip area is large.

Arithmetic Logic Unit

An arithmetic-logic unit (ALU) is the part of a computer processor (CPU) that carries out arithmetic and logic operations on the operands in computer instruction words. In some processors, the ALU is divided into two units, an arithmetic unit (AU) and a logic unit (LU). Some processors contain more than one AU - for example, one for *fixed-point* operations and another for *floating-point* operations. (In personal computers floating point operations are sometimes done by a floating point unit on a separate chip called a numeric coprocessor.)

Typically, the ALU has direct input and output access to the processor controller, main memory (random access memory or RAM in a personal computer), and input/output devices. Inputs and outputs flow along an electronic path that is called a bus. The input consists of an instruction word (sometimes called a machine instruction word) that contains an operation code (sometimes called an "op code"), one or more operands, and sometimes a format code. The operation code tells the ALU what operation to perform and the operands are used in the operation. (For example, two operands might be added together or compared logically.) The format may be combined with the op code and tells, for example, whether this is a fixed-point or a floating-point instruction. The output consists of a result that is placed in a storage *register* and settings that indicate whether the operation was performed successfully. (If it isn't, some sort of status will be stored in a permanent place that is sometimes called the machine status word).

In general, the ALU includes storage places for input operands, operands that are being added, the accumulated result (stored in an *accumulator*), and shifted results. The flow of bits and the operations performed on them in the subunits of the ALU is controlled by gated circuits. The gates in these circuits are controlled by a sequence logic unit that uses a particular algorithm or sequence for each operation code. In the arithmetic unit, multiplication and division are done by a series of adding or subtracting and shifting operations. There are several ways to represent negative numbers. In the logic unit, one of 16 possible logic operations can be performed - such as comparing two operands and identifying where bits don't match.

The design of the ALU is obviously a critical part of the processor and new approaches to speeding up instruction handling are continually being developed.

The three fundamental attributes of an ALU are its operands and results, functional organization, and algorithms.

Operands and Results

The operands and results of the ALU are machine words of two kinds: *arithmetic words,* which represent numerical values in digital form, and *logic words,* which represent arbitrary sets of digitally encoded symbols. Arithmetic words consist of digit vectors (strings of digits).

Operator: Operator is arithmetic or logical operation that is performed on the operand given in instructions.

Flag: ALU uses many types of the flag during processing instructions. All these bits are stored in status or flag registers.

Functional Organization of an ALU

A typical ALU consists of three types of functional parts: storage registers, operations logic, and sequencing logic.

Arithmetic Logical Unit (ALU) Architecture

ALU is formed through the combinational circuit. The combinational circuit used logical gates like AND, OR, NOT, XOR for their construction. The combinational circuit does not have any memory element to store a previous data bit. Adders are the main part of the arithmetic logic unit to perform addition, subtraction by 2's complement.

Control unit generates the selection signals for selecting the function performed by ALU.

Registers: Registers are a very important component in ALU to store instruction, intermediate data, output, and input.

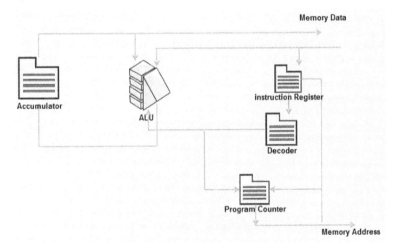

Logic Gates

Logic gates are building a block of ALU. Logic gates are constructed from diode, resistors or transistors. These gates are used in Integrated circuit represent binary input as 'ON' and 'OFF' state. Binary number 0 is represented by 'OFF' and Binary Number '1' is represented by 'ON' state in an integrated circuit.

OR gate: OR gate can take two or more inputs. The output of OR gate is always 1 if any of the inputs is 1 and 0 if all the inputs are false. OR gate performs an addition operation on all operand given in instructions. It can be expressed as X=A+B or X=A+B+C.

OR

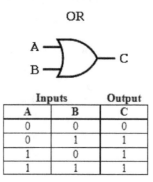

Inputs		Output
A	B	C
0	0	0
0	1	1
1	0	1
1	1	1

AND gate: AND gate takes two or more inputs. The output of AND gate is 1 if all inputs are 1. AND gate gives 0 results if any one of input in given data is 0. AND gate performs multiplication option on all inputs operands. It is represented by '.' symbol. We can write it as- X=A.B or X=A.B.C.

AND

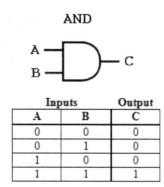

Inputs		Output
A	B	C
0	0	0
0	1	0
1	0	0
1	1	1

NOT gate: NOT gate is used to reverse the result of gates or reverse Boolean state from 0 to 1 and 1 to 0. NOT gate is also used with 'AND' and 'OR' gate. While using with AND or 'OR' gate, NOT gate is representing an as small circle in front of both gates. After using NOT gate, AND gates convert into NAND or 'OR' gate convert into NOR.

NOT

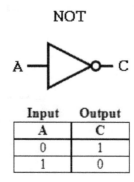

Input	Output
A	C
0	1
1	0

Registers: Registers provide fast memory access as a comparison to cache, RAM, hard disk. They are built on CPU. Register are small in size. Processing Intermediate data stored in registers. A number of registers used for specific purpose. ALU used four general purpose register. All these four registers are 16-bit register is divided into registers. 16-bit register implies that register can store maximum 16 bit of data.

Accumulator: Accumulator is 16 bit by default and general purpose register. By default means that any operand in instruction does not specify a particular register for holding the operand. That time operand will automatically store in AC. AC is used as two separate registers of 7 bit AL and AH. AC located inside the ALU. Intermediate data and result after execution will store in AC.AC used MBR to deal with memory.

Program counter: PC stands for program counter. *It is 16-bit register*. It counts the number of instruction left for execution. It acts as a pointer for instructions and also known as Instruction pointer register. PC holds the address of next instruction to be executed. When an instruction is fetched from the register. Register get automatically incremented by one and point to the address of next instruction.

Flag register: it is also known as a Status register or Program Status register. Flag register holds the Boolean value of status word used by the process.

Auxiliary flag: if two numbers are to be added such that if in the beginning of higher bit there is a carry. This is known as auxiliary bit.

Carry bit: Carry bit is indicate the most significant borrow or carry bit by subtracting a greater number than a smaller number or adding two numbers.

Sign Bit: Sign bit is a most significant bit in 2's complement to show that result is negative or positive. It is also known as negative bit. If the final carry over here after the sum of last most significant bit is 1, it is dropped and the result is positive.

If there is no carry over here then 2's complement will negative and negative bit set as 1.

Overflow bit: Overflow bit used to indicate that stack is overflow or not after processing the instruction. It is set to be 1 means that stack is overflow if it is 0 then its reverse to happen.

Parity bit: Parity bit represent odd or even set of '1' bits in given string. It is used as error detecting code. Parity bit has two types: Even parity bit and an Odd parity bit.

In even parity bit, we count the occurrence of I's in the string. If a number of 1 bit is odd in counting than we will add even parity bit to make it even or if the number of 1 bit are even then even parity bit is 0.

Data	*Number of 1 bits*	*even parity bit*	*Data including Even Parity bit*
1010111	*5*	*1*	*11010111*

Memory Address register: Address register holds the address of memory where data is residing. CPU fetches the address from the register and access the location to acquire data. In the same way, MAR is used to write the data into memory.

Data register: Data registers also Known as Memory Data Register. It holds the content or instruction fetched from memory location for reading and writing purpose. It is 16-bit register means that can store 2^{16} bytes of data. From Data, register instruction moves in Instruction register and data content moves to AC for manipulation.

Instruction register: Instruction holds the instruction to be executed. Control unit of CPU fetch the instruction, decode it and execute the instruction by accessing appropriate content.IR is 16-bit register. It has two fields – Opcode and operand.

PC holds the address of the instruction to be executed. Once the address is fetched it gets incremented by 1.PC hold the address of next instructions. In this situation, IR holds the address of the current instruction.

Input /output register: Input register holds the input from input devices and output register hold the output that has to give to output devices.

Memory Management Unit

A computer's memory management unit (MMU) is the physical hardware that handles its virtual memory and caching operations. The MMU is usually located within the computer's central processing unit (CPU), but sometimes operates in a separate integrated chip (IC). All data request inputs are sent to the MMU, which in turn determines whether the data needs to be retrieved from RAM or ROM storage.

A memory management unit is also known as a paged memory management unit.

The memory management unit performs three major functions:

- Hardware memory management

- Operating system (OS) memory management

- Application memory management.

Hardware memory management deals with a system's RAM and cache memory, OS memory management regulates resources among objects and data structures, and application memory management allocates and optimizes memory among programs.

The MMU also includes a section of memory that holds a table that matches virtual addresses to physical addresses, called the translation look a side buffer (TLB).

Many microprocessors and microcontrollers incorporate a memory management unit (MMU) or have one available as an option. Equally, there are some devices that have no MMU support and many systems are built without one anyway.

We need to think in terms of logical addresses, which are what the software deals with, and physical addresses, which are seen by the hardware (the memory system). If there is no MMU, logical and physical addresses are the same. An MMU changes the mapping between logical and physical addresses.

Obviously, the simplest thing an MMU can do is map the logical addresses straight on to their physical counterparts.

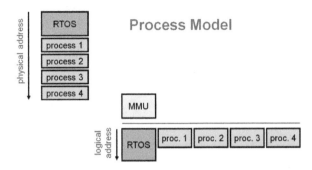

A common use of an MMU is to implement an operating system using process model – like Linux. In this case, each task has one or more dedicated areas of memory for its code and data. When a task is made current by the scheduler, the MMU maps these physical addresses onto a logical address area starting from 0. All the physical memory belonging to other tasks (processes) and to the OS itself is hidden from view and, thus, protected. Each process behaves as if it has free use of the entire CPU. Although this mechanism is safe and elegant, it has the drawback that there is an overhead – the MMU remapping – on every context switch.

Another approach is to implement a lightweight process model (also called "thread protected mode"). In most RTOSes, an MMU has not been traditionally used (or available) and all memory is visible at all times. If the MMU is set up in the trivial way I mentioned earlier, parts of the mapping may be switched off as each task is scheduled. Thus, no remapping of addresses occurs, but only the memory for the current task, and relevant parts of the OS, is visible at any one time. This provides much of the protection of process model, with a lower overhead on each context switch.

CPU Modes

Processor Mode also called as CPU modes or CPU "privilege level". The CPU modes are used by processor to create an operating environment for automatic. Specifically, the CPU mode controls how the processor sees and manages the system memory and task that use it. There are three different modes of operation but one more mode is added for new 64 bit processor:

1. Real Mode.

2. Protected Mode.

3. Virtual Mode Real Mode.

4. 64 bit extension Mode.

Real Mode

The original IBM PC could only address 1MB of system memory and the original versions of DOS created to work on it were designed with this in mind. DOS is it's by nature a single tasking operating system meaning it can only handle one program running at a time. The decision made in this early days have carried forward until now and in each new processor care had to be taken to be able to put the processor in a mode that would be compatible with the original Intel 8088 chip. This is called Real Mode. Real mode is of course used by DOS and "standard" DOS application.

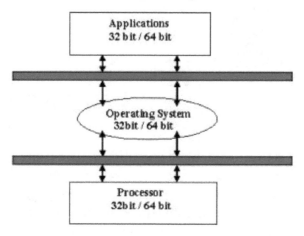

Protected Mode

Starting with the 80286 chip in the IBM AT, a new CPU mode was published called protected mode. This is much more powerful mode of operation than real mode and is used in all modern multitasking operating systems. The advantages of protected mode (compared to real mode) are:

- Full access to all of the system memory. There is no1 MB limitation in mode.

- Ability to multiple tasking meaning having the operating system manages the execution of multiple programs simultaneously.

- Preference to for virtual memory which gives the permission the system to use the hard disk to emulate additional system memory when needed.

- Faster (32 bit) access to memory and faster 32 bit drivers to do I/O transfer.

The name of this mode comes from its primary use which is multitasking operating system. Each program that is running has its own assigned memory location which is protected from conflict with other programs. If a program tries to access a memory address that it isn't allowed to a "protection fault" is generated.

Protected mode is now used by the most people use their PCs.

Virtual Mode

This mode is also called virtual 8086 mode. The third mode of operation is actually an some more capability, an enhancement of protected mode. The use Protected mode is for to run graphical multitasking operating system such as the various types of windows. There is often desire to be able to run DOS program under the window, but DOS programs need to be run in the real mode not protected mode. Virtual real mode is used to solve this problem. Virtual real mode is also used when you use a DOS box or run a DOS game in Windows 95.

64 Bit Extension Mode

This mode is also called Long Mode. 64 bit extension mode is the mode where a 64 bit application can access the 64 bit instruction and registers while 32 bit and 16 bit programs are executed in a compatibility sub mode.

Multi-core Processor

A multicore processor is a single integrated circuit (a.k.a., chip multiprocessor or CMP) that contains multiple core processing units, more commonly known as *cores*. There are many different multicore processor architectures, which vary in terms of:

- Number of cores: Different multicore processors often have different numbers of cores. For example, a quad-core processor has four cores. The number of cores is usually a power of two.

- Number of core types:

  o Homogeneous (symmetric) cores. All of the cores in a homogeneous multicore processor are of the same type; typically the core processing units are general-purpose central processing units that run a single multicore operating system.

  o Heterogeneous (asymmetric) cores. Heterogeneous multicore processors have a mix of core types that often run different operating systems and include graphics processing units.

- Number and level of caches: Multicore processors vary in terms of their instruction and data caches, which are relatively small and fast pools of local memory.

- How cores are interconnected: Multicore processors also vary in terms of their bus architectures.

- Isolation. The amount, typically minimal, of in-chip support for the spatial and temporal isolation of cores:

  o Physical isolation ensures that different cores cannot access the same physical hardware (e.g., memory locations such as caches and RAM).

  o Temporal isolation ensures that the execution of software on one *core* does not impact the temporal behavior of software running on another *core*.

Homogeneous Multicore Processor

The following figure notionally shows the architecture of a system in which 14 software applications are allocated by a single host operating system to the cores in a homogeneous quad-core processor. In this architecture, there are three levels of cache, which are progressively larger but slower: L1 (consisting of an instruction cache and a data cache), L2, and L3. Note that the L1 and L2 caches are local to a single core, whereas L3 is shared among all four cores.

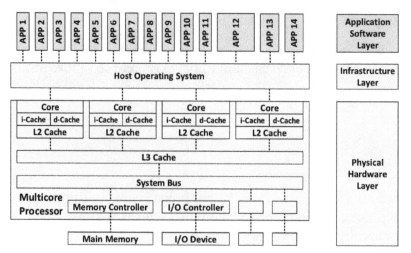

Heterogeneous multicore processor

The following figure notionally shows how these 14 applications could be allocated to four different operating systems, which in turn are allocated to four different cores, in a heterogeneous, quad-core processor. From left to right, the cores include a general-purpose central processing unit core running Windows; a graphical processing unit (GPU) core running graphics-intensive applications on Linux; a digital signal processing (DSP) core running a real-time operating system (RTOS); and a high-performance core also running an RTOS.

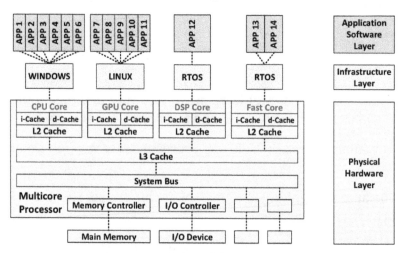

Current trends in multicore processing

Multicore processors are replacing traditional, single-core processors so that fewer single-core processors are being produced and supported. Consequently, single-core processors are becoming technologically obsolete. Heterogeneous multicore processors, such as computer-on-a-chip processors, are becoming more common.

Although multicore processors have largely saturated some application domains (e.g., cloud computing, data warehousing, and on-line shopping), they are just starting to be used in real-time, safety- and security-critical, cyber-physical systems. One area in which multicore processing is becoming popular is in environments constrained by size, weight, and power, and cooling (SWAP-C), in which significantly increased performance is required.

Pros of Multicore Processing

Multicore processing is typically commonplace because it offers advantages in the following seven areas:

1. Energy Efficiency: By using multicore processors, architects can decrease the number of embedded computers. They overcome increased heat generation due to Moore's Law (i.e., smaller circuits increase electrical resistance, which creates more heat), which in turn decreases the need for cooling. The use of multicore processing reduces power consumption (less energy wasted as heat), which increases battery life.

2. True Concurrency: By allocating applications to different cores, multicore processing increases the intrinsic support for actual (as opposed to virtual) parallel processing within individual software applications across multiple applications.

3. Performance: Multicore processing can increase performance by running multiple applications concurrently. The decreased distance between cores on an integrated chip enables shorter resource access latency and higher cache speeds when compared to using separate processors or computers. However, the size of the performance increase depends on the number of cores, the level of real concurrency in the actual software, and the use of shared resources.

4. Isolation: Multicore processors *may* improve (but do *not* guarantee) spatial and temporal isolation (segregation) compared to single-core architectures. Software running on one core is less likely to affect software on another core than if both are executing on the same single core. This decoupling is due to both spatial isolation (of data in core-specific cashes) and temporal isolation, because threads on one core are not delayed by threads on another core. Multicore processing may also improve robustness by localizing the impact of defects to single core. This increased isolation is particularly important in the independent execution of mixed-criticality applications (mission-critical, safety critical, and security-critical).

5. Reliability and Robustness: Allocating software to multiple cores increases reliability and robustness (i.e., fault and failure tolerance) by limiting fault and/or failure propagation from software on one core to software on another. The allocation of software to multiple cores also supports failure tolerance by supporting failover from one core to another (and subsequent recovery).

6. Obsolescence Avoidance: The use of multicore processors enables architects to avoid technological obsolescence and improve maintainability. Chip manufacturers are applying the latest technical advances to their multicore chips. As the number of cores continues to increase, it becomes increasingly hard to obtain single-core chips.

7. Hardware Costs: By using multicore processors, architects can produce systems with fewer computers and processors.

Cons of Multicore Processing

Although there are many advantages to moving to multicore processors, architects must address disadvantages and associated risks in the following six areas:

1. Shared Resources: Cores on the same processor share both *processor-internal* resources (L3 cache, system bus, memory controller, I/O controllers, and interconnects) and *processor-external* resources (main memory, I/O devices, and networks). These shared resources imply (1) the existence of single points of failure, (2) two applications running on the *same* core can interfere with each other, and (3) software running on one core can impact software running on *another* core (i.e., interference can violate spatial and temporal isolation because multicore support for isolation is limited). The diagram below uses the color red to illustrate six shared resources.

2. Interference: Interference occurs when software executing on one core impacts the behavior of software executing on other cores in the same processor. This interference includes failures of both *spatial* isolation (due to shared memory access) and failure of *temporal* isolation (due to interference delays and/or penalties). Temporal isolation is a bigger problem than spatial isolation since multicore processors may have special hardware that can be used to enforce spatial isolation (to prevent software running on different cores from accessing the same processor-internal memory). The number of interference paths increases rapidly with the number of cores and the exhaustive analysis of all interference paths is often impossible. The impracticality of exhaustive analysis necessitates the selection of representative interference paths when analyzing isolation. The following diagram uses the color red to illustrate three possible interference paths between pairs of applications involving six shared resources.

3. Concurrency Defects: Cores execute concurrently, creating the potential for concurrency defects including deadlock, livelock, starvation, suspension, (data) race conditions, priority inversion, order violations, and atomicity violations. Note that these are essentially the same types of concurrency defects that can occur when software is allocated to multiple threads on a single core.

4. Non-determinism: Multicore processing increases non-determinism. For example, I/O Interrupts have top-level hardware priority (also a problem with single core processors). Multicore processing is also subject to lock trashing, which stems from excessive lock conflicts due to simultaneous access of kernel services by different cores (resulting in decreased concurrency and performance). The resulting non-deterministic behavior can be unpredictable, can cause related faults and failures, and can make testing more difficult (e.g., running the same test multiple times may not yield the same test result).

5. Analysis Difficulty: The real concurrency due to multicore processing requires different memory consistency models than virtual interleaved concurrency. It also breaks traditional analysis approaches for work on single core processors. The analysis of maximum time limits is harder and may be overly conservative. Although interference analysis becomes more complex as the number of cores-per-processor increases, overly-restricting the core number may not provide adequate performance.

6. Accreditation and Certification: Interference between cores can cause missed deadlines and excessive jitter, which in turn can cause faults (hazards) and failures (accidents). Verifying a multicore system requires proper real-time scheduling and timing analysis and/or specialized performance testing. Moving from a single-core to a multicore architecture

may require recertification. Unfortunately, current safety policy guidelines are based on single-core architectures and must be updated based on the recommendations that will be listed in the final blog entry in this series.

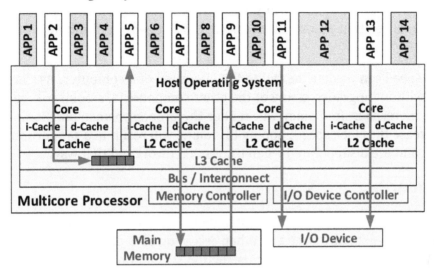

SEI-research on Multicore Processing

Real-time scheduling on multicore processing platforms is a Department of Defense (DoD) technical area of urgent concern for unmanned aerial vehicles (UAVs) and other systems that demand ever-increasing computational power. SEI researchers have provided a range of techniques and tools that improve scheduling on multicore processors. We developed a mode-change protocol for multicores with several operational modes, such as aircraft taxi, takeoff, flight, and landing modes. The SEI developed the first protocol to allow multicore software to switch modes while meeting all timing requirements, thereby allowing software designers add or remove software functions while ensuring safety.

Clock Rate

In a computer, clock speed refers to the number of pulses per second generated by an oscillator that sets the tempo for the processor. Clock speed is usually measured in MHz(megahertz, or millions of pulses per second) or GHz (gigahertz, or billions of pulses per second). Today's personal computers run at a clock speed in the hundreds of megahertz and some exceed one gigahertz. The clock speed is determined by a quartz-crystal circuit, similar to those used in radio communications equipment.

Computer clock speed has been roughly doubling every year. The Intel 8088, common in computers around the year 1980, ran at 4.77 MHz. The 1 GHz mark was passed in the year 2000.

Clock speed is one measure of computer "power," but it is not always directly proportional to the performance level. If you double the speed of the clock, leaving all other hardware unchanged, you will not necessarily double the processing speed. The type of microprocessor, the bus architecture, and the nature of the instruction set all make a difference. In some applications, the amount of random access memory (RAM) is important, too.

Some processors execute only one instruction per clock pulse. More advanced processors can perform more than one instruction per clock pulse. The latter type of processor will work faster at a given clock speed than the former type. Similarly, a computer with a 32-bit bus will work faster at a given clock speed than a computer with a 16-bit bus. For these reasons, there is no simplistic, universal relation among clock speed, "bus speed," and millions of instructions per second (MIPS).

Excessive clock speed can be detrimental to the operation of a computer. As the clock speed in a computer rises without upgrades in any of the other components, a point will be reached beyond which a further increase in frequency will render the processor unstable. Some computer users deliberately increase the clock speed, hoping this alone will result in a proportional improvement in performance, and are disappointed when things don't work out that way.

Megahertz Myth

The megahertz myth addresses the fallacy that higher clock speed translates to better performance. In reality, this picture isn't quite accurate. When assessing CPU performance, certain contributing factors outweigh clock rate. For instance, instruction sets and pipeline depth are valuable in determining performance. However, before you throw clock speed out the window, as it's a valuable metric for comparing CPUs from the same family.

The origins of the myth came about with the competing Apple II and IBM computers, both running PowerPC CPUs. PowerPC CPUs exhibited varying performance yields, despite having the same clock speed. The x86 architecture, with longer pipelines, actually aided CPUs to reach higher frequencies. The Apple variant was significantly slower than the IBM iteration.

To the uninformed consumer, clock speed is the ultimate metric when comparing CPUs. Yet, various factors mean that, say, a 2 GHz CPU can outperform a 2.6 GHz processor. Microarchitecture plays a key role, as does pipeline, and even program design. Thus, clock rate isn't nearly as reliable an indicator of potential performance. Benchmarks instead provide better insight when comparing CPUs.

Modern Adaptations of the Myth

With the advent of multithreading and multicore processors, the myth has stirred up more misconceptions regarding the measurement of performance in multi-core processors. Many people believe that a quad-core processor running at 3 GHz would result in an overall performance of 12 GHz worth of CPU. Others may say that the overall performance is in fact 3 GHz, with each core running at 750 MHz. Both of these ideas are incorrect. Often the same user making these comparisons will be comparing multiple brands of CPU, which will not do the same amount of work per cycle in any case. While micro-architecture traits such as pipeline depth play the same role in performance, the design of parallel processing brings other factor into the picture: software efficiency.

It is true that a poorly written program will run poorly on even a single-core system, but even a well written program that was designed in a linear fashion, will often (if not always) perform better on a single-core system than a multi-core one when run by itself. A system's overall performance cannot be judged by simply comparing the amount of processor cores and clock rates, the software running on the system is also a major factor of observed speed. The myth of the importance of clock rate has confused many people as to how they judge the speed of a computer system.

Challenges to the Myth

Comparisons between PowerPC and Pentium had become a staple of Apple presentations. At the New York City Macworld Expo *Keynote* on July 18, 2001, Steve Jobs described an 867 MHz G4 as completing a task in 45 seconds while a 1.7 GHz Pentium 4 took 82 seconds for the same task, saying that «the name that we've given it is the megahertz myth». He then introduced senior hardware VP Jon Rubinstein who gave a tutorial describing how shorter pipelines gave better performance at half the clock rate. The online cartoon Joy of Tech subsequently presented a series of cartoons inspired by Rubinstein's tutorial.

Intel Reaches its own Speed Limit

From approximately 1995 to 2005, Intel advertised its Pentium mainstream processors primarily on the basis of clock speed alone, in comparison to competitor products such as from AMD. Press articles had predicted that computer processors may eventually run as fast as 10 to 20 gigahertz in the next several decades.

This continued up until about 2005, when the Pentium Extreme Edition was reaching thermal dissipation limits running at speeds of nearly 4 gigahertz. The processor could go no faster without requiring complex changes to the cooling design, such as microfluidic cooling channels embedded within the chip itself to remove heat rapidly.

This was followed by the introduction of the Core 2 desktop processor in 2006, which was a major change from previous Intel desktop processors, allowing nearly a 50% decrease in processor clock while retaining the same performance.

Core 2 had its beginnings in the Pentium M mobile processor, where energy efficiency was more important than raw power, and initially offered power-saving options not available in the Pentium 4 and Pentium D.

Microprocessor

Microprocessor is a controlling unit of a micro-computer, fabricated on a small chip capable of performing ALU (Arithmetic Logical Unit) operations and communicating with the other devices connected to it.

Microprocessor consists of an ALU, register array, and a control unit. ALU performs arithmetical and logical operations on the data received from the memory or an input device. Register array consists of registers identified by letters like B, C, D, E, H, L and accumulator. The control unit controls the flow of data and instructions within the computer.

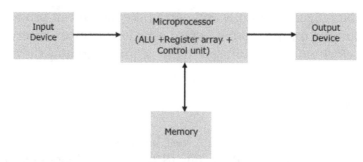

Work of Microprocessor

The microprocessor follows a sequence: Fetch, Decode, and then Execute.

Initially, the instructions are stored in the memory in a sequential order. The microprocessor fetches those instructions from the memory, then decodes it and executes those instructions till STOP instruction is reached. Later, it sends the result in binary to the output port. Between these processes, the register stores the temporarily data and ALU performs the computing functions.

List of Terms used in a Microprocessor

Here is a list of some of the frequently used terms in a microprocessor:

- Instruction Set: It is the set of instructions that the microprocessor can understand.

- Bandwidth: It is the number of bits processed in a single instruction.

- Clock Speed: It determines the number of operations per second the processor can perform. It is expressed in megahertz (MHz) or gigahertz (GHz).It is also known as Clock Rate.

- Word Length: It depends upon the width of internal data bus, registers, ALU, etc. An 8-bit microprocessor can process 8-bit data at a time. The word length ranges from 4 bits to 64 bits depending upon the type of the microcomputer.

- Data Types: The microprocessor has multiple data type formats like binary, BCD, ASCII, signed and unsigned numbers.

Features of a Microprocessor

Here is a list of some of the most prominent features of any microprocessor:

- Cost-effective: The microprocessor chips are available at low prices and results its low cost.

- Size: The microprocessor is of small size chip, hence is portable.

- Low Power Consumption: Microprocessors are manufactured by using metal oxide semiconductor technology, which has low power consumption.

- Versatility: The microprocessors are versatile as we can use the same chip in a number of applications by configuring the software program.

- Reliability: The failure rate of an IC in microprocessors is very low, hence it is reliable.

Microarchitecture

Microarchitecture, abbreviated as μarch or uarch, is the fundamental design of a microprocessor.

Microarchitecture is the logical representation of how a microprocessor is designed so that the interconnections between components – the control unit, the arithmetic logic unit, registers and others – interact in an optimized manner. This includes how buses, the data pathways between components, are laid out to dictate the shortest paths and proper connections. In modern microprocessors there are often several layers to deal with complexity. The basic idea is to lay out a circuit that could execute commands and operations that are defined in an instruction set.

A technique that is currently used in microarchitecture is the pipelined datapath. It is a technique that allows a form of parallelism that is applied in data processing by allowing several instructions to overlap in execution. This is done by having multiple execution pipelines that run in parallel or close to parallel.

Execution units are also a crucial aspect of microarchitecture. Execution units perform the operations or calculations of the processor. The choice of the number of execution units, their latency and throughput is a central micro architectural design consideration. The size, latency, throughput and connectivity of memories within the system are also micro architectural decisions.

Another part of microarchitecture is system-level design. This includes decisions on performance such as level and connectivity of input, as well as output and I/O devices.

Micro architectural design pays closer attention to restrictions than capability. A microarchitecture design decision directly affects what goes into a system; it heeds to issues such as:

- Performance
- Chip area/cost
- Logic complexity
- Ease of debugging
- Testability
- Ease of connectivity
- Power consumption
- Manufacturability.

A good microarchitecture is one that caters to all of these criteria.

Scalar Processor

A scalar processor is a normal processor, which works on simple instruction at a time, which operates on single data items. But in today's world, this technique will prove to be highly inefficient, as the overall processing of instructions will be very slow.

Vector (Array) Processing

There is a class of computational problems that are beyond the capabilities of a conventional computer. These problems require vast number of computations on multiple data items, that will take a conventional computer (with scalar processor) days or even weeks to complete.

Such complex instruction, which operates on multiple data at the same time, requires a better way of instruction execution, which was achieved by Vector processors.

Scalar CPUs can manipulate one or two data items at a time, which is not very efficient. Also, simple instructions like ADD A to B, and store into C are not practically efficient.

Addresses are used to point to the memory location where the data to be operated will be found, which leads to added overhead of data lookup. So until the data is found, the CPU would be sitting ideal, which is a big performance issue.

Hence, the concept of Instruction Pipeline comes into picture, in which the instruction passes through several sub-units in turn. These sub-units perform various independent functions, for example: the first one decodes the instruction, the second sub-unit fetches the data and the third sub-unit performs the math itself. Therefore, while the data is fetched for one instruction, CPU does not sit idle, it rather works on decoding the next instruction set, ending up working like an assembly line.

Vector processor, not only use Instruction pipeline, but it also pipelines the data, working on multiple data at the same time.

A normal scalar processor instruction would be ADD A, B, which leads to addition of two operands, but what if we can instruct the processor to ADD a group of numbers(from 0 to n memory location) to another group of numbers (let's say, n to k memory location). This can be achieved by vector processors.

In vector processor a single instruction, can ask for multiple data operations, which saves time, as instruction is decoded once, and then it keeps on operating on different data items.

Applications of Vector Processors

Computer with vector processing capabilities are in demand in specialized applications. The following are some areas where vector processing is used:

1. Petroleum exploration.

2. Medical diagnosis.

3. Data analysis.

4. Weather forecasting.

5. Aerodynamics and space flight simulations.

6. Image processing.

7. Artificial intelligence.

Superscalar Processors

It was first invented in 1987. It is a machine which is designed to improve the performance of the scalar processor. In most applications, most of the operations are on scalar quantities. Superscalar approach produces the high performance general purpose processors.

The main principle of superscalar approach is that it executes instructions independently in different pipelines. As we already know, that Instruction pipelining leads to parallel processing thereby speeding up the processing of instructions. In Superscalar processor, multiple such pipelines are introduced for different operations, which further improves parallel processing.

There are multiple functional units each of which is implemented as a pipeline. Each pipeline consists of multiple stages to handle multiple instructions at a time which support parallel execution of instructions.

It increases the throughput because the CPU can execute multiple instructions per clock cycle. Thus, superscalar processors are much faster than scalar processors.

A scalar processor works on one or two data items, while the vector processor works with multiple data items. A superscalar processor is a combination of both. Each instruction processes one data item, but there are multiple execution units within each CPU thus multiple instructions can be processing separate data items concurrently.

While a superscalar CPU is also pipelined, there are two different performance enhancement techniques. It is possible to have a non-pipelined superscalar CPU or pipelined non-superscalar CPU. The superscalar technique is associated with some characteristics, these are:

1. Instructions are issued from a sequential instruction stream.

2. CPU must dynamically check for data dependencies.

3. Should accept multiple instructions per clock cycle.

Superscalar Example

Assume 2-way superscalar processor with the following pipeline:

- 1 ADD/SUB ALU pipeline (1-Cycle INT-OP)

- 1 MULT/DIV ALU pipelines (4-Cycle INT-OP such as MULT)

- 2 MEM pipelines (1-Cycle (L1 hit) and 4-Cycle (L1 miss) MEM OP)

Show the pipeline diagram for the following codes assuming the bypass network:

- LD R1 <- A (L1 hit); LD R2 <- B (L1 miss)

- MULT R3, R1, R2; ADD R4, R1, R2

- SUB R5, R3, R4; ADD R4, R4, 1

- ST C <- R5; ST D <- R4

Coprocessor

A coprocessor is an auxiliary processing unit that is used to supplement the processing power of a microprocessor. In short, a coprocessor is an add-on that provides functionally that could not be incorporated in a processor for either economic or technical reasons.

Early microprocessors struggled to provide sufficient functionality on a single silicon chip you got a device that fetched instructions and executed instructions on integers. Floating-point operations, string processing, memory management and many of the functions we expect a processor to perform did not exist.

A processor can be designed to delegate certain operations to one or more external coprocessors. This takes requires two elements: a means of incorporating new instructions into the existing coprocessor architecture and a means of communicating between the processor and coprocessor. Ideally, these tasks should be invisible to the user and a processor-coprocessor pair should appear just as a processor with an enhanced instruction set architecture.

Note that there is a difference between an accelerator and a coprocessor, although both have the same function that is, to enhance performance. The accelerator improves the performance of a system exactly like the coprocessor, but the accelerator is not an extension of the processor's architecture. It is usually a memory-mapped peripheral that can be accessed from the system bus.

The microprocessor itself fetches instructions from memory, and, if an instruction is a coprocessor instruction, the CPU passes it to the coprocessor by means of a bus (which may or may not be dedicated). Moreover, the processor is normally responsible for fetching any data required by the coprocessor.

ARM Coprocessors

Coprocessors for the ARM are connected to it via its data and control buses. When the ARM first encounters an instruction that is not part of its current instruction set, the ARM regards it as a potential coprocessor operation. It is treated only as an illegal instruction exception after it has failed to be accepted buy a coprocessor.

Moreover, because the ARM offers predicated instruction, an op-code that would not be executed because of the predicated condition and state of the condition flags, is not executed irrespective of whether it is a valid coprocessor instruction or not.

When the ARM detects a potential coprocessor instruction, is asserts CPI, coprocessor instruction, which is monitored by all coprocessors in the system. A coprocessor can read the instruction from the data bus and check for both a valid coprocessor ID and a tag (one of 16). If there's a match, the coprocessor responds by asserting CPA, coprocessor absent. Now the coprocessor can assert, CPB, to take control until its operation has been completed.

Hardware Multithreading

A multithreading processor is able to pursue two or more threads of control in parallel within the processor pipeline. The contexts of two or more threads are often stored in separate on-chip register sets.

Formally speaking, CMT(Chip Multi-Threading), is a processor technology that allows multiple hardware threads of execution (also known as strands) on the same chip, through multiple cores per chip, multiple threads per core, or a combination of both.

Multiple Cores per Chip

CMP (Chip Multi-Processing, a.k.a. Multicore), is a processor technology that combines multiple processors (a.k.a. cores) on the same chip.

The idea is very similar to SMP, but implemented within a single chip. Is the most famous paper about this technology?

Multiple Threads per Core

- Vertical Multithreading – Instructions can be issued only from a single thread in any given CPU cycle.

  o Interleaved Multithreading (a.k.a. Fine Grained Multithreading), the instructions of other threads is fetched and fed into the execution pipelines at each processor cycle. So context switches at every CPU cycle.

  o Blocked Multithreading (a.k.a. Coarse Grained Multithreading), the instructions of other threads is executed successively until an event in current execution thread occurs that may cause latency. This delay event induces a context switch.

- Horizontal Multithreading – Instructions can be issued from multiple threads in any given cycle.

  This is so called Simultaneous multithreading (SMT): Instructions are simultaneously issued from multiple threads to the execution units of a superscalar processor. Thus, the wide superscalar instruction issue is combined with the multiple-context approach.

Unused instruction slots, which arise from latencies during the pipelined execution of single-threaded programs by a contemporary microprocessor, are filled by instructions of other threads within a multithreaded processor. The executions units are multiplexed among those thread contexts that are loaded in the register sets.

o Underutilization of a superscalar processor due to missing instruction-level parallelism can be overcome by simultaneous multithreading, where a processor can issue multiple instructions from multiple threads in each cycle. Simultaneous multithreaded processors combine the multithreading technique with a wide-issue superscalar processor to utilize a larger part of the issue bandwidth by issuing instructions from different threads simultaneously.

Types of Multithreading

Block Multi-threading

The simplest type of multi-threading occurs when one thread runs until it is blocked by an event that normally would create a long latency stall. Such a stall might be a cache-miss that has to access off-chip memory, which might take hundreds of CPU cycles for the data to return. Instead of waiting for the stall to resolve, a threaded processor would switch execution to another thread that was ready to run. Only when the data for the previous thread had arrived, would the previous thread be placed back on the list of ready to-run threads.

For example:

1. Cycle i: instruction j from thread A is issued

2. Cycle i+1: instruction j+1 from thread A is issued

3. Cycle i+2: instruction j+2 from thread A is issued, load instruction which misses in all caches

4. Cycle i+3: thread scheduler invoked, switches to thread B

5. Cycle i+4: instruction k from thread B is issued

6. Cycle i+5: instruction k+1 from thread B is issued.

Conceptually, it is similar to cooperative multi-tasking used in real-time operating systems in which tasks voluntarily give up execution time when they need to wait upon some type of the event.

Terminology:

This type of multi-threading is known as Block or Cooperative or Coarse-grained multithreading.

Hardware Cost

The goal of multi-threading hardware support is to allow quick switching between a blocked thread and another thread ready to run. To achieve this goal, the hardware cost is to replicate the program visible registers as well as some processor control registers (such as the program counter). Switching from one thread to another thread means the hardware switches from using one register set to another.

Such additional hardware has these benefits:

- The thread switch can be done in one CPU cycle.

- It appears to each thread that it is executing alone and not sharing any hardware resources with any other threads. This minimizes the amount of software changes needed within the application as well as the operating system to support multithreading.

In order to switch efficiently between active threads, each active thread needs to have its own register set. For example, to quickly switch between two threads, the register hardware needs to be instantiated twice.

Examples:

- Many families of microcontrollers and embedded processors have multiple register banks to allow quick context switching for interrupts. Such schemes can be considered a type of block multithreading among the user program thread and the interrupt threads.

Interleaved Multi-threading

1. Cycle i+1: an instruction from thread B is issued

2. Cycle i+2: an instruction from thread C is issued.

The purpose of this type of multithreading is to remove all data dependency stalls from the execution pipeline. Since one thread is relatively independent from other threads, there's less chance of one instruction in one pipe stage needing an output from an older instruction in the pipeline.

Conceptually, it is similar to pre-emptive multi-tasking used in operating systems. One can make the analogy that the time-slice given to each active thread is one CPU cycle.

Terminology:

This type of multithreading was first called Barrel processing, in which the staves of a barrel represent the pipeline stages and their executing threads. Interleaved or Pre-emptive or Fine-grained or time-sliced multithreading are more modern terminology.

Hardware Costs

In addition to the hardware costs discussed in the Block type of multithreading, interleaved multithreading has an additional cost of each pipeline stage tracking the thread ID of the instruction it is processing. Also, since there are more threads being executed concurrently in the pipeline, shared resources such as caches and TLBs need to be larger to avoid thrashing between the different threads.

Simultaneous Multi-threading

Simultaneous multithreading (SMT) is a technique for improving the overall efficiency of superscalar CPUs with hardware multithreading. SMT permits multiple independent threads of execution to better utilize the resources provided by modern processor architectures.

The most advanced type of multi-threading applies to superscalar processors. A normal superscalar processor issues multiple instructions from a single thread every CPU cycle. In Simultaneous Multi-threading (SMT), the superscalar processor can issue instructions from multiple threads every CPU cycle. Recognizing that any single thread has a limited amount of instruction level parallelism, this type of multithreading tries to exploit parallelism available across multiple threads to decrease the waste associated with unused issue slots.

For example:

1. Cycle i : instructions j and j+1 from thread A; instruction k from thread B all simultaneously issued

2. Cycle i+1: instruction j+2 from thread A; instruction k+1 from thread B; instruction m from thread C all simultaneously issued

3. Cycle i+2: instruction j+3 from thread A; instructions m+1 and m+2 from thread C all simultaneously issued.

Terminology:

To distinguish the other types of multithreading from SMT, the term Temporal multithreading is used to denote when instructions from only one thread can be issued at a time.

Hardware Costs

 In addition to the hardware costs discussed for interleaved multithreading, SMT has the additional cost of each pipeline stage tracking the Thread ID of each instruction being processed. Again, shared resources such as caches and TLBs have to be sized for the large number of active threads being processed.

- Fixed interleave

  o Each of N threads executes one instruction every N cycles

  o If thread not ready to go in its slot, insert pipeline bubble.

- Software-controlled interleave

  o OS allocates S pipeline slots amongst N threads

  o Hardware performs fixed interleave over S slots executing whichever thread is in that slot.

- Hardware-controlled thread scheduling

  o Hardware keeps track of which threads are ready to go

  o Picks next thread to execute based on hardware priority scheme.

CPU Registers

In *computer architecture*, a processor register is a very fast computer memory used to speed the execution of computer programs by providing quick access to commonly used values-typically, the values being in the midst of a calculation at a given point in time.

These registers are the top of the memory hierarchy, and are the fastest way for the system to manipulate data. In a very simple *microprocessor*, it consists of a single memory location, usually called an *accumulator*. Registers are built from fast multi-ported memory cell. They must be able to drive its data onto an internal bus in a single clock cycle. The result of ALU operation is stored here and could be re-used in a subsequent operation or saved into memory.

Registers are normally measured by the number of bits they can hold, for example, an "8-bit register" or a "32-bit register". Registers are now usually implemented as a register file, but they have also been implemented using individual flip-flops, high speed core memory, thin film memory, and other ways in various machines.

CPU Register

The term is often used to refer only to the group of registers that can be directly indexed for input or output of an instruction, as defined by the instruction set. More properly, these are called the "*architected registers*". For instance, the x86 instruction set defines a set of eight 32-bit registers, but a CPU that implements the X86 instruction set will contain many more hardware registers than just these eight.

A brief description of most important CPU's registers and their functions are given below:

1. Memory Address Register (MAR)

This register holds the address of memory where CPU wants to read or write data. When CPU wants to store some data in the memory or reads the data from the memory, it places the address of the required memory location in the MAR.

2. Memory Buffer Register (MBR)

This register holds the contents of data or instruction read from, or written in memory. The contents of instruction placed in this register are transferred to the Instruction Register, while the contents of data are transferred to the accumulator or I/O register.

In other words you can say that this register is used to store data/instruction coming from the memory or going to the memory.

3. I/O Address Register (I/O AR)

I/O Address register is used to specify the address of a particular I/O device.

4. I/O Buffer Register (I/O I3R)

I/O Buffer Register is used for exchanging data between the I/O module and the processor.

5. Program Counter (PC)

Program Counter register is also known as Instruction Pointer Register. This register is used to store the address of the next instruction to be fetched for execution. When the instruction is fetched, the value of IP is incremented. Thus this register always points or holds the address of next instruction to be fetched.

6. Instruction Register (IR):

Once an instruction is fetched from main memory, it is stored in the Instruction Register. The control unit takes instruction from this register, decodes and executes it by sending signals to the appropriate component of computer to carry out the task.

7. Accumulator Register:

The accumulator register is located inside the ALU, It is used during arithmetic & logical operations of ALU. The control unit stores data values fetched from main memory in the accumulator for arithmetic or logical operation. This register holds the initial data to be operated upon, the intermediate results, and the final result of operation. The final result is transferred to main memory through MBR.

8. Stack Control Register:

A stack represents a set of memory blocks; the data is stored in and retrieved from these blocks in an order, i.e. First In and Last Out (FILO). The Stack Control Register is used to manage the stacks in memory. The size of this register is 2 or 4 bytes.

9. Flag Register:

The Flag register is used to indicate occurrence of a certain condition during an operation of the CPU. It is a special purpose register with size one byte or two bytes. Each bit of the flag register constitutes a flag (or alarm), such that the bit value indicates if a specified condition was encountered while executing an instruction.

References

- What-is-cpu-central-processing-unit-and-how-its-work: deskdecode.com, Retrieved 25 June 2018

- Design-of-control-unit, computer-architecture: studytonight.com, Retrieved 10 April 2018

- Memory-management-unit-mmu-4768: techopedia.com, Retrieved 17 May 2018

- Performance-fundamentals-megahertz: cupofmoe.com, Retrieved 19 July 2018

- Hardware-Multithreading-115017034: scribd.com, Retrieved 19 June 2018

Computer Memory and its Management

Computer memory refers to the integrated circuits, which store information form instant use in a computer. There are two kinds of computer memory, volatile and non-volatile memory. Memory management is a type of resource management, which is applied to computer memory, for allocating memory to programs at request or free it for reuse. The topics elaborated in this chapter related to computer memory and memory management, such as random-access memory, read-only memory, virtual memory, memory segmentation, etc. will help in developing a better perspective of the field.

A memory is just like a human brain. It is used to store data and instructions. Computer memory is the storage space in the computer, where data is to be processed and instructions required for processing are stored. The memory is divided into large number of small parts called cells. Each location or cell has a unique address, which varies from zero to memory size minus one. For example, if the computer has 64k words, then this memory unit has $64 * 1024 = 65536$ memory locations. The address of these locations varies from 0 to 65535.

The memory of the computer is divided into two categories are mentioned below.

Primary Memory (Main Memory)

Primary memory holds only those data and instructions on which the computer is currently working. It has a limited capacity and data is lost when power is switched off. It is generally made up of semiconductor device. These memories are not as fast as registers. The data and instruction required to be processed resides in the main memory. It is divided into two subcategories RAM and ROM.

Characteristics of Main Memory

- These are semiconductor memories.
- It is known as the main memory.
- Usually volatile memory.
- Data is lost in case power is switched off.
- It is the working memory of the computer.
- Faster than secondary memories.
- A computer cannot run without the primary memory.

Secondary Memory

This type of memory is also known as external memory or non-volatile. It is slower than the main memory. These are used for storing data/information permanently. CPU directly does not access these memories, instead they are accessed via input-output routines. The contents of secondary memories are first transferred to the main memory, and then the CPU can access it. For example, disk, CD-ROM, DVD, etc.

Characteristics of Secondary Memory

- These are magnetic and optical memories.
- It is known as the backup memory.
- It is a non-volatile memory.
- Data is permanently stored even if power is switched off.
- It is used for storage of data in a computer.
- Computer may run without the secondary memory.
- Slower than primary memories.

Different Types of Secondary Storage Devices

Hard Disc, Compact Disc, DVD, Pen Drive, Flash Drive, etc.

Hard Disc

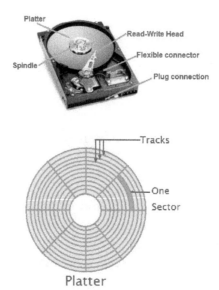

Platter

This is the main storage device of the computer which is fixed inside the CPU box. Its storage capacity is very high that varies from 200 GB to 3 TB. As it is fixed inside the CPU box, it is not easy to move the hard disc from one computer to another.

A hard disc contains a number of metallic discs which are called platters. Information is recorded on the surface of the platters in a series of concentric circles. These circles are called Tracks. For the purpose of addressing information, the surface is considered to be divided into segments called Sectors. This division helps in the proper organisation of data on the platter and helps in maximum utilization of the storage space.

Compact Disc (CD)

Compact Disc(CD)

It is a thin plastic disc coated with metal. Computer can read and write data stored on it. This is an optical storage device with a storage capacity of up to 700 MB and it can store varieties of data like pictures, sounds, movies, texts, etc.

CD-ROM

CD-ROM refers to Compact Disc-Read Only Memory. Data or information is recorded at the time of manufacturing and it can only be read. A CD-ROM cannot be used to record fresh data by the computer.

CD-R

CD-R is the short form of Compact Disc-Recordable. Data can be written on it once and can be read whenever required. The data written once cannot be erased.

CD-RW

CD-RW stands for Compact Disc Re-writable. CD-RW can be used to write information over and over again, i.e., previous information can be erased and new information can be written on it using a CD writer fixed inside the CPU box. CDs are slow in comparison to hard discs to read or write the information on them. They are portable storage devices.

DVD

DVD(Digital Versatile Disc)

DVD stands for Digital Versatile Disc.it is an optical storage device which reads data faster than a CD.A single layer, single sided DVD can store data up to 4.7 GB, i.e., around 6 times than that of CD and a double layer DVD can store data up to 17.08 GB, i.e. around 25 times that of CD. Though DVDs look just like CDs, they can hold much more data, for example, a full length movie.

Flash Drive

Flash Drive

It is an electronic memory device popularly known as pen drive in which data can be stored permanently and erased when not needed.it is a portable storage device that can be easily connected and removed from the CPU to store data in it. its capacity can vary form 2 GB to 256 GB.

Blu-ray Disc

Blu-ray Disc

This is a newly invented optical data storage device whose storage capacity can be form 25 GB up to 200 GB.it is mainly used to store high quality sound and movie data. They are the scratch resistant discs that are why, storing data on these is much safer than a CD OR DVD. So, these are some the common devices we use to store information and data in the computer.

Memory Units

Data in the computer's memory is represented by the two digits 0 and 1.These two digits are called Binary Digits or Bits. A bit is the smallest unit of computer's memory. To represent each character in memory, a set of 8 binary digits is used. This set of 8 bit is called a Byte. So, one Byte is used to represent one character of data.

Bits=0,1

1 Byte= 8 bits(e.g,11001011)

To represent a large amount of data in memory, higher data storage units are used like KB(Kilobyte),MB(megabyte),GB(Gigabyte),TB(terabyte),etc.

But all these unites are formed with the set of bytes like,

1 KB(kilobyte)   = 2^{10} Bytes=1024 Bytes

1 MB(megabyte) = 2^{10} KB=1024 KB

= 1024*1024 Bytes

= 1048576 Bytes

1 GB(Gigabyte) = 2^{10} MB=1024 MB

1 TB(Terabyte)   = 2^{10} GB

= 1024 GB

Volatile Memory

Volatile storage is a type of computer memory that needs power to preserve stored data. If the computer is switched off, anything stored in the volatile memory is removed or deleted.

All random access memory (RAM) other than the CMOS RAM used in the BIOS is volatile. RAM is typically used as a primary storage or main memory in computer systems. Since the primary storage demands extreme speed, it mainly uses volatile memory. Due to the volatile nature of RAM, users often need to save their work to a nonvolatile permanent medium, such as a hard drive, in order to avoid data loss.

Volatile storage is also known as volatile memory or temporary memory.

There are two kinds of volatile RAM: dynamic and static. Even though both types need continuous electrical current for proper functioning, there are some important differences as well.

Dynamic RAM (DRAM) is very popular due to its cost effectiveness. If a computer has 1 gigabyte or 512 megabytes of RAM, the specification describes dynamic RAM (DRAM). DRAM stores each bit of information in a different capacitor within the integrated circuit. DRAM chips need just one single capacitor and one transistor to store each bit of information. This makes it space efficient and inexpensive.

The main advantage of static RAM (SRAM) is that it is much faster than dynamic RAM. Its disadvantage is its high price. SRAM does not need continuous electrical refreshes, but it still requires constant current to sustain the difference in voltage. In general, SRAM needs less power than DRAM, even though the power requirements differ based on the computer's clock speed. At moderate speeds SRAM usually requires just a fraction of the power used by DRAM. When idle, the power requirements of static RAM are low. Every single bit in a static RAM chip needs a cell of six transistors, whereas dynamic RAM requires only one capacitor and one transistor. As a result, SRAM is unable to accomplish the storage capabilities of the DRAM family.

SRAM is most commonly used in networking devices, like switches, routers, cable modems, etc., for buffering the transmitted information.

The physical structure and electronic properties of volatile memory makes it faster compared to electro-mechanical storage devices such as hard drives, which makes it an ideal candidate as the computer's main form of memory.

In terms of security, volatile memory is very secure since it does not retain any record at all after power is removed, so no data can be salvaged. However, this is a double-edged sword since all data is lost if there is power interruption.

- *DRAM:* Dynamic RAM is a form of random access memory. DRAM uses a capacitor to store each bit of data, and the level of charge on each capacitor determines whether that bit is a logical 1 or 0. However these capacitors do not hold their charge indefinitely, and therefore the data needs to be refreshed periodically. As a result of this dynamic refreshing it gains its name of being a dynamic RAM. DRAM is the form of semiconductor memory that is often used in equipment including personal computers and workstations where it forms the main RAM for the computer.

- *SRAM:* Static Random Access Memory. This form of semiconductor memory gains its name from the fact that, unlike DRAM, the data does not need to be refreshed dynamically. It is able to support faster read and write times than DRAM (typically 10 ns against 60 ns for DRAM), and in addition its cycle time is much shorter because it does not need to pause between accesses. However it consumes more power, is less dense and more expensive than DRAM. As a result of this it is normally used for caches, while DRAM is used as the main semiconductor memory technology.

- *SDRAM:* Synchronous DRAM. This form of semiconductor memory can run at faster speeds than conventional DRAM. It is synchronized to the clock of the processor and is capable of keeping two sets of memory addresses open simultaneously. By transferring data alternately from one set of addresses, and then the other, SDRAM cuts down on the delays associated with non-synchronous RAM, which must close one address bank before opening the next.

Non-volatile Memory

A device which can hold data in it even if it is not connected to any power source is called Non Volatile Memory. The typical examples for Non Volatile Memory are your Hard drives and flash drives. Even if you turn off your PC the data in your hard drive or flash drive stays intact.

Hard Drive is a typical example of Non Volatile Memory. It will take some time to access the data in a hard drive and it also will take some time to write data into it but can be retrieved back even if the power supply to it is interrupted. Hibernation is one of the good examples of storing the memory that is there in RAM to Hard drive. If you remember in previous versions of windows we used to enable the hibernation manually and it used to say that it uses additional 2 GB of memory in Hard drive. What happens during hibernation is that all the data that is there on the RAM will be written over to Hard drive thereby storing the system state and system will be turned off. Whenever you turn on the PC again, the data in hard drive will be retrieved back to restore the system state. In linux typically this hard drive partition is SWAP. With the recent trends of making system to boot faster is using cold shutdown than proper shut down where the necessary programs that needed to start OS will be stored on to Hard drive and retrieved back after system start up through which boot time is reduced.

- PROM: Pronounced prom, an acronym for programmable read-only memory. A PROM is a memory chip on which data can be written only once. Once a program has been written onto a PROM, it remains there forever. Unlike RAM, PROMs retain their contents when the computer is turned off. The difference between a PROM and a ROM (read-only memory) is that a PROM is manufactured as blank memory, whereas a ROM is programmed during the manufacturing process. To write data onto a PROM chip, you need a special device called a PROM programmer or PROM burner. The process of programming a PROM is sometimes called burning the PROM. An EPROM (erasable programmable read-only memory) is a special type of PROM that can be erased by exposing it to ultraviolet light. Once it is erased, it can be reprogrammed. An EEPROM is similar to a PROM, but requires only electricity to be erased.

- EPROM: Acronym for erasable programmable read-only memory, and pronounced e-prom, EPROM is a special type of memory that retains its contents until it is exposed to ultraviolet light. The ultraviolet light clears its contents, making it possible to reprogram the memory. To write to and erase an EPROM, you need a special device called a PROM programmer or PROM burner. An EPROM differs from a PROM in that a PROM can be written to only once and cannot be erased. EPROMs are used widely in personal computers because they enable the manufacturer to change the contents of the PROM before the computer is actually shipped. This means that bugs can be removed and new versions installed shortly before delivery. A note on EPROM technology: The bits of an EPROM are programmed by injecting electrons with an elevated voltage into the floating gate of a field-effect transistor where a 0 bit is desired. The electrons trapped there cause that transistor to conduct, reading as 0. To erase the EPROM, the trapped electrons are given enough energy to escape the floating gate by bombarding the chip with ultraviolet radiation through the quartz window. To prevent slow erasure over a period of years from sunlight and fluorescent lights, this quartz window is covered with an opaque label in normal use.

- EEPROM: Acronym for electrically erasable programmable read-only memory. Pronounced double-e-prom or e-e-prom, an EEPROM is a special type of PROM that can be erased by exposing it to an electrical charge. Like other types of PROM, EEPROM retains its contents even when the power is turned off. Also like other types of ROM, EEPROM is not as fast as RAM. EEPROM is similar to flash memory (sometimes called flash EEPROM). The principal difference is that EEPROM requires data to be written or erased one byte at a time whereas flash memory allows data to be written or erased in blocks. This makes flash memory faster.

- FRAM: Short for Ferroelectric Random Access Memory, a type of non-volatile memory developed by Ramtron International Corporation. FRAM combines the access speed of DRAM and SRAM with the non-volatility of ROM. Because of its high speed, it is replacing EEPROM in many devices. The term FRAM itself is a trademark of Ramtron.

- NVRAM: Abbreviation of Non-Volatile Random Access Memory, a type of memory that retains its contents when power is turned off. One type of NVRAM is SRAM that is made non-volatile by connecting it to a constant power source such as a battery. Another type of NVRAM uses EEPROM chips to save its contents when power is turned off. In this case, NVRAM is composed of a combination of SRAM and EEPROM chips.

- Bubble Memory: A type of non-volatile memory composed of a thin layer of material that can be easily magnetized in only one direction. When a magnetic field is applied to circular area of this substance that is not magnetized in the same direction, the area is reduced to a smaller circle, or bubble. It was once widely believed that bubble memory would become one of the leading memory technologies, but these promises have not been fulfilled. Other non-volatile memory types, such as EEPROM, are both faster and less expensive than bubble memory.

- Flash Memory: A special type of EEPROM that can be erased and reprogrammed in blocks instead of one byte at a time. Many modern PCs have their BIOS stored on a flash memory chip so that it can easily be updated if necessary. Such a BIOS is sometimes called a flash BIOS. Flash memory is also popular in modems because it enables the modem manufacturer to support new protocols as they become standardized.

Cache Memory

Cache memory, also called CPU memory, is high-speed static random access memory (SRAM) that a computer microprocessor can access more quickly than it can access regular random access memory (RAM). This memory is typically integrated directly into the CPU chip or placed on a separate chip that has a separate bus interconnect with the CPU. The purpose of cache memory is to store program instructions and data that are used repeatedly in the operation of programs or information that the CPU is likely to need next. The computer processor can access this information quickly from the cache rather than having to get it from computer's main memory. Fast access to these instructions increases the overall speed of the program.

As the microprocessor processes data, it looks first in the cache memory. If it finds the instructions or data it's looking for there from a previous reading of data, it does not have to perform a more time-consuming reading of data from larger main memory or other data storage devices. Cache memory is responsible for speeding up computer operations and processing.

Once they have been opened and operated for a time, most programs use few of a computer's resources. That's because frequently re-referenced instructions tend to be cached. This is why system performance measurements for computers with slower processors but larger caches can be faster than those for computers with faster processors but less cache space.

Multi-tier or multilevel caching has become popular in server and desktop architectures, with different levels providing greater efficiency through managed tiring. Simply put, the less frequently certain data or instructions are accessed, the lower down the cache level the data or instructions are written.

Implementation

Mainframes used an early version of cache memory, but the technology as it is known today began to be developed with the advent of microcomputers. With early PCs, processor performance increased much faster than memory performance, and memory became a bottleneck, slowing systems.

In the 1980s, the idea took hold that a small amount of more expensive, faster SRAM could be used to improve the performance of the less expensive, slower main memory. Initially, the memory cache was separate from the system processor and not always included in the chipset. Early PCs typically had from 16 KB to 128 KB of cache memory.

With 486 processors, Intel added 8 KB of memory to the CPU as Level 1 (L1) memory. As much as 256 KB of external Level 2 (L2) cache memory was used in these systems. Pentium processors saw the external cache memory double again to 512 KB on the high end. They also split the internal cache memory into two caches: one for instructions and the other for data.

Processors based on Intel's P6 microarchitecture, introduced in 1995, were the first to incorporate L2 cache memory into the CPU and enable all of a system's cache memory to run at the same clock speed as the processor. Prior to the P6, L2 memory external to the CPU was accessed at a much slower clock speed than the rate at which the processor ran, and slowed system performance considerably.

Early memory cache controllers used a write-through cache architecture, where data written into cache was also immediately updated in RAM. This approached minimized data loss, but also slowed operations. With later 486-based PCs, the write-back cache architecture was developed, where RAM isn't updated immediately. Instead, data is stored on cache and RAM is updated only at specific intervals or under certain circumstances where data is missing or old.

Cache Memory Mapping

Caching configurations continue to evolve, but cache memory traditionally works under three different configurations:

- Direct mapped cache has each block mapped to exactly one cache memory location. Conceptually, direct mapped cache is like rows in a table with three columns: the data block or cache line that contains the actual data fetched and stored, a tag with all or part of the address of the data that was fetched, and a flag bit that shows the presence in the row entry of a valid bit of data.

- Fully associative cache mapping is similar to direct mapping in structure but allows a block to be mapped to any cache location rather than to a prespecified cache memory location as is the case with direct mapping.

- Set associative cache mapping can be viewed as a compromise between direct mapping and fully associative mapping in which each block is mapped to a subset of cache locations. It is sometimes called *N-way set associative mapping*, which provides for a location in main memory to be cached to any of "N" locations in the L1 cache.

Format of the Cache Hierarchy

Cache memory is fast and expensive. Traditionally, it is categorized as "levels" that describe its closeness and accessibility to the microprocessor.

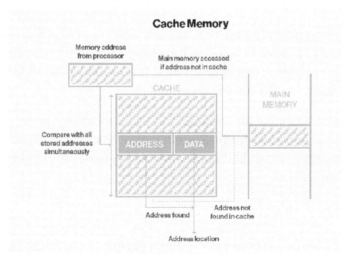

L1 cache, or primary cache, is extremely fast but relatively small, and is usually embedded in the processor chip as CPU cache.

L2 cache, or secondary cache, is often more capacious than L1. L2 cache may be embedded on the CPU, or it can be on a separate chip or coprocessor and have a high-speed alternative system bus connecting the cache and CPU. That way it doesn't get slowed by traffic on the main system bus.

Level 3 (L3) cache is specialized memory developed to improve the performance of L1 and L2. L1 or L2 can be significantly faster than L3, though L3 is usually double the speed of RAM. With multicore processors, each core can have dedicated L1 and L2 cache, but they can share an L3 cache. If an L3 cache references an instruction, it is usually elevated to a higher level of cache.

In the past, L1, L2 and L3 caches have been created using combined processor and motherboard components. Recently, the trend has been toward consolidating all three levels of memory caching on the CPU itself. That's why the primary means for increasing cache size has begun to shift from the acquisition of a specific motherboard with different chipsets and bus architectures to buying a CPU with the right amount of integrated L1, L2 and L3 cache.

Contrary to popular belief, implementing flash or more dynamic RAM (DRAM) on a system won't increase cache memory. This can be confusing since the terms *memory caching* (hard disk buffering) and *cache memory* are often used interchangeably. Memory caching, using DRAM or flash to buffer disk reads, is meant to improve storage I/O by caching data that is frequently referenced in a buffer ahead of slower magnetic disk or tape. Cache memory, on the other hand, provides read buffering for the CPU.

Specialization and Functionality

In addition to instruction and data caches, other caches are designed to provide specialized system functions. According to some definitions, the L3 cache's shared design makes it a specialized cache. Other definitions keep instruction caching and data caching separate, and refer to each as a specialized cache.

Translation look aside buffers (TLBs) are also specialized memory caches whose function is to record virtual address to physical address translations.

Still other caches are not, technically speaking, memory caches at all. Disk caches, for instance, can use RAM or flash memory to provide data caching similar to what memory caches do with CPU instructions. If data is frequently accessed from disk, it is cached into DRAM or flash-based silicon storage technology for faster access time and response.

Specialized caches are also available for applications such as web browsers, databases, network address binding and client-side Network File System protocol support. These types of caches might be distributed across multiple networked hosts to provide greater scalability or performance to an application that uses them.

Locality

The ability of cache memory to improve a computer's performance relies on the concept of locality of reference. Locality describes various situations that make a system more predictable, such as where the same storage location is repeatedly accessed, creating a pattern of memory access that the cache memory relies upon.

There are several types of locality. Two key ones for cache are temporal and spatial. Temporal locality is when the same resources are accessed repeatedly in a short amount of time. Spatial locality refers to accessing various data or resources that are in close proximity to each other.

Cache vs. Main Memory

DRAM serves as a computer's main memory, performing calculations on data retrieved from storage. Both DRAM and cache memory are volatile memories that lose their contents when the power is turned off. DRAM is installed on the motherboard, and the CPU accesses it through a bus connection.

An example of dynamic RAM

DRAM is usually about half as fast as L1, L2 or L3 cache memory, and much less expensive. It provides faster data access than flash storage, hard disk drives (HDDs) and tape storage. It came into use in the last few decades to provide a place to store frequently accessed disk data to improve I/O performance.

DRAM must be refreshed every few milliseconds. Cache memory, which also is a type of random access memory, does not need to be refreshed. It is built directly into the CPU to give the processor the fastest possible access to memory locations, and provides nanosecond speed access time to frequently referenced instructions and data. SRAM is faster than DRAM, but because it's a more complex chip, it's also more expensive to make.

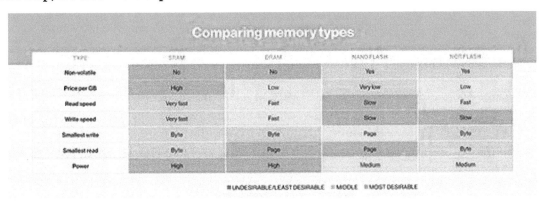

Comparing memory types				
TYPE	SRAM	DRAM	NANDFLASH	NORFLASH
Non-volatile	No	No	Yes	Yes
Price per GB	High	Low	Very low	Low
Read speed	Very fast	Fast	Slow	Fast
Write speed	Very fast	Fast	Slow	Slow
Smallest write	Byte	Byte	Page	Byte
Smallest read	Byte	Page	Page	Byte
Power	High	High	Medium	Medium

■ UNDESIRABLE/LEAST DESIRABLE   = MIDDLE   ■ MOST DESIRABLE

Cache vs. Virtual Memory

A computer has a limited amount of RAM and even less cache memory. When a large program or multiple programs are running, it's possible for memory to be fully used. To compensate for a shortage of physical memory, the computer's operating system (OS) can create virtual memory.

To do this, the OS temporarily transfers inactive data from RAM to disk storage. This approach increases virtual address space by using active memory in RAM and inactive memory in HDDs to form contiguous addresses that hold both an application and its data. Virtual memory lets a computer run larger programs or multiple programs simultaneously, and each program operates as though it has unlimited memory.

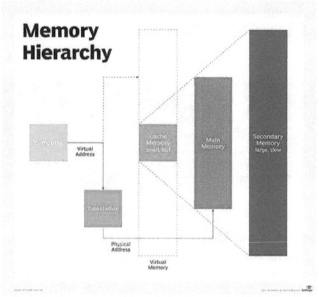

Where virtual memory fits in the memory hierarchy

In order to copy virtual memory into physical memory, the OS divides memory into pagefiles or swap files that contain a certain number of addresses. Those pages are stored on a disk and when they're needed, the OS copies them from the disk to main memory and translates the virtual addresses into real addresses.

Random-access Memory

RAM (Random Access Memory) is the hardware in a computing device where the operating system (OS), application programs and data in current use are kept so they can be quickly reached by the device's processor. RAM is the main memory in a computer, and it is much faster to read from and write to than other kinds of storage, such as a hard disk drive (HDD), solid-state drive (SSD) or optical drive.

Random Access Memory is volatile. That means data is retained in RAM as long as the computer is on, but it is lost when the computer is turned off. When the computer is rebooted, the OS and other files are reloaded into RAM, usually from an HDD or SSD.

Uses of Random Access Memory

Because of its volatility, Random Access Memory can't store permanent data. RAM can be compared to a person's short-term memory, and a hard drive to a person's long-term memory. Short-term memory is focused on immediate work, but it can only keep a limited number of facts in view at any one time. When a person's short-term memory fills up, it can be refreshed with facts stored in the brain's long-term memory.

A computer also works this way. If RAM fills up, the computer's processor must repeatedly go to the hard disk to overlay the old data in RAM with new data. This process slows the computer's operation.

RAM modules

A computer's hard disk can become completely full of data and unable to take any more, but RAM won't run out of memory. However, the combination of RAM and storage memory can be completely used up.

Working of RAM

The term random access as applied to RAM comes from the fact that any storage location, also known as any memory address, can be accessed directly. Originally, the term Random Access Memory was used to distinguish regular core memory from offline memory.

Offline memory typically referred to magnetic tape from which a specific piece of data could only be accessed by locating the address sequentially, starting at the beginning of the tape. RAM is organized and controlled in a way that enables data to be stored and retrieved directly to and from specific locations.

Other types of storage - such as the hard drive and CD-ROM - are also accessed directly or randomly, but the term random access isn't used to describe these other types of storage.

RAM is similar in concept to a set of boxes in which each box can hold a 0 or a 1. Each box has a unique address that is found by counting across the columns and down the rows. A set of RAM boxes is called an array, and each box is known as a cell.

To find a specific cell, the RAM controller sends the column and row address down a thin electrical line etched into the chip. Each row and column in a RAM array has its own address line. Any data that's read flows back on a separate data line.

RAM is physically small and stored in microchips. It's also small in terms of the amount of data it can hold. A typical laptop computer may come with 8 gigabytes of RAM, while a hard disk can hold 10 terabytes.

RAM microchips are gathered together into memory modules, which plug into slots in a computer's motherboard. A bus, or a set of electrical paths, is used to connect the motherboard slots to the processor.

A hard drive, on the other hand, stores data on the magnetized surface of what looks like a vinyl record. And, alternatively, an SSD stores data in memory chips that, unlike RAM, are nonvolatile, don't depend on having constant power and won't lose data once the power is turned off.

Most PCs enable users to add RAM modules up to a certain limit. Having more RAM in a computer cuts down on the number of times the processor must read data from the hard disk, an operation that takes longer than reading data from RAM. RAM access time is in nanoseconds, while storage memory access time is in milliseconds.

Types of Random Access Memory

RAM comes in two primary forms.

Dynamic Random Access Memory (DRAM) makes up the typical computing device's RAM and, as was previously noted, it needs that power to be on to retain stored data.

Each DRAM cell has a charge or lack of charge held in an electrical capacitor. This data must be constantly refreshed with an electronic charge every few milliseconds to compensate for leaks from the capacitor. A transistor serves as a gate, determining whether a capacitor's value can be read or written.

Static Random Access Memory (SRAM) also needs constant power to hold on to data, but it doesn't need to be continually refreshed the way DRAM does.

In SRAM, instead of a capacitor holding the charge, the transistor acts as a switch, with one position serving as 1 and the other position as 0. Static RAM requires several transistors to retain one bit of data compared to dynamic RAM which needs only one transistor per bit. As a result, SRAM chips are much larger and more expensive than an equivalent amount of DRAM.

However, SRAM is significantly faster and uses less power than DRAM. The price and speed differences mean static RAM is mainly used in small amounts as cache memory inside a computer's processor.

RAM vs. Virtual Memory

A computer can run short on memory, especially when running multiple programs simultaneously. Operating systems can compensate for physical memory shortfalls by creating virtual memory.

With virtual memory, data is temporarily transferred from RAM to disk storage, and virtual address space is increased using active memory in RAM and inactive memory in an HDD to form contiguous addresses that hold an application and its data. Using virtual memory, a system can load larger programs or multiple programs running at the same time, letting each operate as if it has infinite memory without having to add more RAM.

Virtual memory is able to handle twice as many addresses as RAM. A program's instructions and data are initially stored at virtual addresses, and once the program is executed, those addresses are turned into actual memory addresses.

One downside to virtual memory is that it can slow a computer because data must be mapped between the virtual and physical memory. With physical memory alone, programs work directly from RAM.

RAM vs. Flash Memory

Flash memory and RAM are both comprised of solid-state chips, but they play different roles in computer systems because of differences in the way they're made, their performance specifications and cost. Flash memory is used for storage memory, while RAM is used as active memory that performs calculations on the data retrieved from storage.

One significant difference between RAM and flash memory is that data must be erased from NAND flash memory in entire blocks, making it slower than RAM, where data can be erased in individual bits.

However, NAND flash memory is less expensive than RAM, and it's also nonvolatile; unlike RAM, it can hold data even when the power is off. Because of its slower speed, no volatility and lower cost, flash is often used for storage memory in SSDs.

RAM vs. ROM

Read-only memory, or ROM, is computer memory containing data that can only be read, not written to. ROM contains boot-up programming that is used each time a computer is turned on. It generally can't be altered or reprogrammed.

The data in ROM is nonvolatile and isn't lost when the computer power is turned off. As a result, read-only memory is used for permanent data storage. Random Access Memory, on the other hand, can only hold data temporarily. ROM is generally several megabytes of storage, while RAM is several gigabytes.

Read-only Memory

Read Only Memory is a kind of meomory, which we can only read but cannot write on it.

This type of memory is non-volatile. The information is stored permanently in such memories during manufacture. A ROM stores such instructions that are required to start a computer. This operation is referred to as bootstrap. ROM chips are not only used in the computer but also in other electronic items like washing machine and microwave oven.

The various types of ROMs and their characteristics are as follows.

MROM (Masked ROM)

The very first ROMs were hard-wired devices that contained a pre-programmed set of data or instructions. These kind of ROMs are known as masked ROMs, which are inexpensive.

PROM (Programmable Read Only Memory)

PROM is read-only memory that can be modified only once by a user. The user buys a blank PROM and enters the desired contents using a PROM program. Inside the PROM chip, there are small fuses which are burnt open during programming. It can be programmed only once and is not erasable.

EPROM: Erasable and Programmable Read Only Memory

EPROM can be erased by exposing it to ultra-violet light for a duration of up to 40 minutes. Usually, an EPROM eraser achieves this function. During programming, an electrical charge is trapped in an insulated gate region. The charge is retained for more than 10 years because the charge has no leakage path. For erasing this charge, ultra-violet light is passed through a quartz crystal window (lid). This exposure to ultra-violet light dissipates the charge. During normal use, the quartz lid is sealed with a sticker.

EEPROM: Electrically Erasable and Programmable Read Only Memory

EEPROM is programmed and erased electrically. It can be erased and reprogrammed about ten thousand times. Both erasing and programming take about 4 to 10 ms (millisecond). In EEPROM, any location can be selectively erased and programmed. EEPROMs can be erased one byte at a time, rather than erasing the entire chip. Hence, the process of reprogramming is flexible but slow.

Advantages of ROM

The advantages of ROM are as follows:

- Non-volatile in nature
- Cannot be accidentally changed
- Cheaper than RAMs
- Easy to test
- More reliable than RAMs
- Static and do not require refreshing
- Contents are always known and can be verified

Memory Management

Memory management is a software utility or term used to describe the process of managing computer memory in the computer. This commonly involves taking segments of memory and assigning them to be used with other applications or moved in-between other portions of memory.

All the programs are loaded in the main memory for execution. Sometimes complete program is loaded into the memory, but sometimes a certain part or routine of the program is loaded into the main memory only when it is called by the program, this mechanism is called Dynamic Loading, this enhance the performance.

Also, at times one program is dependent on some other program. In such a case, rather than loading all the dependent programs, CPU links the dependent programs to the main executing program when its required. This mechanism is known as Dynamic Linking.

Swapping

A process needs to be in memory for execution. But sometimes there is not enough main memory to hold all the currently active processes in a timesharing system. So, excess process are kept on disk and brought in to run dynamically. Swapping is the process of bringing in each process in main memory, running it for a while and then putting it back to the disk.

Contiguous Memory Allocation

In contiguous memory allocation each process is contained in a single contiguous block of memory. Memory is divided into several fixed size partitions. Each partition contains exactly one process. When a partition is free, a process is selected from the input queue and loaded into it. The free blocks of memory are known as *holes*. The set of holes is searched to determine which hole is best to allocate.

Memory Protection

Memory protection is a phenomenon by which we control memory access rights on a computer. The main aim of it is to prevent a process from accessing memory that has not been allocated to it. Hence prevents a bug within a process from affecting other processes, or the operating system itself, and instead results in a segmentation fault or storage violation exception being sent to the disturbing process, generally killing of process.

Memory Allocation

Memory allocation is a process by which computer programs are assigned memory or space. It is of three types:

1. First Fit:

   The first hole that is big enough is allocated to program.

2. Best Fit:

   The smallest hole that is big enough is allocated to program.

3. Worst Fit:

   The largest hole that is big enough is allocated to program.

Fragmentation

Fragmentation occurs in a dynamic memory allocation system when most of the free blocks are too small to satisfy any request. It is generally termed as inability to use the available memory.

In such situation processes are loaded and removed from the memory. As a result of this, free holes exists to satisfy a request but is non-contiguous i.e. the memory is fragmented into large no. of small holes. This phenomenon is known as External Fragmentation.

Also, at times the physical memory is broken into fixed size blocks and memory is allocated in unit of block sizes. The memory allocated to a space may be slightly larger than the requested memory. The difference between allocated and required memory is known as internal fragmentation i.e. the memory that is internal to a partition but is of no use.

Paging

A solution to fragmentation problem is paging. Paging is a memory management mechanism that allows the physical address space of a process to be non-contagious. Here physical memory is divided into blocks of equal size called Pages. The pages belonging to a certain process are loaded into available memory frames.

Page Table

A Page Table is the data structure used by a virtual memory system in a computer operating system to store the mapping between *virtual address* and *physical addresses.*

Virtual address is also known as logical address and is generated by the CPU. While physical address is the address that actually exists on memory.

Segmentation

Segmentation is another memory management scheme that supports the user-view of memory. Segmentation allows breaking of the virtual address space of a single process into segments that may be placed in non-contiguous areas of physical memory.

Segmentation with Paging

Both paging and segmentation have their advantages and disadvantages, it is better to combine these two schemes to improve on each. The combined scheme is known as 'Page the Elements'. Each segment in this scheme is divided into pages and each segment is maintained in a page table. So the logical address is divided into following 3 parts :

- Segment numbers(S)

- Page number (P)

- The displacement or offset number (D)

Demand Paging

The process of loading the page into memory on demand (whenever page fault occurs) is known as demand paging.

The process includes the following steps:

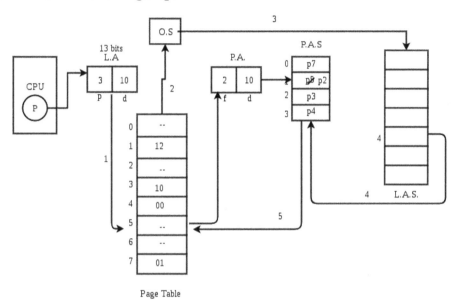

Page Table

1. If CPU try to refer a page that is currently not available in the main memory, it generates an interrupt indicating memory access fault.

2. The OS puts the interrupted process in a blocking state. For the execution to proceed the OS must bring the required page into the memory.

3. The OS will search for the required page in the logical address space.

4. The required page will be brought from logical address space to physical address space. The page replacement algorithms are used for the decision making of replacing the page in physical address space.

5. The page table will updated accordingly.

6. The signal will be sent to the CPU to continue the program execution and it will place the process back into ready state.

Hence whenever a page fault occurs these steps are followed by the operating system and the required page is brought into memory.

Advantages:

- More processes may be maintained in the main memory: Because we are going to load only some of the pages of any particular process, there is room for more processes. This leads to more efficient utilization of the processor because it is more likely that at least one of the more numerous processes will be in the ready state at any particular time.

- A process may be larger than all of main memory: One of the most fundamental restrictions in programming is lifted. A process larger than the main memory can be executed because of demand paging. The OS itself loads pages of a process in main memory as required.

- It allows greater multiprogramming levels by using less of the available (primary) memory for each process.

Manual Memory Management

Manual memory management is where the programmer has direct control over when memory may be recycled. Usually this is either by explicit calls to heap management functions (for example, malloc and free in C), or by language constructs that affect the control stack (such as local variables). The key feature of a manual memory manager is that it provides a way for the program to say, "Have this memory back; I've finished with it"; the memory manager does not recycle any memory without such an instruction.

The advantages of manual memory management are:

- It can be easier for the programmer to understand exactly what is going on;

- Some manual memory managers perform better when there is a shortage of memory.

The disadvantages of manual memory management are:

- The programmer must write a lot of code to do repetitive bookkeeping of memory;

- Memory management must form a significant part of any module interface;

- Manual memory management typically requires more memory overhead per object;

- Memory management bugs are common.

It is very common for programmers, faced with an inefficient or inadequate manual memory manager, to write code to duplicate the behavior of a memory manager, either by allocating large blocks and splitting them for use, or by recycling blocks internally. Such code is known as a sub allocator. Sub allocators can take advantage of special knowledge of program behavior, but are less efficient in general than fixing the underlying allocator. Unless written by a memory management expert, sub allocators may be inefficient or unreliable.

The following languages use mainly manual memory management in most implementations, although many have conservative garbage collection extensions: Algol; C; C++; COBOL; Fortran; Pascal.

Automatic Memory Management

Automatic memory management is a service, either as a part of the language or as an extension, that automatically recycles memory that a program would not otherwise use again. Automatic memory managers (often known as garbage collectors, or simply collectors) usually do their job by recycling blocks that are unreachable from the program variables (that is, blocks that cannot be reached by following pointers).

The advantages of automatic memory management are:

- the programmer is freed to work on the actual problem;

- module interfaces are cleaner;

- there are fewer memory management bugs;

- memory management is often more efficient.

The disadvantages of automatic memory management are:

- memory may be retained because it is reachable, but won't be used again;

- automatic memory managers (currently) have limited availability.

There are many ways of performing automatic recycling of memory, a few of which are discussed in Recycling techniques.

Most modern languages use mainly automatic memory management: BASIC, Dylan, Erlang, Haskell, Java, JavaScript, Lisp, ML, Modula-3, Perl, PostScript, Prolog, Python, Scheme, Smalltalk, etc.

Memory Management Unit and Memory Protection Unit

MMU and MPU are specialized hardware which are used by CPU for memory handling. MMU is used for many functions primarily Virtual Memory (i.e. translation of virtual address to physical address) and memory protection. But MPU is used for memory protection only. In that sense, we can think of MMU as super set of MPU.

Processors which need to run high-end operating systems such as Android, Linux, Windows typically have MMU but processors which need to run RTOS such as ThreadX, Nucleus typically have MPU. Let us mention few of the real world examples of the processors with MMU and MPU. Typically, a smart-phone contains two main processors – one which runs high-end OS (e.g. Android) where Apps are running and second which runs baseband RTOS (e.g. ThredX) where 3G/4G protocol stacks are running. First one is called *Apps processor* while second one is called *Baseband processor*. Apps processor (e.g. ARM Cortex-A series) has MMU while Baseband processor (e.g. ARM Cortex-R series) has MPU.

A quick analogy can be thought of MMU as 'swiss army knife' and MPU as 'knife'! Basically, MMU implementation in HW much more complex than that of MPU. That's why many computer systems (such as real time embedded systems) which don't need Virtual Memory but need memory protection have much simpler MPU instead of full blown MMU.

The MMU has two special registers that are accessed by the CPU's control unit. A data to be sent to main memory or retrieved from memory is stored in the *Memory Data Register* (MDR). The desired logical memory address is stored in the *Memory Address Register* (MAR). The address translation is also called address binding and uses a memory map that is programmed by the operating system.

The job of the operating system is to load the appropriate data into the MMU when a processes is started and to respond to the occasional Page Faults by loading the needed memory and updating the memory map.

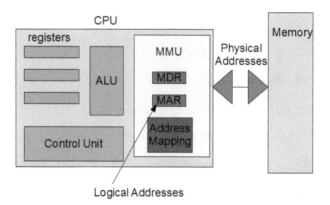

Before memory addresses are loaded on to the system bus, they are translated to physical addresses by the MMU.

Examples

Most modern systems divide memory into pages that are 4-64 KB in size, often with the capability to use huge pages from 2 MB to 1 GB in size. Page translations are cached in a translation lookaside buffer (TLB). Some systems, mainly older RISC designs, trap into the OS when a page translation is not found in the TLB. Most systems use a hardware-based tree walker. Most systems allow the MMU to be disabled, but some disable the MMU when trapping into OS code.

VAX

VAX pages are 512 bytes, which is very small. An OS may treat multiple pages as if they were a single larger page. For example, Linux on VAX groups eight pages together. Thus, the system is viewed as having 4 KB pages. The VAX divides memory into four fixed-purpose regions, each 1 GB in size. They are:

- P0 space

  o Used for general-purpose per-process memory such as heaps.

- P1 space

  o (Or control space) which is also per-process and is typically used for supervisor, ex-ecutive, kernel, user stacks and other per-process control structures managed by the operating system.

- S0 space

  o (Or system space) which is global to all processes and stores operating system code and data, whether paged or not, including pagetables.

- S1 space

  o Which is unused and "Reserved to Digital".

Page tables are big linear arrays. Normally, this would be very wasteful when addresses are used at both ends of the possible range, but the page table for applications is itself stored in the kernel's paged memory. Thus, there is effectively a two-level tree, allowing applications to have sparse memory layout without wasting a lot of space on unused page table entries. The VAX MMU is notable for lacking an accessed bit. OSes which implement paging must find some way to emulate the accessed bit if they are to operate efficiently. Typically, the OS will periodically unmap pages so that page-not-present faults can be used to let the OS set an accessed bit.

ARM

ARM architecture-based application processors implement an MMU defined by ARM's virtual memory system architecture. The current architecture defines PTEs for describing 4 KB and 64 KB pages, 1 MB sections and 16 MB super-sections; legacy versions also defined a 1 KB tiny page. ARM uses a two-level page table if using 4 KB and 64 KB pages, or just a one-level page table for 1 MB sections and 16 MB sections.

TLB updates are performed automatically by page table walking hardware. PTEs include read/write access permission based on privilege, cacheability information, an NX bit, and a non-secure bit.

IBM System/360 Model 67, IBM System/370 and Successors

The IBM System/360 Model 67, which was introduced Aug. 1965, included an MMU that was called a dynamic address translation (DAT) box. It had the unusual feature of storing accessed and dirty bits outside of the page table. They refer to physical memory rather than virtual memory, and are accessed by special-purpose instructions. This reduces overhead for the OS, which would otherwise need to propagate accessed and dirty bits from the page tables to a more physically oriented data structure. This makes OS-level virtualization easier.

Starting in August, 1972, the IBM System/370 had a similar MMU, although it initially supported only a 24-bit virtual address space rather than the 32-bit virtual address space of the System/360 Model 67. It also stored the accessed and dirty bits outside the page table. In early 1983, the System/370-XA architecture expanded the virtual address space to 31 bits, and in 2000, the 64-bit z/Architecture was introduced, with the address space expanded to 64 bits; those continued to store the accessed and dirty bits outside the page table.

DEC Alpha

The DEC Alpha processor divides memory into 8 KB pages. After a TLB miss, low-level firmware machine code (here called PALcode) walks a three-level tree-structured page table. Addresses are broken down as follows: 21 bits unused, 10 bits to index the root level of the tree, 10 bits to index the middle level of the tree, 10 bits to index the leaf level of the tree, and 13 bits that pass through to the physical address without modification. Full read/write/execute permission bits are supported.

MIPS

The MIPS architecture supports one to 64 entries in the TLB. The number of TLB entries is configurable at CPU configuration before synthesis. TLB entries are dual. Each TLB entry maps a virtual page number (VPN2) to either one of two page frame numbers (PFN0 or PFN1), depending on the least significant bit of the virtual address that is not part of the page mask. This bit and the page mask bits are not stored in the VPN2. Each TLB entry has its own page size, which can be any value from 1 KB to 256 MB in multiples of four. Each PFN in a TLB entry has a caching attribute, a dirty and a valid status bit. A VPN2 has a global status bit and an OS assigned ID which participates in the virtual address TLB entry match, if the global status bit is set to zero. A PFN stores the physical address without the page mask bits.

A TLB refill exception is generated when there are no entries in the TLB that match the mapped virtual address. A TLB invalid exception is generated when there is a match but the entry is marked invalid. A TLB modified exception is generated when there is a match but the dirty status is not set. If a TLB exception occurs when processing a TLB exception, a double fault TLB exception, it is dispatched to its own exception handler.

MIPS32 and MIPS32r2 support 32 bits of virtual address space and up to 36 bits of physical address space. MIPS64 supports up to 64 bits of virtual address space and up to 59 bits of physical address space.

Sun 1

The original Sun 1 was a single-board computer built around the Motorola 68000 microprocessor and introduced in 1982. It included the original Sun 1 memory management unit that provided address translation, memory protection, memory sharing and memory allocation for multiple processes running on the CPU. All access of the CPU to private on-board RAM, external Multibus memory, on-board I/O and the Multibus I/O ran through the MMU, where they were translated and protected in uniform fashion. The MMU was implemented in hardware on the CPU board.

The MMU consisted of a context register, a segment map and a page map. Virtual addresses from the CPU were translated into intermediate addresses by the segment map, which in turn were translated into physical addresses by the page map. The page size was 2 KB and the segment size was 32 KB which gave 16 pages per segment. Up to 16 contexts could be mapped concurrently. The maximum logical address space for a context was 1024 pages or 2 MB. The maximum physical address that could be mapped simultaneously was also 2 MB.

The context register was important in a multitasking operating system because it allowed the CPU to switch between processes without reloading all the translation state information. The 4-bit context register could switch between 16 sections of the segment map under supervisor control, which allowed 16 contexts to be mapped concurrently. Each context had its own virtual address space. Sharing of virtual address space and inter-context communications could be provided by writing the same values in to the segment or page maps of different contexts. Additional contexts could be handled by treating the segment map as a context cache and replacing out-of-date contexts on a least-recently used basis.

The context register made no distinction between user and supervisor states. Interrupts and traps did not switch contexts which required that all valid interrupt vectors always be mapped in page 0 of context, as well as the valid supervisor stack.

PowerPC

In PowerPC G1, G2, G3, and G4 pages are normally 4 KB. After a TLB miss, the standard PowerPC MMU begins two simultaneous lookups. One lookup attempts to match the address with one of four or eight data block address translation (DBAT) registers, or four or eight instruction block address translation registers (IBAT), as appropriate. The BAT registers can map linear chunks of memory as large as 256 MB, and are normally used by an OS to map large portions of the address space for the OS kernel's own use. If the BAT lookup succeeds, the other lookup is halted and ignored.

The other lookup, not directly supported by all processors in this family, is via a so-called "inverted page table," which acts as a hashed off-chip extension of the TLB. First, the top four bits of the address are used to select one of 16 segment registers. Then 24 bits from the segment register replace those four bits, producing a 52-bit address. The use of segment registers allows multiple processes to share the same hash table.

The 52-bit address is hashed, then used as an index into the off-chip table. There, a group of eight-page table entries is scanned for one that matches. If none match due to excessive hash collisions, the processor tries again with a slightly different hash function. If this, too, fails, the CPU traps into OS (with MMU disabled) so that the problem may be resolved. The OS needs to discard an entry from the hash table to make space for a new entry. The OS may generate the new entry from a more-normal tree-like page table or from per-mapping data structures which are likely to be slower and more space-efficient. Support for no-execute control is in the segment registers, leading to 256 MB granularity.

A major problem with this design is poor cache locality caused by the hash function. Tree-based designs avoid this by placing the page table entries for adjacent pages in adjacent locations. An operating system running on the PowerPC may minimize the size of the hash table to reduce this problem.

It is also somewhat slow to remove the page table entries of a process. The OS may avoid reusing segment values to delay facing this, or it may elect to suffer the waste of memory associated with per-process hash tables. G1 chips do not search for page table entries, but they do generate the hash, with the expectation that an OS will search the standard hash table via software. The OS can write to the TLB. G2, G3, and early G4 chips use hardware to search the hash table. The latest chips allow the OS to choose either method. On chips that make this optional or do not support it at all, the OS may choose to use a tree-based page table exclusively.

IA-32 / x86

The x86 architecture has evolved over a very long time while maintaining full software compatibility, even for OS code. Thus, the MMU is extremely complex, with many different possible operating modes. Normal operation of the traditional 80386 CPU and its successors (IA-32) is described.

The CPU primarily divides memory into 4 KB pages. Segment registers, fundamental to the older 8088 and 80286 MMU designs, are not used in modern OSes, with one major exception: access to thread-specific data for applications or CPU-specific data for OS kernels, which is done with explicit use of the FS and GS segment registers. All memory access involves a segment register, chosen according to the code being executed. The segment register acts as an index into a table, which provides an offset to be added to the virtual address. Except when using FS or GS, the OS ensures that the offset will be zero.

After the offset is added, the address is masked to be no larger than 32 bits. The result may be looked up via a tree-structured page table, with the bits of the address being split as follows: 10 bits for the branch of the tree, 10 bits for the leaves of the branch, and the 12 lowest bits being directly copied to the result. Some operating systems, such as OpenBSD with its W^X feature, and Linux with the Exec Shield or PaX patches, may also limit the length of the code segment, as specified by the CS register, to disallow execution of code in modifiable regions of the address space.

Minor revisions of the MMU introduced with the Pentium have allowed very large 4 MB pages by skipping the bottom level of the tree (this leaves 10 bits for indexing the first level of page hierarchy with the remaining 10+12 bits being directly copied to the result). Minor revisions of the MMU introduced with the Pentium Pro introduced the physical address extension (PAE) feature, enabling 36-bit physical addresses with 2+9+9 bits for three-level page tables and 12 lowest bits being directly copied to the result. Large pages (2 MB) are also available by skipping the bottom level of the tree (resulting in 2+9 bits for two-level table hierarchy and the remaining 9+12 lowest bits copied directly). In addition, the page attribute table allowed specification of cacheability by looking up a few high bits in a small on-CPU table.

No-execute support was originally only provided on a per-segment basis, making it very awkward to use. More recent x86 chips provide a per-page no-execute bit in the PAE mode. The W^X, Exec Shield, and PaX mechanisms described above emulate per-page non-execute support on machines x86 processors lacking the NX bit by setting the length of the code segment, with a performance loss and a reduction in the available address space.

x86-64

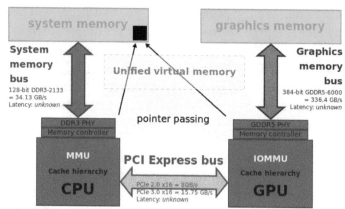

Heterogeneous System Architecture (HSA) creates a unified virtual address space for CPUs, GPUs and DSPs, obsoleting the mapping tricks and data copying.

x86-64 is a 64-bit extension of x86 that almost entirely removes segmentation in favor of the flat memory model used by almost all operating systems for the 386 or newer processors. In long mode, all segment offsets are ignored, except for the FS and GS segments. When used with 4 KB pages, the page table tree has four levels instead of three.

The virtual addresses are divided as follows: 16 bits unused, nine bits each for four tree levels (for a total of 36 bits), and the 12 lowest bits directly copied to the result. With 2 MB pages, there are only three levels of page table, for a total of 27 bits used in paging and 21 bits of offset. Some newer CPUs also support a 1 GB page with two levels of paging and 30 bits of offset.

CPUID can be used to determine if 1 GB pages are supported. In all three cases, the 16 highest bits are required to be equal to the 48th bit, or in other words, the low 48 bits are sign extended to the higher bits. This is done to allow a future expansion of the addressable range, without compromising backwards compatibility. In all levels of the page table, the page table entry includes a no-execute bit.

Unisys MCP Systems (Burroughs B5000)

The Burroughs B5000 from 1961 was the first commercial system to support virtual memory (after the Atlas), even though it has no MMU It provides the two functions of an MMU - virtual memory addresses and memory protection - with a different architectural approach.

First, in the mapping of virtual memory addresses, instead of needing an MMU, the MCP systems are descriptor-based. Each allocated memory block is given a master descriptor with the properties of the block (i.e., the size, address, and whether present in memory). When a request is made to access the block for reading or writing, the hardware checks its presence via the presence bit (pbit) in the descriptor.

A pbit of 1 indicates the presence of the block. In this case, the block can be accessed via the physical address in the descriptor. If the pbit is zero, an interrupt is generated for the MCP (operating system) to make the block present. If the address field is zero, this is the first access to this block, and it is allocated (an init pbit). If the address field is non-zero, it is a disk address of the block, which has previously been rolled out, so the block is fetched from disk and the pbit is set to one and the physical memory address updated to point to the block in memory (another pbit). This makes descriptors equivalent to a page-table entry in an MMU system. System performance can be monitored through the number of pbits. Init pbits indicate initial allocations, but a high level of other pbits indicates that the system may be thrashing.

All memory allocation is therefore completely automatic (one of the features of modern systems) and there is no way to allocate blocks other than this mechanism. There are no such calls as malloc or dealloc, since memory blocks are also automatically discarded. The scheme is also lazy, since a block will not be allocated until it is actually referenced. When memory is nearly full, the MCP examines the working set, trying compaction (since the system is segmented, not paged), deallocating read-only segments (such as code-segments which can be restored from their original copy) and, as a last resort, rolling dirty data segments out to disk.

Another way the B5000 provides a function of a MMU is in protection. Since all accesses are via the descriptor, the hardware can check that all accesses are within bounds and, in the case of a write, that the process has write permission. The MCP system is inherently secure and thus has no need of an MMU to provide this level of memory protection. Descriptors are read only to user processes and may only be updated by the system (hardware or MCP). (Words whose tag is an odd number are read-only; descriptors have a tag of 5 and code words have a tag of 3.)

Blocks can be shared between processes via copy descriptors in the process stack. Thus, some processes may have write permission, whereas others do not. A code segment is read only, thus reentrant and shared between processes. Copy descriptors contain a 20-bit address field giving index of the master descriptor in the master descriptor array. This also implements a very efficient and secure IPC mechanism. Blocks can easily be relocated, since only the master descriptor needs update when a block's status changes.

The only other aspect is performance – do MMU-based or non-MMU-based systems provide better performance? MCP systems may be implemented on top of standard hardware that does have an MMU (for example, a standard PC). Even if the system implementation uses the MMU in some way, this will not be at all visible at the MCP level.

C Dynamic Memory Allocation

Dynamic memory management refers to manual memory management. The process of allocating memory during program execution is called dynamic memory allocation. It allows us to obtain more memory when required and release it when not necessary.

Although C inherently does not have any technique to allocate memory dynamically, there are 4 library functions defined under <stdlib.h> for dynamic memory allocation.

Function	Use of Function
malloc()	Allocates requested size of bytes and returns a pointer first byte of allocated space
calloc()	Allocates space for an array elements, initializes to zero and then returns a pointer to memory
free()	deallocate the previously allocated space
realloc()	Change the size of previously allocated space

C malloc()

The name malloc stands for "memory allocation".

The function malloc() reserves a block of memory of specified size and return a pointer of type void which can be casted into pointer of any form.

Syntax of Malloc()

```
ptr = (cast-type*) malloc(byte-size)
```

Here, ptr is pointer of cast-type. The malloc() function returns a pointer to an area of memory with size of byte size. If the space is insufficient, allocation fails and returns NULL pointer.

```
ptr = (int*) malloc(100 * sizeof(int));
```

This statement will allocate either 200 or 400 according to size of int 2 or 4 bytes respectively and the pointer points to the address of first byte of memory.

C calloc()

The name calloc stands for "contiguous allocation".

The only difference between malloc() and calloc() is that, malloc() allocates single block of memory whereas calloc() allocates multiple blocks of memory each of same size and sets all bytes to zero.

Syntax of Calloc()

```
ptr = (cast-type*)calloc(n, element-size);
```

This statement will allocate contiguous space in memory for an array of n elements. For example:

```
ptr = (float*) calloc(25, sizeof(float));
```

This statement allocates contiguous space in memory for an array of 25 elements each of size of float, i.e, 4 bytes.

C Free()

Dynamically allocated memory created with either calloc() or malloc() doesn't get freed on its own. You must explicitly use free() to release the space.

Syntax of Free()

```
free(ptr);
```

This statement frees the space allocated in the memory pointed by ptr.

Example: Using C malloc() and free()

Write a C program to find sum of n elements entered by user. To perform this program, allocate memory dynamically using malloc() function.

```
#include <stdio.h>

#include <stdlib.h>

int main()

{

        int num, i, *ptr, sum = 0;

        printf("Enter number of elements: ");

        scanf("%d", &num);

        ptr = (int*) malloc(num * sizeof(int)); //memory allocated using malloc

        if(ptr == NULL)

        {
```

```
        printf("Error! memory not allocated.");

        exit(0);

    }

    printf("Enter elements of array: ");

    for(i = 0; i < num; ++i)

    {

        scanf("%d", ptr + i);

        sum += *(ptr + i);

    }

    printf("Sum = %d", sum);

    free(ptr);

    return 0;

}
```

Example: Using C calloc() and free()

Write a C program to find sum of n elements entered by user. To perform this program, allocate memory dynamically using calloc() function.

```
#include <stdio.h>

#include <stdlib.h>

int main()

{

    int num, i, *ptr, sum = 0;

    printf("Enter number of elements: ");

    scanf("%d", &num);

    ptr = (int*) calloc(num, sizeof(int));

    if(ptr == NULL)

    {

        printf("Error! memory not allocated.");

        exit(0);
```

```
        }

        printf("Enter elements of array: ");

        for(i = 0;  i < num;  ++i)

        {

                scanf("%d", ptr + i);

                sum += *(ptr + i);

        }

        printf("Sum = %d", sum);

        free(ptr);

        return 0;

}
```

C Realloc()

If the previously allocated memory is insufficient or more than required, you can change the previously allocated memory size using realloc().

Syntax of Realloc()

```
ptr = realloc(ptr, newsize);
```

Here, ptr is reallocated with size of newsize.

Example: Using Realloc()

```
#include <stdio.h>

#include <stdlib.h>

int main()

{

        int *ptr, i , n1, n2;

        printf("Enter size of array: ");

        scanf("%d", &n1);

        ptr = (int*) malloc(n1 * sizeof(int));

        printf("Address of previously allocated memory: ");
```

```
for(i = 0; i < n1; ++i)

        printf("%u\t",ptr + i);

printf("\nEnter new size of array: ");

scanf("%d", &n2);

ptr = realloc(ptr, n2 * sizeof(int));

for(i = 0; i < n2; ++i)

        printf("%u\t", ptr + i);

    return 0;

}
```

Common Errors

The improper use of dynamic memory allocation can frequently be a source of bugs. These can include security bugs or program crashes, most often due to segmentation faults.

Most common errors are as follows:

- Not Checking for Allocation Failures

  Memory allocation is not guaranteed to succeed, and may instead return a null pointer. Using the returned value, without checking if the allocation is successful, invokes undefined behavior. This usually leads to crash (due to the resulting segmentation fault on the null pointer dereference), but there is no guarantee that a crash will happen so relying on that can also lead to problems.

- Memory Leaks

  Failure to deallocate memory using free leads to buildup of non-reusable memory, which is no longer used by the program. This wastes memory resources and can lead to allocation failures when these resources are exhausted.

- Logical Errors

  All allocations must follow the same pattern: allocation using malloc, usage to store data, deallocation using free. Failures to adhere to this pattern, such as memory usage after a call to free (dangling pointer) or before a call to malloc (wild pointer), calling free twice ("double free"), etc., usually causes a segmentation fault and results in a crash of the program. These errors can be transient and hard to debug – for example, freed memory is usually not immediately reclaimed by the OS, and thus dangling pointers may persist for a while and appear to work.

Implementations

The implementation of memory management depends greatly upon operating system and architecture. Some operating systems supply an allocator for malloc, while others supply functions to control certain regions of data. The same dynamic memory allocator is often used to implement both malloc and the operator new in C++.

Heap-based

Implementation of the allocator is commonly done using the heap, or data segment. The allocator will usually expand and contract the heap to fulfill allocation requests.

The heap method suffers from a few inherent flaws, stemming entirely from fragmentation. Like any method of memory allocation, the heap will become fragmented; that is, there will be sections of used and unused memory in the allocated space on the heap. A good allocator will attempt to find an unused area of already allocated memory to use before resorting to expanding the heap. The major problem with this method is that the heap has only two significant attributes: base, or the beginning of the heap in virtual memory space; and length, or its size. The heap requires enough system memory to fill its entire length, and its base can never change. Thus, any large areas of unused memory are wasted. The heap can get "stuck" in this position if a small used segment exists at the end of the heap, which could waste any amount of address space. On lazy memory allocation schemes, such as those often found in the Linux operating system, a large heap does not necessarily reserve the equivalent system memory; it will only do so at the first write time (reads of non-mapped memory pages return zero). The granularity of this depends on page size.

Dlmalloc

Doug Lea has developed dlmalloc ("Doug Lea's Malloc") as a general-purpose allocator, starting in 1987. The GNU C library (glibc) uses ptmalloc, an allocator based on dlmalloc.

Memory on the heap is allocated as "chunks", an 8-byte aligned data structure which contains a header, and usable memory. Allocated memory contains an 8 or 16 byte overhead for the size of the chunk and usage flags. Unallocated chunks also store pointers to other free chunks in the usable space area, making the minimum chunk size 24 bytes.

Unallocated memory is grouped into "bins" of similar sizes, implemented by using a double-linked list of chunks (with pointers stored in the unallocated space inside the chunk).

For requests below 256 bytes (a "smallbin" request), a simple two power best fit allocator is used. If there are no free blocks in that bin, a block from the next highest bin is split in two.

For requests of 256 bytes or above but below the mmap threshold, recent versions of dlmalloc use an in-place *bitwise trie* algorithm. If there is no free space left to satisfy the request, dlmalloc tries to increase the size of the heap, usually via the brk system call.

For requests above the mmap threshold (a "largebin" request), the memory is always allocated using the mmap system call. The threshold is usually 256 KB. The mmap method averts problems with huge buffers trapping a small allocation at the end after their expiration, but always allocates an entire page of memory, which on many architectures is 4096 bytes in size.

FreeBSD's and NetBSD's Jemalloc

Since FreeBSD 7.0 and NetBSD 5.0, the old malloc implementation (phkmalloc) was replaced by jemalloc, written by Jason Evans. The main reason for this was a lack of scalability of phk-malloc in terms of multithreading. In order to avoid lock contention, jemalloc uses separate "arenas" for each CPU. Experiments measuring number of allocations per second in multi-threading application have shown that this makes it scale linearly with the number of threads, while for both phkmalloc and dlmalloc performance was inversely proportional to the number of threads.

OpenBSD's Malloc

OpenBSD's implementation of the malloc function makes use of mmap. For requests greater in size than one page, the entire allocation is retrieved using mmap; smaller sizes are assigned from memory pools maintained by malloc within a number of "bucket pages," also allocated with mmap. On a call to free, memory is released and unmapped from the process address space using mun-map. This system is designed to improve security by taking advantage of the address space layout randomization and gap page features implemented as part of OpenBSD's mmap system call, and to detect use-after-free bugs—as a large memory allocation is completely unmapped after it is freed, further use causes a segmentation fault and termination of the program.

Hoard Malloc

Hoard is an allocator whose goal is scalable memory allocation performance. Like OpenBSD's allocator, Hoard uses mmap exclusively, but manages memory in chunks of 64 kilobytes called superblocks. Hoard's heap is logically divided into a single global heap and a number of per-pro-cessor heaps. In addition, there is a thread-local cache that can hold a limited number of super-blocks. By allocating only from superblocks on the local per-thread or per-processor heap, and moving mostly-empty superblocks to the global heap so they can be reused by other proces-sors, Hoard keeps fragmentation low while achieving near linear scalability with the number of threads.

Thread-caching Malloc (Tcmalloc)

Every thread has local storage for small allocations. For large allocations mmap or sbrk can be used. TCMalloc, a *malloc* developed by Google, has garbage-collection for local storage of dead threads. The TCMalloc is considered to be more than twice as fast as glibc's ptmalloc for multi-threaded programs.

In-kernel

Operating system kernels need to allocate memory just as application programs do. The imple-mentation of malloc within a kernel often differs significantly from the implementations used by C libraries, however. For example, memory buffers might need to conform to special restrictions imposed by DMA, or the memory allocation function might be called from interrupt context. This necessitates a malloc implementation tightly integrated with the virtual memory subsystem of the operating system kernel.

Overriding Malloc

Because malloc and its relatives can have a strong impact on the performance of a program, it is not uncommon to override the functions for a specific application by custom implementations that are optimized for application's allocation patterns. The C standard provides no way of doing this, but operating systems have found various ways to do this by exploiting dynamic linking. One way is to simply link in a different library to override the symbols. Another, employed by Unix System V.3, is to make malloc and free function pointers that an application can reset to custom functions.

Allocation Size Limits

The largest possible memory block malloc can allocate depends on the host system, particularly the size of physical memory and the operating system implementation. Theoretically, the largest number should be the maximum value that can be held in a size_t type, which is an implementation-dependent unsigned integer representing the size of an area of memory. In the C99 standard and later, it is available as the SIZE_MAX constant from <stdint.h>. Although not guaranteed by ISO C, it is usually 2CHAR_BIT × sizeof(size_t) − 1.

Extensions and Alternatives

The C library implementations shipping with various operating systems and compilers may come with alternatives and extensions to the standard malloc package. Notable among these is:

- alloca, which allocates a requested number of bytes on the call stack. No corresponding deallocation function exists, as typically the memory is deallocated as soon as the calling function returns. alloca was present on Unix systems as early as 32/V (1978), but its use can be problematic in some (e.g., embedded) contexts. While supported by many compilers, it is not part of the ANSI-C standard and therefore may not always be portable. It may also cause minor performance problems: it leads to variable-size stack frames, so that both stack and frame pointers need to be managed (with fixed-size stack frames, one of these is redundant). Larger allocations may also increase the risk of undefined behavior due to a stack overflow. C99 offered variable-length arrays as an alternative stack allocation mechanism - however, this feature was relegated to optional in the later C11 standard.

- POSIX defines a function posix_memalign that allocates memory with caller-specified alignment. Its allocations are deallocated with free.

Malloc() and Calloc()

This function allocates a size byte of memory. It returns a pointer (*) to the first byte, or if there is an error, it returns NULL (to ensure that the situation is out of memory).

The syntax of the function is:

```
Syntax: void *malloc(size_t size);
```

This function accepts a single argument called size which is of type size_t. The size_t is defined as unsigned int in stdlib.h, for now, you can think of it as an alias to unsigned int.

If successful, malloc() returns a void pointer to the first allocated byte of memory. Before you can use the pointer you must cast it to appropriate type. So malloc() function is generally used as follows:

```
p = (datatype *)malloc(size);
```

where the p is a pointer of type (datatype *) and size is memory space in bytes you want to allocate.

Let's take a simple example:

Suppose we want to allocate 20 bytes (for storing 5 integers, where the size of each integer is 4 bytes) dynamically using malloc(). Here is how we can do it:

```
int *p; // p is pointer to int or (int*)
```

```
p = (int*)malloc(20); // allocate 20 bytes
```

This statement allocates 20 contiguous bytes of memory from the heap and assigns the address of the first byte to variable p. Notice how void pointer returned from the malloc() function is type-casted and then assigned to p. Memory allocated contains garbage value so do not try to dereference it before assigning proper values to it.

As we know the size of data types in C vary from system to system, that's why malloc() function is used in conjunction with the size of operator.

```
int *p; // p is pointer to int or (int*)
```

```
p = (int*)malloc(5*sizeof(int)); // allocate sufficient memory for 5 integers
```

We are still allocating 20 bytes of memory but now our program is portable (i.e it can be run on the various operating system without any modification.) and certainly more readable.

Now we have p pointing to the first byte of allocated memory, we can easily access subsequent bytes using pointer arithmetic.

When the heap runs out of free space, malloc() function returns NULL. So before using the pointer variable in any way, we must first always check the value returned by malloc() function.

if(p == NULL)

{

```
 printf("Memory allocation failed");
```

```
 exit(1); // exit the program
```

}

Let's rewrite the program to calculate the average marks of students in a class using the malloc() function.

```
#include<stdio.h>
```

```c
#include<stdlib.h>
int main()
{
    float *p, sum = 0;
    int i, n;
    printf("Enter the number of students: ");
    scanf("%d", &n);
    // allocate memory to store n variables of type float
    p = (float*)malloc(n*sizeof(float));
    // if dynamic allocation failed exit the program
    if(p==NULL)
    {
    printf("Memory allocation failed");
    exit(1); // exit the program
    }
    // ask the student to enter marks
    for(i = 0; i < n; i++)
    {
    printf("Enter marks for %d student: ", i+1);
    scanf("%f", p+i);
    }
    // calculate sum
    for(i = 0; i < n; i++)
    {
    sum += *(p+i);
    }
    printf("\nAverage marks = %.2f\n", sum/n);
    // signal to operating system program ran fine
```

```
        return 0;

}
```

Expected Output:

1st run:

> Enter the number of students: 4
>
> Enter marks for 1 student: 12.12
>
> Enter marks for 2 student: 34.14
>
> Enter marks for 3 student: 43.1
>
> Enter marks for 4 student: 45.87
>
> Average marks = 33.81

2nd run:

> Enter the number of students: 2
>
> Enter marks for 1 student: 13.41
>
> Enter marks for 2 student: 56.31
>
> Average marks = 34.86

Works

In line 6, we have declared a pointer to float p and a float variable s, where it is initialized to 0.

In line 7, we have declared two variables i and n of type int.

In line 9, printf() function prints "Enter the number of students: " to the console.

In line 10, scanf() is used to read input from the user, which is then stored in a variable n.

Line 12 uses malloc() function to dynamically allocate memory to store n numbers of type float. The variable p is of type pointer to float or (float*), that's why the result of malloc() function is type casted using (float*).

In line 15, the if condition checks whether the pointer returned by malloc() is null pointer or not. If p is NULL then memory allocation failed and the program terminates.

In line 21, we have a for loop which repeatedly asks the user to enter marks n times. Notice that in scanf()statement p + i is used without & sign because p is a pointer.

In line 29, we have another for loop which accumulates the marks of n students in a variable sum.

In line 34, Average marks are displayed by dividing total marks by a total number of students.

The C library function void *calloc(size_t nitems, size_t size) allocates the requested memory and returns a pointer to it. The difference in malloc and calloc is that malloc does not set the memory to zero where as calloc sets allocated memory to zero.

Declaration

Following is the declaration for calloc() function.

```
void *calloc(size_t nitems, size_t size)
```

Parameters

- Nitems – This is the number of elements to be allocated.

- Size – This is the size of elements.

Return Value

This function returns a pointer to the allocated memory, or NULL if the request fails.

Example

The following example shows the usage of calloc() function.

```
#include <stdio.h>

#include <stdlib.h>

int main () {

        int i, n;

        int *a;

        printf("Number of elements to be entered:");

        scanf("%d",&n);

        a = (int*)calloc(n, sizeof(int));

        printf("Enter %d numbers:\n",n);

        for( i=0 ; i < n ; i++ ) {

        scanf("%d",&a[i]);

        }

        printf("The numbers entered are: ");

        for( i=0 ; i < n ; i++ ) {

        printf("%d ",a[i]);
```

```
    }

    free( a );


    return(0);

}
```

Let us compile and run the above program that will produce the following result:

```
Number of elements to be entered:3

Enter 3 numbers:

22

55

14

The numbers entered are: 22 55 14
```

Difference between Malloc and Calloc

Malloc	Calloc
The name malloc stands for *memory allocation*.	The name calloc stands for *contiguous allocation*.
void *malloc(size_t n) returns a pointer to n bytes of uninitialized storage, or NULL if the request cannot be satisfied. If the space assigned by malloc() is overrun, the results are undefined.	void *calloc(size_t n, size_t size)returns a pointer to enough free space for an array of n objects of the specified size, or NULL if the request cannot be satisfied. The storage is initialized to zero.
malloc() takes one argument that is, *number of bytes.*	calloc() take two arguments those are: *number of blocks* and *size of each block.*
syntax of malloc(): void *malloc(size_t n); Allocates n bytes of memory. If the allocation succeeds, a void pointer to the allocated memory is returned. Otherwise NULL is returned.	syntax of calloc(): void *calloc(size_t n, size_t size); Allocates a contiguous block of memory large enough to hold n elements of sizebytes each. The allocated region is initialized to zero.
malloc is faster than calloc.	calloc takes little longer than mallocbecause of the extra step of initializing the allocated memory by zero. However, in practice the difference in speed is very tiny and not recognizable.

Similarities between Malloc and Calloc

The pointer returned by malloc or calloc has the proper alignment for the object in question, but it must be cast into the appropriate type.

Proper alignment means the value of the returned address is guaranteed to be an even multiple of alignment. The value of alignment must be a power of two and must be greater than or equal to the size of a word.

The malloc(), calloc() functions will fail if:

- The physical limits of the system are exceeded by n bytes of memory which cannot be allocated.

- There is not enough memory available to allocate n bytes of memory; but the application could try again later.

Memory Pool

A *memory pool* is a kernel object that allows memory blocks to be dynamically allocated from a designated memory region. The memory blocks in a memory pool can be of any size, thereby reducing the amount of wasted memory when an application needs to allocate storage for data structures of different sizes. The memory pool uses a "buddy memory allocation" algorithm to efficiently partition larger blocks into smaller ones, allowing blocks of different sizes to be allocated and released efficiently while limiting memory fragmentation concerns.

Any number of memory pools can be defined. Each memory pool is referenced by its memory address.

A memory pool has the following key properties:

- A minimum block size, measured in bytes. It must be at least 4X bytes long, where X is greater than 0.

- A maximum block size, measured in bytes. This should be a power of 4 times larger than the minimum block size. That is, "maximum block size" must equal "minimum block size" times 4^Y, where Y is greater than or equal to zero.

- The number of maximum-size blocks initially available. This must be greater than zero.

- A buffer that provides the memory for the memory pool's blocks. This must be at least "maximum block size" times "number of maximum-size blocks" bytes long.

The memory pool's buffer must be aligned to an N-byte boundary, where N is a power of 2 larger than 2 (i.e. 4, 8, 16, ...). To ensure that all memory blocks in the buffer are similarly aligned to this boundary, the minimum block size must also be a multiple of N.

A thread that needs to use a memory block simply allocates it from a memory pool. Following a successful allocation, the *data* field of the block descriptor supplied by the thread indicates the starting address of the memory block. When the thread is finished with a memory block, it must release the block back to the memory pool so the block can be reused.

If a block of the desired size is unavailable, a thread can optionally wait for one to become available. Any number of threads may wait on a memory pool simultaneously; when a suitable memory block becomes available, it is given to the highest-priority thread that has waited the longest.

Unlike a heap, more than one memory pool can be defined, if needed. For example, different applications can utilize different memory pools; this can help prevent one application from hijacking resources to allocate all of the available blocks.

Internal Operation

A memory pool's buffer is an array of maximum-size blocks, with no wasted space between the blocks. Each of these "level 0" blocks is a *quad-block* that can be partitioned into four smaller "level 1" blocks of equal size, if needed. Likewise, each level 1 block is itself a quad-block that can be partitioned into four smaller "level 2" blocks in a similar way, and so on. Thus, memory pool blocks can be recursively partitioned into quarters until blocks of the minimum size are obtained, at which point no further partitioning can occur.

A memory pool keeps track of how its buffer space has been partitioned using an array of *block set* data structures. There is one block set for each partitioning level supported by the pool, or (to put it another way) for each block size. A block set keeps track of all free blocks of its associated size using an array of *quad-block status* data structures.

When an application issues a request for a memory block, the memory pool first determines the size of the smallest block that will satisfy the request, and examines the corresponding block set. If the block set contains a free block, the block is marked as used and the allocation process is complete. If the block set does not contain a free block, the memory pool attempts to create one automatically by splitting a free block of a larger size or by merging free blocks of smaller sizes; if a suitable block can't be created, the allocation request fails.

The memory pool's merging algorithm cannot combine adjacent free blocks of different sizes, nor can it merge adjacent free blocks of the same size if they belong to different parent quad-blocks. As a consequence, memory fragmentation issues can still be encountered when using a memory pool.

When an application releases a previously allocated memory block it is combined synchronously with its three "partner" blocks if possible, and recursively so up through the levels. This is done in constant time, and quickly, so no manual "defragmentation" management is needed.

Implementation

A memory pool is defined using a variable of type struct k_mem_pool. However, since a memory pool also requires a number of variable-size data structures to represent its block sets and the status of its quad-blocks, the kernel does not support the run-time definition of a memory pool. A memory pool can only be defined and initialized at compile time by calling K_MEM_POOL_DE-FINE.

The following code defines and initializes a memory pool that has 3 blocks of 4096 bytes each, which can be partitioned into blocks as small as 64 bytes and is aligned to a 4-byte boundary. (That is, the memory pool supports block sizes of 4096, 1024, 256, and 64 bytes.) Observe that the macro defines all of the memory pool data structures, as well as its buffer.

K_MEM_POOL_DEFINE(my pool, 64, 4096, 3, 4);

Allocating a Memory Block

A memory block is allocated by calling k_mem_pool_alloc().

The following code builds on the example above, and waits up to 100 milliseconds for a 200 byte memory block to become available, then fills it with zeroes. A warning is issued if a suitable block is not obtained.

Note that the application will actually receive a 256 byte memory block, since that is the closest matching size supported by the memory pool.

```
struct k_mem_block block;

if (k_mem_pool_alloc(&my_pool, &block, 200, 100) == 0)) {

 memset(block.data, 0, 200);

 ...

} else {

 printf("Memory allocation time-out");

}
```

Releasing a Memory Block

A memory block is released by calling k_mem_pool_free().

The following code builds on the example above, and allocates a 75 byte memory block, then releases it once it is no longer needed. (A 256 byte memory block is actually used to satisfy the request).

```
struct k_mem_block block;

k_mem_pool_alloc(&my_pool, &block, 75, K_FOREVER);

... /* use memory block */

k_mem_pool_free(&block);
```

Suggested uses

Use a memory pool to allocate memory in variable-size blocks.

Use memory pool blocks when sending large amounts of data from one thread to another, to avoid unnecessary copying of the data.

APIs

The following memory pool APIs are provided by kernel.h:

- *K_MEM_POOL_DEFINE*

- *k_mem_pool_alloc()*

- *k_mem_pool_free()*

Example

Now that we know what benefits we get from the pool, let's create one.

The first thing we need to do is to define the memory layout. As said before, we will split our memory in chunks. Every chunk has a small header that contains a pointer to the *next chunk*, a pointer to the *previous chunk*, the *user data size* and a *flag* to say if the chunk is free or not.

The header consists of 16 bytes (we assume pointers to be 4 bytes, this won't work on a 64 bits architecture).

First 8 bytes are needed to store where is the next and where is the previous chunk in the pool. If the current chunk is the first one or the last one prev/next pointers will be NULL.

Other 4 bytes are used to store the user data size; this is needed because we want to know how big is the chunk of data after the header.

The last thing we save in the header is a boolean flag that states whether the chunk is free or used. This will take 1 more byte, plus 3 bytes of padding means other4 bytes which takes our grand total to *16 bytes*.

The Chunk class looks as follow:

```
class Chunk

{

public:

        Chunk(DWORD userDataSize) :      m_next(NULL),
                                         m_prev(NULL),
                                         m_userdataSize(userDataSize),
                                         m_free(true) {};

        void write(void* dest)

        {
```

```
    memcpy(dest, this, sizeof(Chunk) );

    }

    void read(void* src)

    {

    memcpy(this, src, sizeof(Chunk) );

    }

    Chunk* m_next;
    Chunk* m_prev;
    DWORD m_userdataSize;
    bool m_free;

};
```

Now that we have defined the smalles unit in our memory management system we can write the memory pool itself.

We want our memory pool object to allow us to allocate a new block and free an existing block. We also require any pool to be able to check the pool's integrity and to dump the whole pool to a txt file.

We call our heap like pool StandardMemoryPool which inherits from MemoryPool. This will allow us to add new memory pools with different behaviours, like *fixed size chunk pools* or *virtual memory pools*.

First of all, let's give a good look at the abstract memory pool class. Our header file starts with some thrasing options.

```
#ifdef _DEBUG

#define TRASH_POOLS 1

#else

#define TRASH_POOLS 0

#endif
```

Trashing the pool is a useful feature that we want to have in our pools. The idea here is to copy a pattern in the user data block on allocation and on deallocation. Doing this we can easily see if the chunk has been used or not and in what state it was left.

The trashing feature is useful in a debug environment, but since it requires a memory copy every time we don't really want to be active in release.

```
/**

* Abstract memory pool class
```

```
*/

class MemoryPool

{

public:

        // Methods

        //-----------------------------------------

        inline virtual void* allocate(DWORD size) = 0;

        inline virtual void free(void* ptr) = 0;

        inline virtual bool integrityCheck() const = 0;

        inline virtual void dumpToFile(const std::string& fileName,

        const DWORD itemsPerLine) const = 0;
```

These four methods are the core of every memory pool and they are all pure virtual. These methods are the most important bits of this class; the rest is pretty straightforward:

```
        inline DWORD getFreePoolSize() const { return m_freePoolSize; }

        inline DWORD getTotalPoolSize() const { return m_totalPoolSize; }

        inline bool hasBoundsCheckOn() const { return m_boundsCheck; }

        // Static

        //-----------------------------------------

        static const BYTE s_trashOnCreation = 0xCC;

        static const BYTE s_trashOnAllocSignature = 0xAB;

        static const BYTE s_trashOnFreeSignature = 0xFE;

        static const BYTE s_boundsCheckSize = 16;

        static const BYTE s_startBound[s_boundsCheckSize];

        static const BYTE s_endBound[s_boundsCheckSize];

protected:

  // Ctor/Dtor

  //-----------------------------------------

  MemoryPool()
```

```
        : m_totalPoolSize(0)

        , m_freePoolSize(0)

        , m_trashOnCreation(TRASH_POOLS)

        , m_trashOnAlloc(TRASH_POOLS)

        , m_trashOnFree(TRASH_POOLS)

        , m_boundsCheck(0)

        {};

    virtual ~MemoryPool(){};

    // Variables

    //-----------------------------------------

    DWORD m_totalPoolSize;

    DWORD m_freePoolSize;

    // Bitfield

    unsigned m_trashOnCreation : 1;

    unsigned m_trashOnAlloc : 1;

    unsigned m_trashOnFree : 1;

    unsigned m_boundsCheck : 1;

};
```

You have probably noticed the m_boundsCheck flag and the two s_startBound ands_end-Bound constants; these are used by any pool to enforce a bound check mechanism that will allow us to trace any eventual memory stomp.

Finally we can create our first pool. First of all we write our constructor to set up the pool for us:

```
// Ctors/Dtor

//-----------------------------------------

StandardMemoryPool(DWORD sizeInBytes, bool boundCheck)

{

    //Set the bound check

    if(boundCheck) m_boundsCheck = 1;

    //Allocate the total memory
```

```
m_poolMemory = ::new unsigned char[sizeInBytes];
```

First important thing, we allocate as many bytes as required. This is the only allocation we will perform for this pool; once we have the memory back from the OS we will handle it manually.

```
m_freePoolSize = sizeInBytes - sizeof(Chunk);
```

```
m_totalPoolSize = sizeInBytes;
```

Since we are writing the Chunk header information straight into the pool this will consume memory. This means that our actual free space is always smaller then the total space. The more chunks we have, the more memory we need to "waste".

```
    // Trash it if required

    if(m_trashOnCreation)

    memset(m_poolMemory, s_trashOnCreation, sizeInBytes);

    //Allocate the first free block

    if(m_boundsCheck)

    {

        m_freePoolSize -= s_boundsCheckSize * 2;

        Chunk freeChunk(sizeInBytes - sizeof(Chunk) - 2 * s_boundsCheckSize);

        freeChunk.write(m_poolMemory + s_boundsCheckSize);

        memcpy( m_poolMemory, s_startBound, s_boundsCheckSize );

        memcpy( m_poolMemory + sizeInBytes - s_boundsCheckSize ,

        s_endBound, s_boundsCheckSize );

    }

    else

    {

        Chunk freeChunk(sizeInBytes - sizeof(Chunk));

        freeChunk.write(m_poolMemory);

    }

}

    ~StandardMemoryPool()

{
```

```
        //Deallocate

        ::delete[] m_poolMemory;

}
```

We finally create the first big block. Obviously this block is free since nothing has been allocated yet. It's important to notice the two memcpys call in the "boundsCheck" version of the code. This is done to put the two guards in place. Having this guards in place will also require more memory for every chunk.

Let's now have a look at how a 64 bytes pool looks like after creation. Notice how different is the free size in the version with bounds check on. We've highlighted the next, prev, size and flag + padding position in memory.

```
Memory pool --------------------------------

Type: Standard Memory

Total Size: 64

Free Size: 48

Free:  0x001e8680 [Bytes:48]

Memory Dump:

Start: 0x001e8680

0x001e8680: 00:00:00:00:00:00:00:00:30:00:00:00:01:cc:cc:cc     0 ÌÌÌ

0x001e8690: cc:cc:cc:cc:cc:cc:cc:cc:cc:cc:cc:cc:cc:cc:cc:cc ÌÌÌÌÌÌÌÌÌÌÌÌÌÌÌÌ

0x001e86a0: cc:cc:cc:cc:cc:cc:cc:cc:cc:cc:cc:cc:cc:cc:cc:cc ÌÌÌÌÌÌÌÌÌÌÌÌÌÌÌÌ

0x001e86b0: cc:cc:cc:cc:cc:cc:cc:cc:cc:cc:cc:cc:cc:cc:cc:cc ÌÌÌÌÌÌÌÌÌÌÌÌÌÌÌÌ

Memory pool --------------------------------

Type: Standard Memory

Total Size: 64

Free Size: 16

Free:  0x001e8aa8 [Bytes:16]

Memory Dump:

Start: 0x001e8a98

0x001e8a98: 5b:42:6c:6f:63:6b:2e:2e:2e:2e:53:74:61:72:74:5d [Block....Start]

0x001e8aa8: 00:00:00:00:00:00:00:00:10:00:00:00:01:cc:cc:cc ÌÌÌ
```

```
0x001e8ab8:  cc:cc:cc:cc:cc:cc:cc:cc:cc:cc:cc:cc:cc:cc:cc:cc  ÌÌÌÌÌÌÌÌÌÌÌÌÌÌÌÌ

0x001e8ac8:  5b:42:6c:6f:63:6b:2e:2e:2e:2e:2e:2e:45:6e:64:5d  [Block......End]
```

Now the interesting part, how to implement those four core functions in our heap like memory pool. Let's go straight to the code!

First of all we write our allocation function. The *allocation function* must find a block big enough to allocate the required memory. Once found it will update the neighbour blocks to point to the newcome and then it will return a pointer to the user data.

```
inline void* StandardMemoryPool::allocate(DWORD _size)

{

        DWORD requiredSize = _size + sizeof(Chunk);

        // If guards are required, add their size

        if(m_boundsCheck)

        requiredSize += s_boundsCheckSize * 2;

        // Now search for a block big enough

        Chunk* block = (Chunk*)( m_boundsCheck == 1 ? m_poolMemory +

        s_boundsCheckSize : m_poolMemory);

        while(block)

        {

        if(block->m_free && block->m_userdataSize >= requiredSize ) break;

        block = block->m_next;

}

BYTE* blockData = (BYTE*)block;

// If no block is found, return NULL

if(!block) return NULL;
```

Straightforward so far. Notice how the required block size increases when bounds check is on. Once we have found a free block we create a new used block with part of the free memory and we update the neighbour blocks' pointers:

```
// If the block is valid, create a new free block with

// what remains of the block memory

DWORD freeUserDataSize = block->m_userdataSize - requiredSize;
```

```
if( freeUserDataSize > s_minFreeBlockSize)

{

        Chunk freeBlock(freeUserDataSize);

        freeBlock.m_next = block->m_next;

        freeBlock.m_prev = block;

        freeBlock.write( blockData + requiredSize );

        if(freeBlock.m_next)

        freeBlock.m_next->m_prev = (Chunk*)(blockData + requiredSize);

        if(m_boundsCheck)

        memcpy( blockData + requiredSize - s_boundsCheckSize, s_startBound,

        s_boundsCheckSize );

        block->m_next = (Chunk*)(blockData + requiredSize);

        block->m_userdataSize = _size;

}

// If a block is found, update the pool size

m_freePoolSize -= block->m_userdataSize;

// Set the memory block

block->m_free = false;
```

So, if the size is enough we have the memory we need. The free block we found will be marked as used and its size will be modified to be what required. Then we create a new free block which will inherith the remaining memory.

This is 128 bytes pool before allocation:

```
0x00268ed0:  00:00:00:00:00:00:00:00:70:00:00:00:01:cc:cc:cc  p Ìc
0x00268ee0:  cc:cc:cc:cc:cc:cc:cc:cc:cc:cc:cc:cc:cc:cc:cc:cc  ÌÌÌÌÌÌÌÌÌÌÌÌÌÌÌÌ
0x00268ef0:  cc:cc:cc:cc:cc:cc:cc:cc:cc:cc:cc:cc:cc:cc:cc:cc  ÌÌÌÌÌÌÌÌÌÌÌÌÌÌÌÌ
0x00268f00:  cc:cc:cc:cc:cc:cc:cc:cc:cc:cc:cc:cc:cc:cc:cc:cc  ÌÌÌÌÌÌÌÌÌÌÌÌÌÌÌÌ
0x00268f10:  cc:cc:cc:cc:cc:cc:cc:cc:cc:cc:cc:cc:cc:cc:cc:cc  ÌÌÌÌÌÌÌÌÌÌÌÌÌÌÌÌ
0x00268f20:  cc:cc:cc:cc:cc:cc:cc:cc:cc:cc:cc:cc:cc:cc:cc:cc  ÌÌÌÌÌÌÌÌÌÌÌÌÌÌÌÌ
0x00268f30:  cc:cc:cc:cc:cc:cc:cc:cc:cc:cc:cc:cc:cc:cc:cc:cc  ÌÌÌÌÌÌÌÌÌÌÌÌÌÌÌÌ
```

```
0x00268f40: cc:cc:cc:cc:cc:cc:cc:cc:cc:cc:cc:cc:cc:cc:cc:cc  ÌÌÌÌÌÌÌÌÌÌÌÌÌÌÌÌ
```

Same pool after allocation:

```
0x00268ed0: 00:8f:26:00:00:00:00:00:20:00:00:00:00:cc:cc:cc  & ÌÌÌ

0x00268ee0: ab:ab:ab:ab:ab:ab:ab:ab:ab:ab:ab:ab:ab:ab:ab:ab  «««««««««««««««««

0x00268ef0: ab:ab:ab:ab:ab:ab:ab:ab:ab:ab:ab:ab:ab:ab:ab:ab  «««««««««««««««««

0x00268f00: 00:00:00:00:d0:8e:26:00:40:00:00:00:01:cc:cc:cc  ÐŽ& @ ÌÌÌ

0x00268f10: cc:cc:cc:cc:cc:cc:cc:cc:cc:cc:cc:cc:cc:cc:cc:cc  ÌÌÌÌÌÌÌÌÌÌÌÌÌÌÌÌ

0x00268f20: cc:cc:cc:cc:cc:cc:cc:cc:cc:cc:cc:cc:cc:cc:cc:cc  ÌÌÌÌÌÌÌÌÌÌÌÌÌÌÌÌ

0x00268f30: cc:cc:cc:cc:cc:cc:cc:cc:cc:cc:cc:cc:cc:cc:cc:cc  ÌÌÌÌÌÌÌÌÌÌÌÌÌÌÌÌ

0x00268f40: cc:cc:cc:cc:cc:cc:cc:cc:cc:cc:cc:cc:cc:cc:cc:cc  ÌÌÌÌÌÌÌÌÌÌÌÌÌÌÌÌ
```

Notice the next pointer and the prev pointer which are not null anymore. Also check the flag for the first block: now it's zero because the block is in use. The first block's user data has been trashed with the 0xab pattern, so we can easily see where the user data is and we can assume that it was just initialized.

The last part of the allocation function deals with bounds check and trashing.

```
// Move the memory around if guards are needed

if(m_boundsCheck)

{

    memcpy( blockData - s_boundsCheckSize, s_startBound, s_boundsCheckSize );

    memcpy( blockData + sizeof(Chunk) + block->m_userdataSize, s_endBound,

    s_boundsCheckSize );

}

    //Trash on alloc if required

    if(m_trashOnAlloc)

        memset(blockData + sizeof(Chunk), s_trashOnAllocSignature,

            block->m_userdataSize);

  return (blockData + sizeof(Chunk));
```

Now the *free function*. The thing is worth noticing in this function is that it will try to merge any free block before and after the block we are trying to free. This grants us that we won't have any free block followed (or preceded) by another free block.

```
inline void StandardMemoryPool::free(void* ptr)

{

    // is a valid node?

    if(!ptr) return;

    Chunk* block = (Chunk*)( (BYTE*)ptr - sizeof(Chunk) );

    ASSERT(block->m_free == false, "This block is already free");

    if(block->m_free) return;
```

The pointer we are given is pointing to user data. We need to move it back of the size of the header to have the Chunk structure.

```
    DWORD fullBlockSize = block->m_userdataSize + sizeof(Chunk) +

    (m_boundsCheck == 1 ? s_boundsCheckSize * 2 : 0);

    m_freePoolSize += block->m_userdataSize;

    Chunk* headBlock = block;

    Chunk* prev = block->m_prev;

    Chunk* next = block->m_next;
```

headBlock will be the head of the free block. prev and next are pointers relative toheadBlock. Initially headBlock is the block we want to free but if the previous block is also free then we set this one to be the headBlock and we increase the size to cover both blocks.

```
    // If the node before is free I merge it with this one

    if(block->m_prev && block->m_prev->m_free)

    {

        headBlock = block->m_prev;

        prev = block->m_prev->m_prev;

        next = block->m_next;

        // Include the prev node in the block size so we trash it as well

        fullBlockSize += m_boundsCheck == 1 ?

            block->m_prev->m_userdataSize +

            sizeof(Chunk) + s_boundsCheckSize * 2 : block->m_prev->m_userdataSize +

            sizeof(Chunk);
```

```
    // If there is a next one, we need to update its pointer

if(block->m_next)

{

   // We will re point the next

   block->m_next->m_prev = headBlock;

   // Include the next node in the block size if it is

   // free so we trash it as well

   if( block->m_next->m_free )

   {

    // We will point to next's next

    next = block->m_next->m_next;

    if(block->m_next->m_next)

       block->m_next->m_next->m_prev = headBlock;

    fullBlockSize +=m_boundsCheck == 1 ?

    block->m_next->m_userdataSize+

    sizeof(Chunk) +

    s_boundsCheckSize * 2 :

    block->m_next->m_userdataSize +

    sizeof(Chunk);

   }

 }

}
```

If the previous one is not free while the next one is not used then we include it in the current head-Block.

```
else

// If next node is free lets merge it to the current one

if(block->m_next && block->m_next->m_free)

{
```

```
headBlock = block;

prev = block->m_prev;

next = block->m_next->m_next;

// Include the next node in the block size so we trash it as well

fullBlockSize +=m_boundsCheck == 1 ?

  block->m_next->m_userdataSize+

  sizeof(Chunk) + s_boundsCheckSize * 2 :

  block->m_next->m_userdataSize +

  sizeof(Chunk);

}
```

Now that we have modified all the pointers we create the free block itself.

```
    // Create the free block

    BYTE* freeBlockStart = (BYTE*)headBlock;

    if(m_trashOnFree)

      memset( m_boundsCheck == 1 ? freeBlockStart -

        s_boundsCheckSize : freeBlockStart,

        s_trashOnFreeSignature, fullBlockSize );

    DWORD freeUserDataSize = fullBlockSize - sizeof(Chunk);

    freeUserDataSize = (m_boundsCheck == 1) ? freeUserDataSize -

         s_boundsCheckSize * 2 : freeUserDataSize;

    Chunk freeBlock(freeUserDataSize);

    freeBlock.m_prev = prev;

    freeBlock.m_next = next;

    freeBlock.write(freeBlockStart);

    // Move the memory around if guards are needed

    if(m_boundsCheck)

    {

      memcpy( freeBlockStart - s_boundsCheckSize, s_startBound,
```

```
            s_boundsCheckSize );

        memcpy( freeBlockStart + sizeof(Chunk) + freeUserDataSize,

            s_endBound, s_boundsCheckSize );

    }

}
```

Now, since we want to handle several pools, we may want to have an XML file to store all this information. This means that we need a manager class and some XML parsing stuff. To parse the XML We've used a small opensource parser called TinyXML. It's included in the compressed file.

The memory pool manager class is simply a Singleton that contains a hashtable with all the pools. When constructed the manager will search for "pool.xml" and will generate all the pools as specified in that file. We can then get the pool by name as follow:

```
MemoryPool* pool = MemoryPoolManager::it().getPool(name);
```

To make it easy to use we probably want to override new and delete. This is done in Allocation.h. This file also contains some useful defines that allow us to simply invoke a macro to allocate and deallocate as follows:

```
MyClass* object = NEW(POOL("MyPool")) MyClass(param1, param2);

DELETE(POOL("MyPool"), object);
```

Virtual Memory

Virtual memory is a storage allocation scheme in which secondary memory can be addressed as though it were part of main memory. The addresses a program may use to reference memory are distinguished from the addresses the memory system uses to identify physical storage sites, and program generated addresses are translated automatically to the corresponding machine addresses. The size of virtual storage is limited by the addressing scheme of the computer system and amount of secondary memory is available not by the actual number of the main storage locations.

It is a technique that is implemented using both hardware and software. It maps memory addresses used by a program, called virtual addresses, into physical addresses in computer memory.

1. All memory references within a process are logical addresses that are dynamically translated into physical addresses at run time. This means that a process can be swapped in and out of main memory such that it occupies different places in main memory at different times during the course of execution.

2. A process may be broken into number of pieces and these pieces need not be continuously located in the main memory during execution. The combination of dynamic run-time address translation and use of page or segment table permits this.

If these characteristics are present then, it is not necessary that all the pages or segments are present in the main memory during execution. This means that the required pages need to be loaded into memory whenever required. Virtual memory is implemented using Demand Paging or Demand Segmentation.

Virtual Memory Compression

Virtual memory compression is a memory management.

Memory compression is a memory management technique that reduces the size of inactive data in the random access memory (RAM) to free up unused space and allow more programs to run at once. It is designed to fully use the available physical memory and thereby increase the system's performance. Memory compression can be applied to computers, smartphones and embedded systems.

Most computer equipment and gadgets have limited amounts of RAM in which to run applications. Memory compression enables the efficient utilization of the entire physical memory so that several programs can run concurrently and efficiently. There are various hardware- and software-based memory management techniques; which to use depends on the operating system, the application and type of computer or gadget.

In memory compression, portions of inactive applications in the memory are compressed to 50% or less of their original size. This frees up the RAM and leaves space for other programs and data. And, because the compression and decompression in the RAM are almost instant, the process saves on time that would otherwise have been used to transfer data between the memory and the computer storage. Memory compression is available for several operating systems such as Windows, Apple OS X, Linux and others. WK dm is a typical dictionary based technique available for most platforms; it combines the dictionary and statistical techniques to provide efficient, fast data compression and decompression operations.

Most memory compression processes are automatic, and only become active when the memory begins to fill up.

Page Table

Page tables is the job operating system is to keep track of which of virtual-page points to which physical frame. This information is kept in a *page-table* which, in its simplest form, could simply be a table where each row contains its associated frame — this is termed a *linear page-table*. If you were to use this simple system, with a 32 bit address-space and 4 KiB pages there would be 1048576 possible pages to keep track of in the page table ($2^{32} \div 4096$); hence the table would be 1048576 entries long to ensure we can always map a virtual page to a physical page.

Page tables can have many different structures and are highly optimized, as the process of finding a page in the page table can be a lengthy process.

The page-table for a process is under the exclusive control of the operating system. When a process requests memory, the operating system finds it a free page of physical memory and records the virtual-to-physical translation in the processes page-table. Conversely, when the process gives up memory, the virtual-to-physical record is removed and the underlying frame becomes free for allocation to another process.

Single-level Page Tables

The most straightforward approach would simply have a single linear array of page-table entries (PTEs). Each PTE contains information about the page, such as its physical page number ("frame" number) as well as status bits, such as whether or not the page is valid.

If we have a 32-bit architecture with 4k pages, then we have 220 pages. If each PTE is 4 bytes, then each page table requires 4 Mbytes of memory. And remember that each process needs its own page table, and there may be on the order of 100 processes running on a typical personal computer. This would require on the order of 400 Mbytes of RAM just to hold the page tables on a typical desktop.

Furthermore, many programs have a very sparse virtual address space. The vast majority of their PTEs would simply be marked invalid.

Multi-level Page Tables

Multi-level page tables are tree-like structures to hold page tables. As an example, consider a two-level page table, again on a 32-bit architecture with $2^{12} = 4$ kbyte pages. Now, we can divide the virtual address into three parts: say 10 bits for the level-0 index, 10 bits for the level-1 index, and again 12 bits for the offset within a page.

The entries of the level-0 page table are pointers to a level-1 page table, and the entries of the level-1 page table are PTEs Note that on a 32-bit architecture, pointers are 4 bytes (32 bits), and PTEs are typically 4 bytes.

So, if we have one valid page in our process, now our two-level page table only consumes (2^{10} level-0 entries) $\cdot$ (22 bytes/entry) + 1 $\cdot$ (2^{10} level-1 entries) $\cdot$ (2^2 bytes/entry) = 2 $\cdot$ 2 ^{12} bytes = 8 kbytes. For processes with sparse virtual memory maps, this is clearly a huge savings, made possible by the additional layer of indirection.

Note that for a process which uses its full memory map, that this two-level page table would use slightly more memory than the single-level page table (4k+4M versus 4M). The worst-case memory usage, in terms of efficiency, is when all 2^{10} level-1 page tables are required, but each one only has a single valid entry In practice, most page tables are 3-level or 4-level tables. The size of the indices for the different levels are optimized empirically by the hardware designers, then these sizes are permanently set in hardware for a given architecture.

Page-table Lookups

The CPU has a page table base register (PTBR) which points to the base (entry 0) of the level-0 page table. Each process has its own page table, and so in a context switch, the PTBR is updated along with the other context registers. The PTBR contains a physical address, not a virtual address.

When the MMU receives a virtual address which it needs to translate to a physical address, it uses the PTBR to go to the the level-0 page table. Then it uses the level-0 index from the most-significant bits (MSBs) of the virtual address to find the appropriate table entry, which contains a pointer to the base address of the appropriate level-1 page table. Then, from that base address, it uses the level-1 index to find the appropriate entry. In a 2-level page table, the level-1 entry is a PTE, and points to the physical page itself. In a 3-level (or higher) page table, there would be more steps: there are N memory accesses for an N-level page table.

This sounds pretty slow: N page table lookups for every memory access. But is it necessarily slow? A special cache called a TLB1 caches the PTEs from recent lookups, and so if a page's PTE is in the TLB cache, this improves a multi-level page table access time down to the access time for a single-level page table.

When a scheduler switches processes, it invalidates all the TLB entries. The new process then starts with a "cold cache" for its TLB, and takes a while for the TLB to "warm up". The scheduler therefore should not switch too frequently between processes, since a "warm" TLB is critical to making memory accesses fast. This is one reason that threads are so useful: switching threads within a process does not require the TLB to be invalidated; switching to a new thread within the same process lets it start up with a "warm" TLB cache right away.

The main drawback is that they need to be extremely fast, fully associative caches. Therefore TLBs are very expensive in terms of power consumption, and have an impact on chip real estate, and increasing chip real estate drives up price dramatically. The TLB can account a significant fraction of the total power consumed by a microprocessor, on the order of 10% or more. TLBs are therefore kept relatively small, and typical sizes are between 8 and 2048 entries.

An additional point is that for TLBs to work well memory accesses have to show locality, i.e. accesses aren't made randomly all over the address map, but rather tend to be close to other addresses which were recently accessed.

Memory Segmentation

Memory is one of the most important resources on a computing system, and its management is primary in every environment. In a bid to use memory efficiently and effectively a number of techniques have been developed to properly manage it. One of these memory management techniques is known as Memory Segmentation (MS). Memory Segmentation is defined as a system of segmenting processes and loading them into different non-contiguous addressed spaces in memory. They are referenced using memory addresses. The processes are first ‹segmented' (or split) most commonly into three segments, one to house the data, another to house the code and a third to house the stack.

Programmers may use different variables to achieve this in their program development. The data segment represents all the variables which will be used in running the program. The code segment is the actual execution of the process, while the stack segment monitors the progress and status of the different elements of the program. Now, depending on how complex a program is or its level of sophistication the program may be comprised of many more segments.

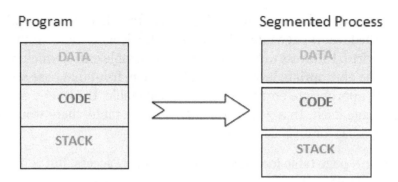

Once the process of segmentation occurs, the entire process can be loaded into different areas in memory instead of one contiguous space. This allows for the loading of smaller segments of the process into memory, allowing the physical memory to be used more efficiently. This loading is done by a placement algorithm with processes provided the exact memory space they require as in dynamic partitioning. This technique allows for better memory management, reducing the occurrences of fragmentation. Programmers armed with this technique segment their programs according to the corresponding program logic. This makes segmentation more realistic to the programmer. How does this all work with memory?

Segmentation and Process Loading

Figure is a graphic representation of memory. We know that memory is divided into different sections. The operating system, as the diagram indicates, occupies a dedicated section in memory

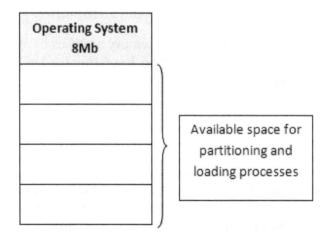

A program's processes are divided into segments as seen in Figure. The processes are loaded into memory using a special placement algorithm similar to dynamic partitioning. If you are familiar with dynamic partitioning, you know that it is a system of loading the process into memory with memory allocations matching the exact size of processes eliminating internal fragmentation.

Now the processes of the program are loaded into memory using a placement algorithm. The algorithm determines which process segment is loaded into which memory location. As such, the different processes that comprise the program can be loaded into different parts of memory. They are referenced using memory addresses in their non-contiguous spaces as seen in figure. Segmentation does not incur internal memory fragmentation but does incur external fragmentation.

Memory Controller

The memory controller manages the data flow going into and from main memory. Traditionally memory controllers were planted on the motherboard's northbridge. However, now it can be located on a separate chip or integrated into the dies of a microprocessor to reduce memory latency.

The Purpose of a Memory Controller

Memory controllers operate a logical format reading and writing dynamic random access memory (DRAM). They also perform a "refresh" operation. By sending a current through the entire device, the DRAM has the system's most up to date data.

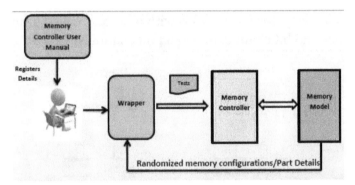

This is important because without constant refreshes DRAM capacitors leak their charge within a fraction of a second and will lose the data written to it. But the underside is that even though this has the potential to increase the system's performance, it locks the microprocessor into a specific type of memory. This in turn forces a chip or motherboard redesign that will support newer memory technologies.

There are many memory-controller features that need to be considered during the design phase. You have access priority of the data and error checking and correcting (ECC) operations. There is also read-write support, as well as byte-write implementations. Furthermore, because data can also fall out of order, there must be some access support for such data. In addition, you also have FIFO options, latency, and bandwidth elements that must be considered to make the memory controller fully functional.

Things that Makes the Memory Controller Work

Multiplexers and demultiplexers make the reading and writing to DRAM possible. They select the row and column address from the memory unit. These are the inputs for the multiplexer circuit. The demultiplexer on the DRAM unit can select the correct memory location and return the data to that location. A multiplexer is the preferred choice device in order to reduce the number of wires required to construct the system.

The memory controller uses a bus to communicate with the memory cell. This width comes from the number of parallel circuit lines available in order to electronically communicate with the memory cell. There is a variety of bus widths available.

The bus width available for a memory controller can range from 8-bit in older systems, to 512-bit in more complicated systems and video cards. These are usually activated as four 64-bit, simultaneous, memory controllers operating in parallel. In some cases, though, some bus widths are designed to operate in a manner where two 64-bit memory controllers access a 128-bit memory device.

Memory Controller: Ganged vs Unganged Mode

One of most important developments in the past 10 years has been how how memory speeds have improved. In a decade the speeds went from 133 Mhz SDR DIMM RAM to 1333 Mhz DDR3 DIMM RAM. However, CPU speeds have gotten even faster. Nevertheless, as fast as RAM speeds have improved there has been a latency that has not been overcome. This affects the speed of the CPU.

One way to improve the latency, (or reduce it) is with a process called granularity. Here, the process involves splitting one 128 bit channel in two 64 bit channels. This is "gang" mode.

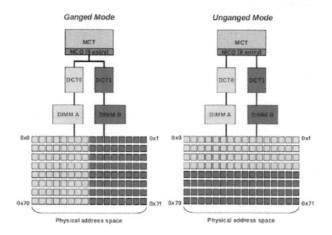

In ganged mode, there is a 128 bit wide logical DIMM that maps the first 64 bits on the physical DDR channel A and the last 64 bit on DDR channel B. The physical address space, in other words, is interleaved between the two DIMMs in 64 bit steps

In unganged mode, each DCT can operate independently with its own 64 bit wide address space. So the processor can be programmed to interleave the single, physical address space on the two normalized address spaces associated with the two memory channels.

The position that AMD takes is to enable unganged mode to get the benefits from increased parallelism. Note that some CPU models, the 8 and 12 core Magny Cours G34 processors, can only use the ungangedmode. This method is one of several that allow the CPU to have faster access to memory.

Variants

Double Data Rate Memory

Double data rate (DDR) memory controllers are used to drive DDR SDRAM, where data is transferred on both rising and falling edges of the system's memory clock. DDR memory controllers are significantly more complicated when compared to single data rate controllers, but they allow for twice the data to be transferred without increasing the memory cell's clock rate or bus width.

Dual-channel Memory

Dual Channel memory controllers are memory controllers where the DRAM devices are separated on to two different buses to allow two memory controllers to access them in parallel. This doubles the theoretical amount of bandwidth of the bus. In theory, more channels can be built (a channel for every DRAM cell would be the ideal solution), but due to wire count, line capacitance, and the need for parallel access lines to have identical lengths, more channels are very difficult to add.

Fully Buffered Memory

Fully buffered memory systems place a memory buffer device on every memory module (called an FB-DIMM when Fully Buffered RAM is used), which unlike traditional memory controller devices, use a serial data link to the memory controller instead of the parallel link used in previous RAM designs. This decreases the number of the wires necessary to place the memory devices on a motherboard (allowing for a smaller number of layers to be used, meaning more memory devices can be placed on a single board), at the expense of increasing latency (the time necessary to access a memory location). This increase is due to the time required to convert the parallel information read from the DRAM cell to the serial format used by the FB-DIMM controller, and back to a parallel form in the memory controller on the motherboard.

In theory, the FB-DIMM's memory buffer device could be built to access any DRAM cells, allowing for memory cell agnostic memory controller design, but this has not been demonstrated, as the technology is in its infancy.

Flash Memory Controller

Many flash memory devices, such as USB memory sticks, include a flash memory controller on chip. Flash memory is inherently slower to access than RAM and often becomes unusable after a few million write cycles, which generally makes it unsuitable for RAM applications.

Memory Protection

Memory protection is required to ensure that different processes do not mix with each other's code or data.

- Every memory address used by a process should be first checked to see whether it falls within the range of memory area that is allocated to the process.

- Two special purpose registers-*lower bound register* (LBR) and *upper bound register* (UBR) are used to implement memory protection.

- These registers store the start address and end address of the memory area allocated to a process.

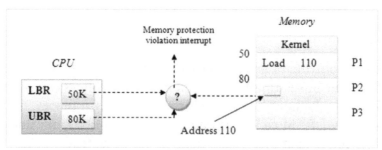

- The kernel loads appropriate values in LBR and UBR at execution time.

- The memory protection hardware compares every address used by a process with LBR and UBR registers.

- If the address is smaller than the address in LBR or larger than the address in UBR, a memory protection violation interrupt is generated.

- A *page table* of the process also stores memory address allocated to that process which maps logical address to its physical address to prevent from accessing any unallocated memory area to be used by that process.

- The relocation register scheme provides an effective way to allow operating system size to change dynamically.

References

- Godse, Atul P.; Godse, Deepali A. (2008). Advanced C Programming. p. 6-28: Technical Publications. p. 400. ISBN 978-81-8431-496-0

- Memory-of-the-computer: informationq.com, Retrieved 11 June 2018

- Tanenbaum, Andrew S.; Herder, Jorrit N.; Bos, Herbert (May 2006). "Can We Make Operating Systems Reliable and Secure?". Computer. 39 (5): 44–51. doi:10.1109/MC.2006.156

- Volatile-storage-9966: techopedia.com, Retrieved 31 March 2018

- "AMD64 Architecture Programmer's Manual Volume 2: System Programming" (PDF). March 2017. Retrieved 2017-12-05

- What-is-the-difference-between-volatile-and-non-volatile-memory-1229: technophileshub.com, Retrieved 24 May 2018

- Stroustrup, Bjarne (2008). Programming: Principles and Practice Using C++. 1009, §27.4 Free store: Addison Wesley. p. 1236. ISBN 978-0-321-54372-1

- Memory-management, operating-system: studytonight.com, Retrieved 10 July 2018

- Kaempf, Michel (2001). "Vudo malloc tricks". Phrack (57): 8. Archived from the original on 22 January 2009. Retrieved 29 April 2009

- Virtual-memory-operating-systems: geeksforgeeks.org, Retrieved 16 June 2018

Varied Principles of Computer Architecture

Study of the principles of computer architecture is vital for an all-inclusive understanding of the subject. The following chapter elucidates the concepts of Amdahl's law, Gustafson's law, Sun-Ni law, Rent's rule, Moore's law, Grosch's law, etc. for an extensive understanding of computer architecture.

Amdahl's Law

It is named after computer scientist Gene Amdahl (a computer architect from IBM and Amdahl corporation), and was presented at the AFIPS Spring Joint Computer Conference in 1967. It is also known as *Amdahl's argument*. It is a formula which gives the theoretical speedup in latency of the execution of a task at a fixed workload that can be expected of a system whose resources are improved. In other words, it is a formula used to find the maximum improvement possible by just improving a particular part of a system. It is often used in *parallel computing* to predict the theoretical speedup when using multiple processors.

Speedup

Speedup is defined as the ratio of performance for the entire task using the enhancement and performance for the entire task without using the enhancement or speedup can be defined as the ratio of execution time for the entire task without using the enhancement and execution time for the entire task using the enhancement.

If Pe is the performance for entire task using the enhancement when possible, Pw is the performance for entire task without using the enhancement, Ew is the execution time for entire task without using the enhancement and Ee is the execution time for entire task using the enhancement when possible then,

Speedup = Pe/Pw

or

Speedup = Ew/Ee

Amdahl's law uses two factors to find speedup from some enhancement:

- Fraction enhanced: The fraction of the computation time in the original computer that can be converted to take advantage of the enhancement. For example- if 10 seconds of the execution time of a program that takes 40 seconds in total can use an enhancement, the fraction is 10/40. This obtained value is *Fraction Enhanced. Fraction enhanced is always less than 1.*

- Speedup enhanced: The improvement gained by the enhanced execution mode; that is, how much faster the task would run if the enhanced mode were used for the entire program. For example – If the enhanced mode takes, say 3 seconds for a portion of the program, while it is 6 seconds in the original mode, the improvement is 6/3. This value is Speedup enhanced. *Speedup Enhanced is always greater than 1.* The overall Speedup is the ratio of the execution time:

$$\text{Overall Speedup} = \frac{\text{Old execution time}}{\text{New execution time}}$$

$$= \frac{1}{\left(\left(1 - \text{Fraction}_{enhanced}\right) + \frac{\text{Fraction}_{enhanced}}{\text{Speedup}_{enhanced}} \right)}$$

Proof:

Let Speedup be "S", old execution time be "T", new execution time be "T'", execution time that is taken by portion A(that will be enhanced) is "t", execution time that is taken by portion A(after enhancing) is "t'", execution time that is taken by portion that won't be enhanced is "tn", Fraction enhanced is "f", Speedup enhanced is "S'".

Now from the above equation,

$S=T/T'$

$T=tn+t$

$T'=tn+t'$

$f=t/T$

$=t/(t+tn)$

$1-f=1-(t/(t+tn))$

$= tn/(t + tn)$

$S'=t/t'$

$t'=t/s'$

$=(T*f)/S'$

$=((tn+t)*f)/S'$

$t'/(tn + t) = f'/S'$

$S = T/T$

$= (tn+t)/(tn+t')$

$= 1/((tn+t')/(tn+t'))$

$= 1/((tn/(tn + t)) + (t'/(tn + t))$

$S = 1/(1 - f' + (f'/S'))$

Overall Speedup = 1/(1 – fraction enhanced + (fraction enhanced/Speedup enhanced)) Hence proved.

Parallel Programs

If 30% of the execution time may be the subject of a speedup, p will be 0.3; if the improvement makes the affected part twice as fast, s will be 2. Amdahl's law states that the overall speedup of applying the improvement will be:

$$S_{latency} = \frac{1}{1 - p + \dfrac{p}{s}} = \frac{1}{1 - 0.3 + \dfrac{0.3}{2}} = 1.18.$$

For example, assume that we are given a serial task which is split into four consecutive parts, whose percentages of execution time are $p1 = 0.11$, $p2 = 0.18$, $p3 = 0.23$, and $p4 = 0.48$ respectively. Then we are told that the 1st part is not sped up, so $s1 = 1$, while the 2nd part is sped up 5 times, so $s2 = 5$, the 3rd part is sped up 20 times, so $s3 = 20$, and the 4th part is sped up 1.6 times, so $s4 = 1.6$. By using Amdahl's law, the overall speedup is,

$$S_{latency} = \frac{1}{\dfrac{p1}{s1} + \dfrac{p2}{s2} + \dfrac{p3}{s3} + \dfrac{p4}{s4}} = \frac{1}{\dfrac{0.11}{1} + \dfrac{0.18}{5} + \dfrac{0.23}{20} + \dfrac{0.48}{1.6}} = 2.19.$$

Notice how the 20 times and 5 times speedup on the 2nd and 3rd parts respectively don't have much effect on the overall speedup when the 4th part (48% of the execution time) is accelerated by only 1.6 times.

Serial Programs

Assume that a task has two independent parts, A and B. Part B takes roughly 25% of the time of the whole computation. By working very hard, one may be able to make this part 5 times faster, but this reduces the time of the whole computation only slightly. In contrast, one may need to perform less work to make part A perform twice as fast. This will make the computation much faster than by optimizing part B, even though part B's speedup is greater in terms of the ratio, (5 times versus 2 times).

Two independent parts A B

Original process

Make B 5x faster

Make A 2x faster

For example, with a serial program in two parts A and B for which $T_A = 3$ s and $T_B = 1$ s,

- If part B is made to run 5 times faster, that is $s = 5$ and $p = T_B/(T_A + T_B) = 0.25$, then

$$S_{\text{latency}} = \frac{1}{1 - 0.25 + \dfrac{0.25}{5}} = 1.25;$$

- If part A is made to run 2 times faster, that is $s = 2$ and $p = T_A/(T_A + T_B) = 0.75$, then

$$S_{\text{latency}} = \frac{1}{1 - 0.75 + \dfrac{0.75}{2}} = 1.60.$$

Therefore, making part A to run 2 times faster is better than making part B to run 5 times faster. The percentage improvement in speed can be calculated as

$$\text{percentage improvement} = 100\left(1 - \frac{1}{S_{\text{latency}}}\right).$$

- Improving part A by a factor of 2 will increase overall program speed by a factor of 1.60, which makes it 37.5% faster than the original computation.

- However, improving part B by a factor of 5, which presumably requires more effort, will achieve an overall speedup factor of 1.25 only, which makes it 20% faster.

Optimizing the Sequential Part of Parallel Programs

If the non-parallelizable part is optimized by a factor of O, then,

$$T(O,s) = (1 - p)\frac{T}{O} + \frac{p}{s}T.$$

It follows from Amdhal's law that the speedup due to parallelism is given by,

$$S_{\text{latency}}(O,s) = \frac{T(O)}{T(O,s)} = \frac{(1 - p)\dfrac{1}{O} + p}{\dfrac{1 - p}{O} + \dfrac{p}{s}}.$$

When $s=1$, we have $S_{\text{latency}}(O,s)=1$, meaning that the speedup is measured with respect to the execution time after the non-parallelizable part is optimized.

When $s=\infty$,

$$S_{\text{latency}}(O,\infty)=\frac{T(O)}{T(O,s)}=\frac{(1-p)\dfrac{1}{O}+p}{\dfrac{1-p}{O}+\dfrac{p}{s}}=1+\frac{p}{1-p}O.$$

If $1-p=0.4$, $O=2$ and $s=5$, then:

$$S_{\text{latency}}(O,s)=\frac{T(O)}{T(O,s)}=\frac{0.4\dfrac{1}{2}+0.6}{\dfrac{0.4}{2}+\dfrac{0.6}{5}}=2.5.$$

Transforming Sequential Parts of Parallel Programs into Parallelizable

Next, we consider the case wherein the non-parallelizable part is reduced by a factor of O', and the parallelizable part is correspondingly increased. Then,

$$T'(O',s)=(1-p)\frac{T}{O'}+\left(1-\frac{1-p}{O'}\right)\frac{T}{s}.$$

It follows from Amdhal's law that the speedup due to parallelism is given by

$$S'_{\text{latency}}(O',s)=\frac{T'(O')}{T'(O',s)}=\frac{1}{(1-p)\dfrac{1}{O'}+\left(1-\dfrac{1-p}{O'}\right)\dfrac{1}{s}}.$$

The derivation above is in agreement with Jakob Jenkov's analysis of the execution time vs. speed-up tradeoff.

Relation to the Law of Diminishing Returns

Amdahl's law is often conflated with the law of diminishing returns, whereas only a special case of applying Amdahl's law demonstrates law of diminishing returns. If one picks optimally (in terms of the achieved speedup) what to improve, then one will see monotonically decreasing improvements as one improves. If, however, one picks non-optimally, after improving a sub-optimal component and moving on to improve a more optimal component, one can see an increase in the return. Note that it is often rational to improve a system in an order that is "non-optimal" in this sense, given that some improvements are more difficult or require larger development time than others.

Amdahl's law does represent the law of diminishing returns if on considering what sort of return one gets by adding more processors to a machine, if one is running a fixed-size computation that will use all available processors to their capacity. Each new processor added to the system will add less usable power than the previous one. Each time one doubles the number of processors the speedup ratio will diminish, as the total throughput heads toward the limit of $1/(1 - p)$.

This analysis neglects other potential bottlenecks such as memory bandwidth and I/O bandwidth. If these resources do not scale with the number of processors, then merely adding processors provides even lower returns.

An implication of Amdahl's law is that to speedup real applications which have both serial and parallel portions, heterogeneous computing techniques are required. For example, a CPU-GPU heterogeneous processor may provide higher performance and energy efficiency than a CPU-only or GPU-only processor.

Amdahl's Law and Multiprocessing

The original formulation of Amdahl's law states the impact of inherently sequential portion of a task on the speedup during multiprocessing. Suppose f represents the fraction of the task that is inherently sequential the using N processors the speedup is given by

$$S = \frac{1}{\left(f + (1-f)/N \right)}$$

When f=0, S = N, resulting in an ideal linear speedup.

When f=0.2, S<5, independent of N

When f=0.5, S<2, independent of N

For large N, S =(1/f), independent of N.

This relationship generates pessimism regarding the viability of massively parallel processing especially if we overestimate the value of the fraction f. But, researchers in parallel computation community started suspecting the usefulness and validity of Amdahl's law after observing impressive linear speedups in some large applications. Gustafson reported near-linear speedups on1024-processor hypercube for three practical applications: beam stress analysis, surface wave simulation, and unstable fluid flow. This lead to suspecting the nature of Amdahl's original formulation. For example, Gustafson argues that Amdahl's law is inappropriate for current approaches to massively parallel processing and suggests an alternate scaled speedup measure. E. Barsis proposed a scaled speedup formula, which is often referred to as Gustafson's law. This is stated as follows: if the fraction of time spent by the sequential part on a parallel system is g, then with N processors the scaled speedup is S = g + (1-g)*N, a simple linear relationship. A note by Stephen J. Williard elaborates on this law.

Yuan Shi (1996), in an illuminating article, shows that the Gustafson's law and Amdahl's law are not two separate laws and in fact proved the equivalence of the two laws. Gustafsonhad mistakenly used the value of g as the value for finAmdahl' slaw and incorrectly suspected the Amdahl's law. The two fractions, f and g, are shown to be related as

$$S = \frac{1}{1 + (1-g)*N/g}$$

For example, Gustafson used g=0.004 and calculated the scaled speedup as 1020 with N=1024, but using Amdahl's law got a speedup of 201 using the value of g for f. If he had used the correct value forf corresponding to g=.004, which is 0.0000039, then he would have gotten the same speedup of 1020 using Amdahl's law! Thus there is nothing pessimistic about Amdahl's law. In practice, for several applications, the fraction of the serial part happens to be very, very small thus leading to near linear speedups.

It is also very easy to use wrong performance measures and arrive at super-linear speedups during multiprocessing. This often leads to suspecting the Amdahl's law. For example, consider the sorting problem based on element comparisons. Suppose we use selection sort on a list of N elements. Worst case number of comparisons is N^2 for this sequential algorithm.

Suppose we use K-fold parallel processing by dividing the listing oK sub lists, each of size N/K. The parallel implementation of sorting by performing selection sort on each sub lists (in parallel) and merging the K sub lists needs the following number of comparisons:

$$N + (N/K)^2 + N^* (K-1)$$

This gives a speedup of

$$S = \frac{N^2}{N+(N/K)^2+N^*(K-1)} = \frac{1}{1/N+1/K^2+(K-!)/N}$$

For large N, S = K^2 which seems to "break" the law yielding super-linear speedup.

The fallacy here is that we are comparing two different types of algorithms. The parallel implementation version is essentially a merge sort while the sequential version is a selection sort. The total number steps performed in the parallel version and the sequential version are not the same? Indeed, if they were the same, we would get the correct sub-linear speedup. The same divide-and-conquer method if run on a single processor would take N + K*(N/K)² + N*(K-1) steps. This gives a correct speedup of

$$S = \frac{N + K^*(N/K)^2 + N^*(K-1)}{N + (N/K)^2 + N^*(K-1)} = K \text{ For large N}$$

Use in Memory Hierarchy Design

One of the goals in computer design is to provide a large memory and a fast memory. Though this appears to be a difficult task, incorporating a hierarchy of memory systems has solved this problem. The principle of locality (both temporal and spatial) has been successfully exploited in the memory hierarchy of modern computer systems. With the growing size of software applications run on current machines, there is a corresponding demand for larger main memory (hundreds of MBs) and cache memory (hundreds of KBs.) In fact, to meet the fast clock speeds (gigahertz) of modern processors multilevel cache memory is used to enhance the performance of the traditional single-level cache. Level I cache is part of the processor chip module and Level II cache is typically on an off-chip module.

Amdahl's law can be applied to get a rough estimate of the performance of the memory systems in the hierarchy. For example, the speedup of main memory access due to a single-level cache memory is given by the formula

$$S = \frac{á}{H + (1-h) *\alpha}$$

h: cache hit ratio

$\alpha : T_m/T_c$

T_m: main memory access time

T_c : cache memory access time

If h=0.5, then S < 2, independent of how fast the cache is. Thus the hit ratio limits the performance of the access. This may sound pessimistic but, in practice, software applications depict a remarkably high degree of spatial and temporal localities leading to very high cache hit rates. This in turn results in good speedup and performance. David O'Neal of National Center for Supercomputing Applications presents some interesting performance results for multilevel cache memory systems.

Use in Instruction Set and Processor Design

To predict the performance enhancement due to an improved feature it is convenient to restate the essence of Amdahl's law as follows:

$$Speedup = \frac{\text{Execution time before a feature is improved}}{\text{Execution time after the improved feature}}$$

Here, the fraction of task that does not use the feature limits the performance or speedup. This should guide the designers in the design process. For example, before an attempt is made to improve the speed of multiplication operation, one should know roughly the fraction of time a task performs multiply operations. Suppose a task takes 100 seconds to run on a processor. Say 40% of this time is consumed by multiply operations (which we will try to improve). Since 60% of the task is unaffected by the improvement, the speedup is given by

S = 100 / (60+(40/K)) where multiply operation is made K-times faster.

Thus, S < 1.67 independent of K. This provides useful feedback to the designer. A guiding rule is that frequently used instructions should be improved. But the designer should be aware of the performance limits due to other slower instructions in the program. Whether to improve the performance of integer arithmetic operations or floating point arithmetic operations involves similar investigation.

Gustafson's Law

Gustafson demonstrated with a 1024-processor system that the basic presumptions in Amdahl's Law are inappropriate for massive parallelism. Gustafson found that the underlying principle that "the problem size scales with the number of processors, or with a more powerful processor, the problem expands to make use of the increased facilities is inappropriate".

Gustafson's empirical results demonstrated that the parallel or vector part of a program scales with the problem size. Times for vector start-up, program loading, serial bottlenecks, and I/O that make up the serial component of the run do not grow with the problem size.

Gustafson formulated that if the serial time, s, and parallel time, $p = (1 - s)$, on a parallel system with n processors, then a serial processor would require the time:

It can be seen that Gustafson presents a much more optimistic picture of speedup due to parallelism than does Amdahl. Unlike the curve for Amdahl's Law, Gustafson's Law is a simple line, "one with a much more moderate slope: $1 - n$. It is thus much easier to achieve parallel performance than is implied by Amdahl's paradigm".

A different take on the flaw of Amdahl's Law can be observed as "a more efficient way to use a parallel computer is to have each processor perform similar work, but on a different section of the data. where large computations are concerned this method works surprisingly well". Doing the same task but on a different range of data circumvents an underlying presumption in Amdahl's Law, that is, "the assumption that a fixed portion of the computation. Must be sequential. This estimate sounds plausible, but it turns out not to be true of most computations".

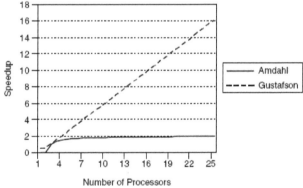

Figure: Liner speedup of Gustafson compared to "diminishing return" speedup of Amdahl with 50% of code available for parallelization. Notice as number of processors increase, speedup does not increase indefinitely for Amdahl due to serial component

Derivation

A task executed by a system whose resources are improved compared to an initial similar system can be split into two parts:

- A part that does not benefit from the improvement of the resources of the system;
- A Part that benefits from the improvement of the resources of the system.

Example: A computer program that processes files from disk. A part of that program may scan the directory of the disk and create a list of files internally in memory. After that, another part of the program passes each file to a separate thread for processing. The part that scans the directory and creates the file list cannot be sped up on a parallel computer, but the part that processes the files can.

The execution workload of the whole task before the improvement of the resources of the system is denoted W. It includes the execution workload of the part that does not benefit from the improvement of the resources and the execution workload of the one that benefit from it. The fraction of the execution workload that would benefit from the improvement of the resources is denoted by p the fraction concerning the part that would not benefit from it is therefore $1-p$. Then

$$W = (1-p)W + pW.$$

It is the execution of the part that benefits from the improvement of the resources that is sped up by a factor s after the improvement of the resources. Consequently, the execution workload of the part that does not benefit from it remains the same. The theoretical execution workload $W(s)$ of the whole task after the improvement of the resources is then

$$W(s) = (1-p)W + spW.$$

Gustafson's law gives the theoretical speedup in latency of the execution of the whole task *at fixed time T*, which yields

$$S_{\text{latency}}(s) = \frac{TW(s)}{TW} = \frac{W(s)}{W} = 1 - p + sp.$$

Applications

Application in Research

Amdahl's law presupposes that the computing requirements will stay the same, given increased processing power. In other words, an analysis of the same data will take less time given more computing power.

Gustafson, on the other hand, argues that more computing power will cause the data to be more carefully and fully analyzed: pixel by pixel or unit by unit, rather than on a larger scale. Where it would not have been possible or practical to simulate the impact of nuclear detonation on every building, car, and their contents (including furniture, structure strength, etc.) because such a calculation would have taken more time than was available to provide an answer, the increase in computing power will prompt researchers to add more data to more fully simulate more variables, giving a more accurate result.

Application in Everyday Computer Systems

Amdahl's Law reveals a limitation in, for example, the ability of multiple cores to reduce the time it takes for a computer to boot to its operating system and be ready for use. Assuming the boot process was mostly parallel, quadrupling computing power on a system that took one minute to load might reduce the boot time to just over fifteen seconds. But greater and greater parallelization would eventually fail to make boot up go any faster, if any part of the boot process were inherently sequential.

Gustafson's law argues that a fourfold increase in computing power would instead lead to a similar increase in expectations of what the system will be capable of. If the one-minute load time is acceptable to most users, then that is a starting point from which to increase the features and functions of the system. The time taken to boot to the operating system will be the same, i.e. one minute, but the new system would include more graphical or user-friendly features.

Limitations

Some problems do not have fundamentally larger datasets. As an example, processing one data point per world citizen gets larger at only a few percent per year. The principal point of Gustafson's law is that such problems are not likely to be the most fruitful applications of parallelism.

Algorithms with nonlinear runtimes may find it hard to take advantage of parallelism "exposed" by Gustafson's law. Snyder points out an $O(N^3)$ algorithm means that double the concurrency gives only about a 26% increase in problem size. Thus, while it may be possible to occupy vast concurrency, doing so may bring little advantage over the original, less concurrent solution—however in practice there have still been considerable improvements.

Hill and Marty emphasize also that methods of speeding sequential execution are still needed, even for multicore machines. They point out that locally inefficient methods can be globally efficient when they reduce the sequential phase. Furthermore, Woo and Lee studied the implication of energy and power on future many-core processors based on Amdahl's law, showing that an asymmetric many-core processor can achieve the best possible energy efficiency by activating an optimal number of cores given the amount of parallelism is known prior to execution.

Sun-Ni law

The Sun-Ni law is an approach used in parallel processing that attempts to improve performance. It is also called memory bounded speedup and was proposed by Professors Xian-He Sun and Lionel M. Ni. This law scales up the problem size and tries to find a solution limited only by the amount of memory available. It is a generalization of two other approaches used in parallel computing called Amdahl's law and Gustafson's law.

One of the challenges in parallel computing is to figure out how the performance of the system improves when it is scaled up. As this can be hard to measure, one of the most well-known scalability metrics studied is speedup. Speedup relates the execution of parallel programs running on a certain number of processors and the execution time it takes for the fastest sequential program to solve that problem. One type of speedup approach is to keep the problem size constant, allowing the number of processors that work on the problem to be increased. This is called Amdahl's law and is known as fixed-size speedup.

Amadhl's law thus attempts to reduce the execution time using more parallel processors and fixes the computational workload as a constant. It essentially tries to solve the problem in lesser and lesser time. In contrast, Gustafson's law, also known as fixed-time speedup, tries to obtain a result within a fixed time and scales up the problem size, carrying out more operations to get an accurate solution. This is applied to problems where there is a time constraint, but it is not vital to solve them in the shortest possible time.

The memory bounded speedup approach, or the Sun-Ni law, is concerned with memory size and how it affects performance. The problem size that can be tackled is affected by the amount of memory available. A limited physical memory means that more time is spent figuring out workarounds to solve a problem within the parallel computing architecture. The approach the Sun-Ni law takes is, if the time limit specified by the fixed-time speedup is met and there is enough memory space, the problem should be scaled to make adequate use of all the available memory.

This is what the Sun-Ni law does, and the formula considers memory size and relates it to performance. Every processor in a parallel computing architecture has a fixed memory, and the formula relates the problem size to the total available memory capacity. The memory bounded speedup laid out in the Sun-Ni law is, in essence, a generalization of both the fixed-time and fixed-size speedups. Given that the total memory size increases when the numbers of processors increase, the Sun-Ni law attempts to utilize all that memory space more efficiently.

Derivation of Sun-Ni's Law

Let W^* be the scaled workload under a memory space constraint. The memory bounded speedup can be defined as:

```
Sequential Time to Solve W*/Parallel Time to Solve W*
```

Suppose f is the portion of the workload that can be parallelized and $(1-f)$ is the sequential portion of the workload.

Let $y = g(x)$ be the function that reflects the parallel workload increase factor as the memory capacity increases m times.

Let: $W = g(M)$ and: $W^* = g(m \cdot M)$ where M is the memory capacity of one node.

Thus, $W^* = g(m \cdot g^{-1}(W))$

The memory bounded speedup is then:

$$\frac{(1-f)W + f \cdot g(m \cdot g^{-1}(W))}{(1-f)W + \dfrac{f \cdot g(m \cdot g^{-1}(W))}{m}}$$

For any power function $g(x) = ax^b$ and for any rational numbers a and b, we have:

$$g(mx) = a(mx)^b = m^b \cdot ax^b = m^b g(x) = \bar{g}(m)g(x)$$

where $\bar{g}(m)$ is the power function with the coefficient as 1.

Thus by taking the highest degree term to determine the complexity of the algorithm, we can rewrite memory bounded speedup as:

$$\frac{(1-f)W + f \cdot \bar{g}(m)W}{(1-f)W + \dfrac{f \cdot \bar{g}(m)W}{m}} = \frac{(1-f) + f \cdot \bar{g}(m)}{(1-f) + \dfrac{f \cdot \bar{g}(m)}{m}}$$

In this equation, $\bar{g}(m)$ represents the influence of memory change on the change in problem size.

Suppose $\bar{g}(m)=1$, Then the memory-bounded speedup model reduces to Amdahl's law, since problem size is fixed or independent of resource increase.

Suppose $\bar{g}(m)=m$, Then the memory-bounded speedup model reduces to Gustafson's law, which means when memory capacity increases m times and the workload also increases m times all the data needed is local to every node in the system.

Often, for simplicity and for matching the notation of Amdahl's Law and Gustafson's Law, the letter G is used to represent the memory bound function $\bar{g}(m)$, and n replaces m. Using this notation we get:

$$Speedup_{\text{memory-bounded}} = \frac{(1-f)+f \cdot G(n)}{(1-f)+\dfrac{f \cdot G(n)}{n}}$$

Examples

Suppose one would like to determine the memory-bounded speedup of matrix multiplication. The memory requirement of matrix multiplication is roughly $x=3N^2$ where N is the dimension of the two $N \times N$ source matrices. And the computation requirement is $2N^3$.

Thus we have:

$$g(x)=2(x/3)^{3/2} = \frac{2}{3^{3/2}}x^{3/2} \text{ and } \bar{g}(x)=x^{3/2}$$

Thus the memory-bounded speedup is for matrix multiplication is:

$$\frac{(1-f)+f \cdot \bar{g}(m)}{(1-f)+\dfrac{f \cdot \bar{g}(m)}{m}} = \frac{(1-f)+f \cdot m^{3/2}}{(1-f)+f \cdot m^{1/2}}$$

The following is another matrix multiplication example which illustrates the rapid increase in parallel execution time. The execution time of a $N \times N$ matrix for a uniprocessor is: $O(n^3)$. While the memory usage is: $O(n^2)$.

Suppose a 10000-by-10000 matrix takes 800 MB of memory and can be factorized in 1 hour on a uniprocessor. Now for the scaled workload suppose is possible to factorize a 320,000-by-320,000 matrix in 32 hours. The time increase is quite large, but the increase in problem size may be more valuable for someones whose premier goal is accuracy. For example, an astrophysicist may be more interested in simulating an N-body problem with as the number of particles as large as possible. This example shows for computation intensive applications, memory capacity does not need to proportionally scale up with computing power.

Applications/Effects of Sun-Ni's Law

The memory-bounded speedup model is the first work to reveal that memory is the performance constraint for high-end computing and presents a quantitative mathematical formulation for the trade-off between memory and computing. It is based on the memory-bounded function, $W=G(n)$, where W is the work and thus also the computation for most applications. M is the memory requirement in terms of capacity, and G is the reuse rate. $W=G(M)$ gives a very simple, but effective, description of the relation between computation and memory requirement. From an architecture viewpoint, the memory-bounded model suggests the size, as well as speed, of the cache(s) should match the CPU performance. Today, modern microprocessors such as the Pentium Pro, Alpha 21164, Strong Arm SA110, and Longson-3A use 80% or more of their transistors for the on-chip cache rather than computing components. From an algorithm design viewpoint, we should reduce the number of memory accesses. That is, reuse the data when it is possible. The function $G()$ gives the reuse rate. Today, the term memory bound functions has become a general term which refers to functions which involve extensive memory access. Memory complexity analysis has become a discipline of computer algorithm analysis.

Rent's Rule

Almost thirty years have passed since the publication of Landman and Russo's paper on the use of a function they called Rent's rule for predicting the average number of terminals a group of modules on a circuit board requires for communication with the rest of the system. In the intervening years, there have been many papers published on the meaning of Rent's rule and its consequences for SSI, LSI, VLSI, and, most recently, GSI design.

Although Rent's rule is widely known, misinterpretations have often led to conclusions which are not in accordance with other published results. We attempt to explain where the discrepancies in interpretations originate and to show that there indeed exists a common ground to the various models that have been built on Rent's rule. At the same time, it reviews the current state of knowledge concerning Rent's rule and the assumptions used in derived expressions which are widely used for modeling gate placement.

Interpretation of Rent's Rule

Rent's rule is essentially an accounting tool which enumerates the number of nets crossing a known boundary between groups of gates. It is therefore helpful to consider the bounded region defining a statistically homogeneous functional circuit block within an arbitrarily large system. In this context, homogeneous means that quantities such as the average wire length per gate and the average number of terminals per gate are independent of the position within the boundary and also in the immediate vicinity of the boundary. It is important to note that, in this stage, it is not necessary to specify the dimension of the gate layout or the details of the bounding box geometry.

The boundary defines a region composed of G gates which require T terminals for communication with the rest of the system. Consider the effect of a slight change, or perturbation, of the boundary geometry so that additional $\ddot{A}G$ gates are enclosed. In the absence of any other information, it is only possible to estimate the additional number of terminals by assuming that the additional $\ddot{A}G$

gates require the same level of communication as the original G gates in the circuit. Since each of the initial G gates requires, on average, T/G terminals, then

$$\Delta T = \left(\frac{T}{G}\right)\Delta G$$

If ΔG and ΔT are small compared with G and T, respectively, we may approximate this difference equation by a simple first order differential equation

$$\frac{dT}{T} = \frac{dG}{G}$$

which may be solved to yield

$$T = tG$$

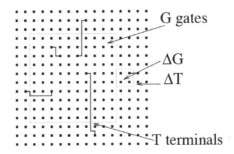

G gates

ΔG

ΔT

T terminals

Figure: Perturbation of a bounding box to assess the change in terminals requirement

where t is generated as a constant of integration. This constant is interpreted as the average number of terminals required by a single gate since $T=t$ when $G=1$.

This analysis is somewhat pessimistic in its estimate of the number of terminals required for communication since it does not allow for the optimization of the gate placement. Procedures based on the Fiduccia -Mattheyses and simulated annealing algorithms, for example, are commonly employed to rearrange gate positions in a manner which favors short- over long-range communication. The fact that the incremental region containing ΔG gates is contiguous with the larger region containing G gates is therefore not accurately reflected in the analysis. After optimization, it is much more likely that wires leaving the perturbed region will implement short-range communication links within the original bounded region, and these nets will not contribute to an increase in the number of terminals for the circuit as a whole.

The level of optimization present within the boundary is characterized by a parameter pi, which modifies our estimate of the number of extra terminals required by the addition of ΔG gates

$$\Delta T = pi\left(\frac{T}{G}\right)\Delta G$$

Values of pi less than unity represent some level of placement optimization within the circuit which favors short over long range communication. It should also be noted that the level of placement optimization, and hence the parameter pi, largely depends on the topology of the circuit's interconnection structure since this topology can make optimizations either easy or very hard to obtain. Approximating the modified difference equation above by its corresponding differential equation and applying the boundary condition used previously yields

$$T = t\, G^{pi}$$

which we recognize as Rent's rule, with the (internal) Rent exponent pi representing the level of placement optimization within a statistically homogeneous circuit characterized by a certain interconnection topology with an average of t terminals per gate. For $pi = 1$, there is no placement optimization, and the circuit is interpreted as a random gate arrangement. This is also the upper bound for pi since the maximum number of terminals for any region containing G gates in a homogeneous system is given by equation $T = tG$. The lower bound on pi is defined by the interconnection topology since it generally is not possible to place all connected gates close together however optimal the placement scheme is. We will denote this lower bound by p^* and call it the intrinsic Rent exponent, a notion first introduced by.

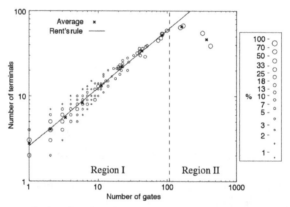

Figure: Terminal-gate relationship for a hierarchical bi-partitioning of a benchmark Netlist .
The diameters of thecircles correspond to the percentage of partitioning modules that have
T terminals out of all modules around an average number of gates G

Figure shows typical Rent data extracted from a benchmark net list. The terminal-gate relationship was obtained using a recursive bi-partitioning process (which corresponds to an optimization of a partitioning based placement) with data collected at each partition level. The geometric average of the data is accurately represented by equation. for the majority of gate sizes, and this region of the graph is labeled region I. However, as the number of gates approaches the total number of gates on the chip, the number of terminals becomes constrained by the limited number of input/output terminals at the chip periphery. This results in a rapid decrease in the number of estimated terminals, and this region is defined as region II. It is possible to define an external, or package level, Rent exponent

$$T_{io} = tG_T^{pe}$$

where T_{io} is the number of input/output pins and G_T is the total number of gates on the chip. Of course, the statistical meaning of the external Rent exponent is open to question since each chip can only provide one data point. Nevertheless, it was recently shown that if one plots the number of pins on the X86 series of Intel microprocessors versus the number of gates on each chip, an external Rent exponent of $p_e = 0.36$ is obtained. It is important to note that this external Rent exponent is very different from the (internal) Rent exponent (a distinction that often has been omitted in literature!).

Rent Exponent Prediction

Given its definition as an exponent, small variations in the Rent exponent can have disproportionate effects on secondary, derived quantities, such as average wire length. It is therefore important to have accurate estimates for the internal and external Rent exponents. Current placement models are not yet at a level of sophistication which allows them to utilize the information contained in region II of the Rent graph. Only an estimate of the internal Rent exponent will therefore be required, and, henceforth, the Rent exponent will be written without a subscript.

In the absence of a general method for determining Rent exponents from first principles, these values have generally been estimated from previously constructed circuits or by reference to one of several influential papers. In 1978, Chiba published a survey which indicated that Rent exponents in the approximate range $0.5 < p < 0.6$ were appropriate. In a critical assessment of these data, Ferry has argued that modern systems (which he refers to as functionally partitioned for $p < 1/2$) are characterized by a much smaller Rent exponent of 0.21. A widely quoted survey provided by Bakoglu indicates that the Rent exponent is characteristic of a given architecture with microprocessors, gates arrays, and high-speed computers characterized by Rent exponents of $p = 0.45, 0.5,$ and 0.63, respectively.

Faced with such contradictory data, a more pragmatic approach would be to actually measure the Rent exponent of the net list directly. However, the reason Rent's rule is used in the first place is because gate placement is NP hard and takes an inordinate amount of processing time. It is therefore usual to estimate by rapidly sampling the properties of a net list. Since t is fixed for a given net list, p may be estimated by supplying just one data point within region I of the Rent graph. This may be achieved by performing a couple of circuit partitions until one reaches the beginning of region I (note that this can be detected), and then one uses the obtained point together with to estimate p. This requires a much smaller amount of processing time than a complete net list placement and provides good Rent exponent estimates. Since this Rent exponent now depends on the quality of the partitioning algorithm, we will denote it as p'. Estimating p by using p' will be sufficiently accurate if there are close relations between the partitioning method and the placement method (which is especially the case for partitioning-based placement). However, the latter approach requires access to the net list, and in many cases this is not possible because the net list does not yet exist, or, for reasons concerned with protecting intellectual property, access to the net list is not permitted. In such a situation, the value of the Rent exponent must be predicted using a projected statistical wiring "signature" of the net list.

Application of Rent's Rule

Although it stems from work in the early 60s, Rent's rule and the resulting wire length estimations have not been widely applied until they received more attention recently. Applications of Rent's rule are mainly seen in the following areas: layout parameter estimations in Electronic Design

Automation, studies of new computer architectures, and the generation of synthetic circuit benchmarks. The increasing problem sizes in electronic design and the sub-micron design challenges have placed the need for a priori estimates of chip layout parameters in the forefront. The generality and predictive power of Rent's rule are perfect for such estimates. Rent's rule has therefore been used in such estimators as Suspens, Ripe, Genesys Bacpac, and GTX. Another application of Rent's rule tries to assess the merits of new chip or computer architectures before they have to be built, using wire length estimates based on Rent's rule and a generic model for the architecture. This research has gained attention especially due to the possibilities of using optical interconnections to build three-dimensional chips. Finally, Rent's rule has also been used to generate synthetic circuit benchmarks.

Apart from this last application (which uses Rent's rule in a direct way), all applications use Rent's rule to obtain wire length estimates. Starting from the premise that the circuit to be modeled and its placement are characterized by a known, constant value of the Rent exponent, the number of nets of length ℓ, $N(\ell)$ may be estimated by writing.

$$N(\ell) = q(\ell)D(\ell)$$

Where $D(\ell)$ is the number of valid two-pin net placement sites and $q(\ell)$ is the probability that a placement site is occupied, which will be referred to as the occupation probability.

This factorization of the problem is useful because the occupation probability $q(\ell)$ may be calculated directly from Rent's rule and is largely independent of system details, while the site function $D(\ell)$ represents information specific to a particular problem, such as the extent of the system and its hierarchical structure.

A. Occupation Probability

The occupation probability can be derived by applying a technique proposed by Davis et al., called conservation of terminals, to the arrangement of gates shown in Fig. (In the following analysis a lower case n is used to denote the length distribution associated with a single gate, while an upper case denotes the length distribution for the entire circuit.) The group of gates defined by a constant distance from a single central gate A, indicated by the shaded region, are labeled , while gates occupying the intervening region are labeled B. Note that it is not necessary at this stage to specify the dimensionality or the geometrical details of the gate placement.

The number of terminals, $T_{A \to C}$, required for communication between the gate at A and the gates within region is calculated first. The area of each circle represents the number of terminals associated with each of the regions, as defined by Rent's rule:

$$T_A = t \qquad T_B = tG_B^p \qquad etc.$$

The total overlapping area of circles, for example, $T_{AB} = t(1 + G_B)^p$, represents the number of terminals associated with their corresponding regions' combined gate count. The intersection of circles represents the number of terminals required for communication between those regions. In particular, $T_{A \to C}$

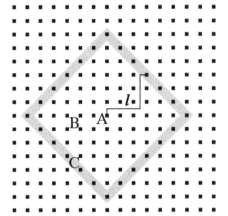

Figure: Definition of regions A, B, and C for an infinite two-dimensional gate array

represents the intersection of regions A and C but excluding any region associated with since we do not allow for the possibility of a net connecting regions A, B, and C. figure above. illustrates the relationship

$$T_{A \to C} = T_{AB} + T_{BC} - T_B - T_{ABC}$$

so that, after applying Rent's rule, the number of terminals required for communication between gate A and the gates in region C is given by

$$T_{A \to C} = t\left[\left(1+G_B\right)^p + \left(G_B + G_C\right)^p - G_B^p - \left(1 + G_B + G_C\right)^p\right]$$

In order to calculate the number of nets associated with the cental gate, rather than the number of terminals, a factor α must be introduced so that the average number of nets connecting gate A with region C is estimated to be

$$n_{A \to C} = \alpha T_{A \to C}$$

Most nets in processing circuits connect pairs of gates together, and so $\alpha \approx 1/2$. Of course, this value represents the median value of a distribution of -terminal nets, but it is assumed that the range of the distribution is very narrow for signal nets and that the effect of bus and clock nets must be considered separately.

In order to proceed further, information is required about the dimensionality and layout of the gates, i.e., information that has been deliberately factored into the site function $D(\ell)$. The unknown layout details are therefore obtained by assuming that the gates are arranged in an infinite two-dimensional plane, with distances measured using a Manhattan metric. This approximation is suggested by the fact that a constant Rent exponent is based on the properties of a homogeneous system, which implicitly does not allow for the possibility of the edges associated with a finite array.

Figure is now interpreted as representative of the physical layout of the gates and the physical geometry of the bounding box (which is a locus of gates at a constant Manhattan distance from gate A). The number of gates in region C, a distance ℓ from A, is seen by inspection to be simply 4ℓ. The appropriate expression

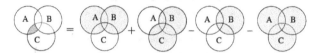

Figure Diagram for calculating terminal requirements

for G_B and G_C are therefore

$$G_B = \sum_{\ell=1}^{\ell-1} 4\ell = 2\ell(\ell-1) \qquad G_C = 4\ell$$

so that Equation $n_{A \to C} = \alpha T_{A \to C}$ may be rewritten (with the subscript $A \to C$ replaced by ℓ) as

$$n(\ell) = \alpha t\{ \left[1 + 2\ell(\ell-1)\right]^p + \left[2\ell(\ell-1) + 4\ell\right]^p - \left[2\ell(\ell-1)\right]^p - \left[1 + 2\ell(\ell-1) + 4\ell\right]^p \}$$

It is straightforward to show by numerical summation that the expression within parentheses sums to unity

$$\sum_{\ell=1}^{\infty} \{ \left[1 + 2\ell(\ell-1)\right]^p + \left[2\ell(\ell-1) + 4\ell\right]^p - \left[2\ell(\ell-1)\right]^p - \left[1 + 2\ell(\ell-1) + 4\ell\right]^p \} = 1$$

and therefore

$$\left[1 + 2\ell(\ell-1)\right]^p + \left[2\ell(\ell-1) + 4\ell\right]^p - \left[2\ell(\ell-1)\right]^p - \left[1 + 2\ell(\ell-1) + 4\ell\right]^p$$

may be interpreted as a probability. However, this represents the probability that gate A has a net of length ℓ. In order to recast this as the site occupancy probability $q(\ell)$, Equation $\left[1 + 2\ell(\ell-1)\right]^p + \left[2\ell(\ell-1) + 4\ell\right]^p - \left[2\ell(\ell-1)\right]^p - \left[1 + 2\ell(\ell-1) + 4\ell\right]^p$ must be divided by the number of placement sites of length ℓ uniquely associated with gate A. The number of gates at a distance ℓ from A has previously been identified as simply 4ℓ. The number of two-terminal placements sites of length ℓ will be half this number, since each site is shared by two gates. The expression for the occupancy probability for gate A is therefore

$$q(\ell) = \frac{1}{2\ell}\{ \left[1 + 2\ell(\ell-1)\right]^p + \left[2\ell(\ell-1) + 4\ell\right]^p - \left[2\ell(\ell-1)\right]^p - \left[1 + 2\ell(\ell-1) + 4\ell\right]^p \}$$

This function is plotted as a solid line in figure below. for $p = 0.6$.

Davis have proposed that a more tractable form for equation may be obtained by expanding the terms in square parentheses as a truncated binomial series. After some simplification, the net length probability is given by

$$q'(\ell) \approx p(1-p)2^{-(1-p)}(\ell)^{-(4-2p)}$$

and this function is plotted in figure. as a dashed line for $p = 0.6$. We see that for all but nearest-neighbor nets $(\ell = 1)$, the occupancy probability is well approximated by a simple powerlaw function of the form $(\ell)^{-(4-2p)}$, a result first reported in (though not expressed in this notation) and re-derived in,

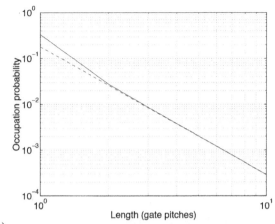

Figure: Probability $q(\ell)$ that a net has a length ℓ as a function of net length for $p = 0.6$. (solid line). Approximation to probability function obtained using a truncated binomial series (dashed line)

using different techniques. Since $q(\ell)$ is interpreted as a probability, it is important to ensure appropriate normalization. The approximation used in deriving equation $q'(\ell) \approx p(1-p)2^{-(1-p)}(\ell)^{-(4-2p)}$ results in a probability distribution which is incorrectly normalized,

$$\sum_{\ell=1}^{\infty} 2\ell q'(\ell) \neq 1$$

an observation reinforced by the difference in the areas under the two curves in Figure.

Number of Net Placement Sites

The preceding analysis employed Rent's rule to derive an expression for the probability that a placement site available to a single gate is occupied by a net. It was necessary to restrict the analysis to an infinite gate array because the edges associated with a finite system represent a source of inhomogeneity which would invalidate the power-law form of Rent's rule used in the analysis.

For many modeling tasks, however, it is precisely the effect of the finite size of the circuit that we are interested in. For example, an accurate estimate of the size and number of the longest nets in the circuit is critical for determining critical path delays, and this is, in part, determined by the area required by the gates in the circuit. The number of placement sites $D(\ell)$ is used to incorporate this information into the statistical wiring model. However, the determination of $D(\ell)$ is a matter of geometry and is not directly related to Rent's rule. To the knowledge of the authors, all the equations represent exact results and are not approximations. The interested reader may determine this by comparing the predictions of the formula with numbers obtained by direct enumeration for a small number of gates.

$D_\alpha(\ell)$ represents the number of available 2-terminal net sites within an infinite two-dimensional array. Although the gate array is assumed to be unbounded, the finite size of the circuit is imposed by limiting the maximum net length to twice the length L of the side of a finite gate array, i.e., for a square array of G gates, $\ell_{max} = 2L = 2\sqrt{G}$. This site density function for the finite two-dimensional plane is highly unsatisfactory, however, because it greatly overestimates the number of long nets.

This is because it assumes that all gates are at the center of the circuit and does not acknowledge the edges that restrict the availability of long 2-terminal net sites.

The correct function for the number of 2-terminal net placement sites within the boundary of a finite, two-dimensional array of gates is given by $D_b(\ell)$. Note that the sum of $D_b(\ell)$ overall ℓ is found to be $G(G-1)/2$ which represents the maximum number of 2-terminal nets that may be placed within a square array of G gates.

The placement of gates within a finite plane is not the only geometrical arrangement of interest. In many cases, the circuit layout reflects a hierarchical bottom-up design style in which larger circuits are formed by the recursive clustering of cells. Alternatively, many placement algorithms are implemented as top-down, min-cut partitioning procedures in which the circuit is recursively bi-partitioned along its x- and y- axes. We are therefore often interested in determining the number of valid placement sites that originate in one quadrant of a group of gates and terminate in another quadrant. This is given by $D_c(\ell)$. We note that the sum of $D_c(\ell)$ overall is $6(G/4)^2$, which represents the maximum number of 2-terminal nets that may be placed within the quadratically partitioned array (the factor of six accounts for the four pairs of adjacent cells and two pairs of diagonal cells). Similar site functions can be obtained for three dimensional placements.

Robustness Principle

Postel's Iaw was formulated by Jon Postel, an early pioneer of the Internet. The law was really a guideline for creators of software protocols. Such protocols were used by computers to communicate with one another on the Internet. The basic idea was that different implementations of the protocol should interoperate.

Although first stated with reference to TCP/IP, the Law has been applied in other areas, from the parsing of HTML to the acceptance of user inputs. The growth and success of the Internet has been attributed in part to this Law.

Postel's law is also known as the Robustness Principle.

Although the Robustness Principle was specifically described for implementations of TCP, it was quickly accepted as a good proposition for implementing network protocols in general. Some have applied it to the design of APIs and even programming language design. It's simple, easy to understand, and intuitively obvious. But is it correct?

For many years the Robustness Principle was accepted dogma, failing more when it was ignored rather than when it was practiced. In recent years, however, that principle has been challenged. This isn't because implementers have gotten more stupid, but rather because the world has become more hostile. Two general problem areas are impacted by the Robustness Principle: orderly interoperability and security.

Standards and Interoperability

Interoperability in network protocol implementations is a Hard Problem. There are many reasons for this, all coming down to the fundamental truth that computers are unforgiving. For example, the specification may be ambiguous: two engineers build implementations that meet the spec, but those implementations still won't talk to each other. The spec may in fact be unambiguous but worded in a way that some people misinterpret it. Arguably some of the most important specs fall into this class because they are written in a form of legalese that is unnatural to most engineers. The specification may not have taken certain situations (for example, hardware failures) into account, which can result in cases where making an implementation work in the real world requires violating the spec.

In a similar vein, the specification may make implicit assumptions about the environment (for example, maximum size of network packets supported by the hardware or how a related protocol works), and those assumptions are incorrect or the environment changes. Finally, and very commonly, some implementers may find a need to enhance the protocol to add new functionality that isn't defined by the spec.

Writing standards (that is, any specification that defines interoperability between different implementations) is an art. Standards are essentially contracts, in the legal sense, but the law has the advantage (or perhaps disadvantage) of a long history of definition, redefinition, and refinement of definition, usually in case law. The goal of a standard is to make interoperability possible. That requires both precision (to avoid ambiguity) and clarity (to avoid misinterpretation). Failure in either way results in a lack of interoperability. Unfortunately, these two goals are sometimes at odds, as noted.

Our normal human language is often ambiguous; in real life we handle these ambiguities without difficulty (or use them as the basis for jokes), but in the technical world they can cause problems. Extremely precise language, however, is so unnatural to us that it can be hard to appreciate the subtleties. Standards often use formal grammar, mathematical equations, and finite-state machines in order to convey precise information concisely, which certainly helps, but these do not usually stand on their own—for example, grammar describes syntax but not semantics, equations have to be translated into code, and finite-state machines are notoriously difficult for humans to understand.

Standards often include diagrams and examples to aid understandability, but these can actually create problems. Consider the possibility that a diagram does not match the descriptive text. Which one is correct? For that matter, any time the same thing is described in two places there is a danger that the two descriptions may say subtly different things. For example, RFC 821 and RFC 822 both describe the syntax of an email address, but unfortunately they differ in minor ways (these standards have since been updated to fix this and other problems). A common solution is always to include necessary duplicate language "by reference" (that is, including a reference to another document rather than an actual description). Of course, taken to an extreme, this can result in a rat's nest of standards documents. For example, the OSI recommendations (standards) for message handling (email) are contained in about 20 different documents filled with cross-references:

> "For many years the Robustness Principle was accepted dogma, failing more when it was ignored rather than when practiced. In recent years, however, that principle has been challenged."

Even using examples can be controversial. Examples are never *normative* (standards buzzword for *authoritative*); that is, if there is a conflict between an example and the body of the text, the text wins. Also, examples are seldom complete. They may demonstrate some piece of the protocol but not all the details. In theory if you removed all the examples from a standard, then the meaning of that standard would not change at all—the sole *reason for* being to aid comprehension. The problem is that some implementers read the examples (which are often easier to understand than the actual text of the standard) and implement from those, thus missing important details of the standard. This has caused some authors of standards to eschew the use of examples altogether.

Some (usually vendor-driven) standards use the "reference implementation" approach—that is, a single implementation that is defined to be correct; all other implementations are in turn correct if and only if they work against the reference implementation. This method is fraught with peril. For one thing, no implementation is ever completely bug-free, so finding and fixing a bug in the reference implementation essentially changes the standard.

Similarly, standards usually have various "undefined" or "reserved" elements—for example, multiple options with overlapping semantics are specified at the same time. Other implementations will find how these undefined elements work and then rely on that unintended behavior. This creates problems when the reference implementation is extended to add functionality; these undefined and reserved elements are typically used to provide the new functions. Also, there may be two independent implementations that each work against the reference implementation but not against each other. All that said, the reference implementation approach could be useful in conjunction with a written specification, particularly as that specification is being refined.

The original InterOp conference was intended to allow vendors with Network File System (NFS) implementations to test interoperability and ultimately demonstrate publicly that they could interoperate. The first 11 days were limited to a small number of engineers so they could get together in one room and actually make their stuff work together. When they walked into the room, the vendors worked mostly against only their own systems and possibly Sun's (since as the original developer of NFS, Sun had the reference implementation at the time). Long nights were devoted to battles over ambiguities in the specification. At the end of those 11 days the doors were thrown open to customers, at which point most (but not all) of the systems worked against every other system. By the end of that session the NFS protocol was much better understood, many bugs had been fixed, and the standard was improved. This is an inevitable path for implementation-driven standards.

Another approach to standards is to get a bunch of smart people in a room to brainstorm what the standard should do, and only after the standard is written should the code be implemented. This most closely matches conventional software engineering, where a specification is written before the code. Taken to extreme, this is the waterfall model. The problem with producing standards this way is the same as occurs with the waterfall model: the specification (standard) sometimes mandates things that are only marginally useful but are difficult or impossible to implement, and the cost of going back and modifying the specification goes up exponentially with time.

Perhaps the best situation of all is where the standards and implementations are being developed in parallel. Ambiguities in the standard were exposed quickly, as were well-meaning features that were unnecessarily difficult to implement. Unfortunately, this is a rare case today, at least in part because the world has gotten sufficiently complex that such quick updates in standards are no longer easy.

Ambiguity and Extensibility in Standards

As an example of ambiguity, consider the following excerpt from a (mythical) standard.

If the A option is specified in the packet, field X contains the value of the parameter.

This assumes a protocol that has a fixed-size header. A is probably a bit in some flags field, and X is some field in the packet. On the surface this description seems pretty clear, but it does not specify what field X means if the A option is *not* specified. A better way to word this might be.

If the A option is specified in the packet, field X contains the value of the parameter; otherwise field X must be zero.

You might be thinking that this wording should be unnecessary—*of course X* should be zero, so why bother being that explicit? But without this detail, it could also mean: "If the A option is not specified in the packet, field X is ignored"—or, perhaps, "field X is undefined." Both of these are substantially different from the "must be zero" interpretation. Furthermore, the difference between these two wordings is trivial but significant. In the former case "ignored" might mean "must be ignored" (that is, under no circumstances should field X be used if option A is not specified). But the latter case allows the possibility that field X might be reused for some other purpose.

Which (finally) brings us back to the Robustness Principle. Given the "must be zero" specification, to be most robust any implementation would be sure to zero the X field before sending a packet (be conservative in what it sends) but would not check the X field upon receipt (be liberal in what it accepts).

Now suppose our standard is revised (version 2) to add a B option (which cannot be used in conjunction with option A) that also uses the X field. The Robustness Principle has come to our rescue: since "robust" version 1 implementations should not check the value of field X unless option A has been specified, there will be no problem adding an option B. Of course, version 1 receivers won't be able to provide the option B functionality, but neither will they be upset when they receive a version 2 packet. This is a good thing: it allows us to expand protocols without breaking older implementations.

This also clarifies what to do when passing on a packet—implementations should *not* clear field X, even though that is the most "conservative" thing to do, because that would break the case of a version 1 implementation forwarding a packet between two version 2 implementations. In this case the Robustness Principle must include a corollary: implementations should silently ignore and pass on anything that they do not understand. In other words, there are two definitions of "conservative" that are in direct conflict.

Now let's suppose that our mythical standard has another field Y that is intended for future use—that is, in a protocol extension. There are many ways to describe such fields, but common examples are to label them "reserved" or "must be zero." The former does not say what value a compliant implementation should use to initialize reserved fields, whereas the latter does, but it is usually assumed that zero is a good initializer. Applying the Robustness Principle makes it easy to see that when version 3 of the protocol is released using field Y there will be no problem, since all older implementations will be sending zero in that field.

Security

The Robustness Principle was formulated in an Internet of cooperators. The world has changed a lot since then. Everything, even services that you may think you control, is suspect. It's not just user input that needs to be checked—attackers can potentially include arbitrary data in DNS (Domain Name System) results, database query results, HTTP reply codes, you name it. Everyone knows to check for buffer overflows, but checking incoming data goes far beyond that.

- You might be tempted to trust your own corporate database, but consider how the data was added in the first place. Do you trust every piece of software that might update that database to do strict checking? If not, you should do your own checking.

- Do you get your data over a TCP connection that goes through your firewall? Have you considered the possibility of connection hijacking? Security-critical data should be accepted only over encrypted, signed connections. Other data should be carefully checked.

- Do you trust connections that come in from computers inside your firewall? Have you ever heard of viruses? Even machines that you think are under your control may have been subverted.

- Do you trust command-line flags and environment variables? If someone has managed to get an account on your system, these might be used for privilege escalation.

The atmosphere of the Internet has changed so much that the Robustness Principle has to be severely reinterpreted. Being liberal in what you accept can contribute to security problems. Sometimes interoperability and security are at odds with each other. In today's climate they are both essential. Some balance must be drawn.

Kerckhoffs's Principle

Kerckhoff's principle is the concept that a cryptographic system should be designed to be secure, even if all its details, except for the key, are publicly known.

The principle, sometimes referred to as Kerckhoff's axiom or law, forms the basis of open security and security by design and contrasts directly with the deprecated security through obscurity model.

After a message has been subjected to a cryptographic algorithm, it is expected to remain secure even if an intruder has or gains full access to the encrypted message and has knowledge of what algorithm was used. The point is that, even if a system's design and details are not made open to begin with, they may be detected by an unauthorized party and, as such, should be inherently secure.

Auguste Kerckhoff, a Dutch linguist and cryptographer, published the principle in an 1883 article, La Cryptographie Militaire (Military Cryptography). The mathematician Claude Shannon further refined Kerckhoff's principle. According to Shannon's maxim, "one ought to design systems under the assumption that the enemy will immediately gain full familiarity with them".

That is, the security should depend *only* on the secrecy of the key, *not* on the secrecy of the methods employed. Keeping keys secret, and changing them from time to time, are reasonable propositions. Keeping your methods secret is more difficult, perhaps impossible in the long term against a determined enemy. Changing the methods once a system is deployed is also difficult, sometimes impossible. The solution is to design the system assuming the enemy will know how it works.

Any serious enemy — one with strong motives and plentiful resources — *will* learn all the internal details of any widely used system. In war, the enemy will capture some of your equipment and some of your people, and will use spies. If your method involves software, enemies can do memory dumps, run it under the control of a debugger, and so on. If it is hardware, they can buy or steal some of the devices and build whatever programs or gadgets they need to test them, or dismantle them and look at chip details with microscopes. They may bribe, blackmail or threaten your staff or your customers. The enemy may *be* a customer if your product is used by two rival organizations and one wants to spy on the other, or if it is available so a potential attacker can buy a copy for analysis. One way or another, sooner or later they *will* know exactly how it all works.

Using secure cryptography is supposed to replace the difficult problem of keeping messages secure with a much more manageable one, keeping relatively small keys secure. A system that requires long-term secrecy for something large and complex — the whole design of a cryptographic system — obviously cannot achieve that goal. It only replaces one hard problem with another. However, if you can design a system that is secure even when the enemy knows everything except the key, then all you need to manage is keeping the keys secret.

Implications for Analysis

For purposes of analyzing ciphers, Kerckhoffs' Principle neatly divides any design into two components. The key can be assumed to be secret for purposes of analysis; in practice various measures will be taken to protect it. Everything else is assumed to be knowable by the opponent, so everything except the key should be revealed to the analyst. Perhaps not all opponents will know everything, but the analyst should because the goal is to create a system that is secure against *any* enemy except one that learns the key.

> "That the security of a cipher system should depend on the key and not the algorithm has become a truism in the computer era, and this one is the best-remembered of Kerckhoff's dicta. ... Unlike a key, an algorithm can be studied and analyzed by experts to determine if it is likely to be secure. An algorithm that you have invented yourself and kept secret has not had the opportunity for such review."

Using this distinction is the only known method of building ciphers that it is reasonable to trust — everything except the key is published and analyzed, so we can be reasonably confident that it is secure, and keys are carefully managed so we can reasonably hope they are secret.

Cryptographers will generally dismiss out-of-hand all security claims for a system whose internal details are kept secret. Without analysis, no system should be trusted, and without details, it cannot be properly analyzed. Of course, there are some exceptions; if a major national intelligence agency claims that one of their secret systems is secure, the claim will be taken seriously because they have their own cipher-cracking experts. However, no-one else making such a claim is likely to be believed.

If you want your system trusted — *or even just taken seriously* — the first step is to publish all the internal details. Anyone who makes security claims for some system without providing complete details is showing that he is unaware of one of the basic principles of cryptography, so most experts will assume the system is worthless. Sensational claims about a system whose details are secret are one of the common indicators of cryptographic snake oil.

In many cases, auditing is an issue — for example, a financial institution's auditors should want to know if the security systems in place are adequate. In other situations, approval may be required — for example, a military organisation generally will not use any cryptosystem until their signals intelligence people have given it the nod. Such auditing or analysis absolutely requires full details of the system; they need not be made public but they *must* be revealed to the auditor or analyst.

Security through Obscurity

It is moderately common for companies — and sometimes even standards bodies as in the case of the CSS encryption on DVDs — to keep the inner workings of a system secret. Some even claim this security by obscurity makes the product safer. Such claims are utterly bogus; of course keeping the innards secret may improve security in the short term, but in the long run only systems which have been published and analyzed should be trusted.

Steve Bellovin commented:

"The subject of security through obscurity comes up frequently. I think a lot of the debate happens because people misunderstand the issue.

"It helps, I think, to go back to Kerckhoffs' second principle, translated as "The system must not require secrecy and can be stolen by the enemy without causing trouble", per http://petitcolas.net/fabien/kerckhoffs/). Kerckhoffs said neither "publish everything" nor "keep everything secret"; rather, he said that the system should still be secure *even if the enemy has a copy*.

"In other words -- design your system assuming that your opponents know it in detail. (A former official at NSA's National Computer Security Center told me that the standard assumption there was that serial number 1 of any new device was delivered to the Kremlin.) After that, though, there's nothing wrong with trying to keep it secret -- it's another hurdle factor the enemy has to overcome. (One obstacle the British ran into when attacking the German Engima system was simple: they didn't know the unkeyed mapping between keyboard keys and the input to the rotor array.) But -- *don't rely on secrecy*.

"That is, it is an error to rely on the secrecy of a system. In the long run, security through obscurity cannot possibly be an effective technique."

Modern-day Twist

A modern-day twist to Kerckhoffs's tenets is the idea that the security of a cryptosystem should depend solely on the secrecy of the key and the private randomizer. Another way of putting it is that a method of secretly coding and transmitting information should be secure even if everyone knows how it works. Of course, despite the attacker's familiarity with the system in question, the attacker lacks knowledge as to which of all possible instances is being presently observed.

This twist does not appeal to some cryptographers, who opine that Kerckhoffs had no fetish for the secrecy of keys and was not opposed to keeping other components (i.e. tables, hashes, algorithms, protocols, etc.) of encryption systems "secret" so long as the system remains "indecipherable".

Advantage of Secret Keys

Using secure cryptography is supposed to replace the difficult problem of keeping messages secure with a much more manageable one, keeping relatively small keys secure. A system that requires long-term secrecy for something as large and complex as the whole design of a cryptographic system obviously cannot achieve that goal. It only replaces one hard problem with another. However, if a system is secure even when the enemy knows everything except the key, then all that is needed is to manage keeping the keys secret.

There are a large number of ways the internal details of a widely used system could be discovered. The most obvious is that someone could bribe, blackmail, or otherwise threaten staff or customers into explaining the system. In war, for example, one side will probably capture some equipment and people from the other side. Each side will also use spies to gather information.

If a method involves software, someone could do memory dumps or run the software under the control of a debugger in order to understand the method. If hardware is being used, someone could buy or steal some of the hardware and build whatever programs or gadgets needed to test it. Hardware can also be dismantled so that the chip details can be examined under the microscope.

Maintaining Security

A generalization some make from Kerckhoffs's principle is: "The fewer and simpler the secrets that one must keep to ensure system security, the easier it is to maintain system security." Bruce Schneier ties it in with a belief that all security systems must be designed to fail as gracefully as possible:

> "Kerckhoffs's principle applies beyond codes and ciphers to security systems in general: every secret creates a potential failure point. Secrecy, in other words, is a prime cause of brittleness—and therefore something likely to make a system prone to catastrophic collapse. Conversely, openness provides ductility."

Any security system depends crucially on keeping some things secret. However, Kerckhoffs's principle points out that the things kept secret ought to be those least costly to change if inadvertently disclosed.

For example, a cryptographic algorithm may be implemented by hardware and software that is widely distributed among users. If security depends on keeping that secret, then disclosure leads to major logistic difficulties in developing, testing, and distributing implementations of a new algorithm – it is "brittle". On the other hand, if keeping the algorithm secret is not important, but only the *keys* used with the algorithm must be secret, then disclosure of the keys simply requires the simpler, less costly process of generating and distributing new keys.

Wirth's Law

Wirth's law is a famous quote from Niklaus Wirth, a Swiss computer scientist. In 1995, he proposed an adage that: "Software is getting slower more rapidly than hardware is getting faster".

The law implies that while hardware progress has been rapid over the years, the same cannot be said of software. It also states that software complexity increases at a higher rate than hardware complexity. Slow software growth can be attributed to software creeping featuritis. Also, extra features added in the software may exceed its main function and code cruft, and the amount of irrelevant code is high in the developed code.

The problem is not entirely caused by bloated software applications. An advanced operating system run on less powerful hardware will run slowly. For example, running Windows 7 on a computer meant for running Windows XP will slow the system. Similarly, the user invoking a large number of applications simultaneously will experience slow software performance. Similarly, the presence of adware, spyware, malware, viruses and Trojans can slow a system down. Therefore, the statement that software speed is slowed down due to bloated software size is not entirely accurate.

Wirth's law contradicts Moore's law by stating that the numbers of transistors present on an integrated chip doubles every year. The main statement made within Wirth's law is: "Software expands to fill memory and software is getting slower more rapidly than hardware is getting faster".

Even though hardware has evolved over the previous decades, software has not necessarily become faster. Some software still runs much slower than previous versions or similar earlier software. For example, a word processor in 1970s took only 10kb of memory, while the same application takes over 100MB today. The advantage is that the processing speed has increased considerably compared to the previous applications. This obeys Moore's law. The increasing complexity of software over the years has been termed as software bloat. Since more and more processing power gets added to the hardware devices, software developers increase the complexity of the software, consistent with the first statement made by Wirth.

A lot of unwanted features are added to basic software supporting core essential features to gain publicity during marketing campaigns, and creeping featuritis arises. In the name of user-friendly software, complexity and code cruft is added by the developer. In short, Wirth's law concludes that the fewer calculations made by the processor for performing a task, the more efficient the design and the more Moore's Law can be obeyed.

Conway's Law

Conway's law was coined by the American computer scientist Melvin Edward Conway and indicates the following:

> "Any organization that designs a system (defined broadly) will produce a design whose structure is a copy of the organization's communication structure."

It is important to know that this law is meant to apply not only to software but to any kind of design. The communication structures that Conway mentions, do not have to be identical to the organization chart. Often there are informal communication structures, which also have to be considered in this context. In addition, the geographical distribution of teams can influence communication. After all it is much simpler to talk to a colleague who works in the same room or at least in the same office than with one working in a different city or even in a different time zone.

Reasons for the Law

Conway's law derives from the fact that each organizational unit designs a specific part of the architecture. If two architectural parts have an interface, coordination in regards to this interface is required—and, consequently, a communication relationship between the organizational units that are responsible for the respective parts of the architecture.

From Conway's law it can also be deduced that design modularization is sensible. Via such a design, it is possible to ensure that not every team member has to constantly coordinate with every other team member. Instead the developers working on the same module can closely coordinate their efforts, while team members working on different modules only have to coordinate when they develop an interface—and even then only in regards to the specific design of the external features of this interface.

However, the communication relationships extend beyond that. It is much easier to collaborate with a team within the same building than with a team located in another city, another country, or even within a different time zone. Therefore, architectural parts having numerous communication relationships are better implemented by teams that are geographically close to each other, because it is easier for them to communicate with each other. In the end, the Conway's law focuses not on the organization chart but on the real communication relationships.

By the way, Conway postulated that a large organization has numerous communication relationships. Thus communication becomes more difficult or even impossible in the end. As a consequence, the architecture can be increasingly affected and finally break down. In the end, having too many communication relationships is a real risk for a project.

The Law as Limitation

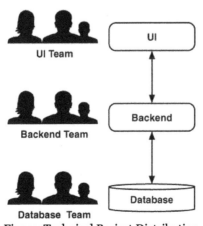

Figure: Technical Project Distribution

Normally Conway's law is viewed as a limitation, especially from the perspective of software development. Let us assume that a project is modularized according to technical aspects. All developers with a UI focus are grouped into one team, the developers with backend focus are put into a second team, and data bank experts make up the third team. This distribution has the advantage that all three teams consist of experts for the respective technology. This makes it easy and transparent to create this type of organization. Moreover, this distribution also appears logical. Team members can easily support each other, and technical exchange is also facilitated.

According to Conway's law, it follows from such a distribution that the three teams will implement three technical layers: a UI, a backend, and a database. The chosen distribution corresponds to the organization, which is in fact sensibly built. However, this distribution has a decisive disadvantage: a typical feature requires changes to UI, backend, and database. The UI has to render the new features for the clients, the backend has to implement the logic, and the database has to create structures for the storage of the respective data. This results in the following disadvantages:

- The person wishing to have a feature implemented has to talk to all three teams.

- The teams have to coordinate their work and create new interfaces.

- The work of the different teams has to be coordinated in a manner that ensures that their efforts temporally fit together. The backend, for instance, cannot really work without getting input from the database, and the UI cannot work without input from the backend.

- When the teams work in sprints, these dependencies cause time delays: The database team generates in its first sprint the necessary changes, within the second sprint the backend team implements the logic, and in the third sprint the UI is dealt with. Therefore, it takes three sprints to implement a single feature.

In the end this approach creates a large number of dependencies as well as a high communication and coordination overhead. Thus this type of organization does not make much sense if the main goal is to implement new features as rapidly as possible.

Many teams following this approach do not realize its impact on architecture and do not consider this aspect further. This type of organization focuses instead on the notion that developers with similar skills should be grouped together within the organization. This organization becomes an obstacle to a design driven by the domain like micro services, whose development is not compatible with the division of teams into technical layers.

The Law as Enabler

However, Conway's law can also be used to support approaches like micro services. If the goal is to develop individual components as independently of each other as possible, the system can be distributed into domain components. Based on these domain components, teams can be created. Figure 3.3 illustrates this principle: There are individual teams for product search, clients, and the order process. These teams work on their respective components, which can be technically divided into UI, backend, and database. By the way, the domain components are not explicitly named in the figure, for they are identical to the team names. Components and teams are synonymous. This approach corresponds to the idea of so-called cross-functional teams, as proposed by methods such as Scrum. These teams should encompass different roles so that they can cover a large range of tasks. Only a team designed along such principles can be in charge of a component—from engineering requirements via implementation through to operation.

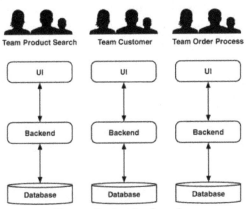

Figure: Project by domains

The division into technical artifacts and the interface between the artifacts can then be settled within the teams. In the easiest case, developers only have to talk to developers sitting next to them to do so. Between teams, coordination is more complex. However, inter-team coordination is not required very often, since features are ideally implemented by independent teams. Moreover, this approach creates thin interfaces between the components. This avoids laborious coordination across teams to define the interface.

Ultimately, the key message to be taken from Conway's law is that architecture and organization are just two sides of the same coin. When this insight is cleverly put to use, the system will have a clear and useful architecture for the project. Architecture and organization have the common goal to ensure that teams can work in an unobstructed manner and with as little coordination overhead as possible.

The clean separation of functionality into components also facilitates maintenance. Since an individual team is responsible for individual functionality and component, this distribution will have long-term stability, and consequently the system will remain maintainable.

The teams need requirements to work upon. This means that the teams need to contact people who define the requirements. This affects the organization beyond the projects, for the requirements come from the departments of the enterprise, and these also according to Conway's law have to correspond to the team structures within the project and the domain architecture. Conway's law can be expanded beyond software development to the communication structures of the entire organization, including the users. To put it the other way round: the team structure within the project and consequently the architecture of a micro service system can follow from the organization of the departments of the enterprise.

The Law and Micro Services

The relationship between architecture and organization of a project only in a general manner. It would be perfectly conceivable to align the architecture along functionalities and devise teams, each of which are in charge for a separate functionality without using micro services. In this case the project would develop a deployment monolith within which all functionalities are implemented.

However, micro services support this approach. In conjunction with the division by domains, the teams become even more independent of each other and have even less need to coordinate their work. The technical coordination as well as the coordination concerning the domains can be reduced to the absolute minimum. This makes it far easier to work in parallel on numerous features and also to bring the features in production.

Micro services as a technical architecture are especially well suited to support the approach to devise a Conway's law–based distribution of functionalities. In fact, exactly this aspect is an essential characteristic of a micro services-based architecture.

Moore's Law

Moore's law is the observation made by Intel co-founder Gordon Moore that the number of transistors on a chip doubles every year while the costs are halved. In 1965, Gordon Moore noticed that the number of transistors per square inch on integrated circuits had doubled every year since their invention. Moore's law predicts that this trend will continue into the foreseeable future.

Although the recent pace has slowed for Moore's law, the doubling of installed transistors on silicon chips occurs closer to every 18 months instead of annually. The 18-month mark is the current definition of Moore's law.

Moore's law suggests exponential growth. Thus, it is unlikely to continue indefinitely. Most experts expect Moore's law to hold for another two decades. Many experts believe Moore's law hit its physical and economical limitations in 2017 and has slowed.

The extension of Moore's law is that computers, machines that run on computers and computing power all become smaller and faster with time, as transistors on integrated circuits become more efficient. Transistors are simple electronic on/off switches embedded in microchips, processors and tiny electrical circuits. The faster microchips process electrical signals, the more efficient a computer becomes.

Costs of these higher-powered computers eventually came down too, usually about 30 percent per year. When designers increased the performance of computers with better-integrated circuits, manufacturers could create better machines that could automate certain processes. This automation created lower-priced products for consumers, as the hardware created lower labour costs.

Contemporary Society

Fifty years after Moore's law, contemporary society sees dozens of benefits from his vision. Mobile devices, such as smartphones and tablet computers, would not work without tiny processors. Smaller and faster computers improve transportation, health care, education and energy production. Just about every facet of a high-tech society benefits from the concept of Moore's law put into practice.

Major Enabling Factors

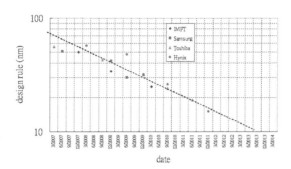

The trend of scaling for NAND flash memory allows doubling of components manufactured
in the same wafer area in less than 18 months

Numerous innovations by scientists and engineers have sustained Moore's law since the beginning of the integrated circuit (IC) era. Some of the key innovations are listed below, as examples of breakthroughs that have advanced integrated circuit technology by more than seven orders of magnitude in less than five decades:

- The foremost contribution, which is the *reason* for Moore's law, is the invention of the integrated circuit, credited contemporaneously to Jack Kilby at Texas Instruments and Robert Noyce at Fairchild Semiconductor.

- The invention of the complementary metal-oxide-semiconductor (CMOS) process by Frank Wanlassin 1963, and a number of advances in CMOS technology by many workers in the semiconductor field since the work of Wanlass, have enabled the extremely dense and high-performance ICs that the industry makes today.

- The invention of dynamic random-access memory (DRAM) technology by Robert Dennard at IBM in 1967 made it possible to fabricate single-transistor memory cells, and the invention of flash memory by Fujio Masuoka at Toshiba in the 1980s led to low-cost, high-capacity memory in diverse electronic products.

- The invention of chemically-amplified photoresist by Hiroshi Ito, C. Grant Willson and J. M. J. Fréchet at IBM c. 1980 that was 5-10 times more sensitive to ultraviolet light. IBM introduced chemically amplified photoresist for DRAM production in the mid-1980s.

- The invention of deep UV excimer laser photolithography by Kanti Jain at IBM c.1980 has enabled the smallest features in ICs to shrink from 800 nanometers in 1990 to as low as 10 nanometers in 2016. Prior to this, excimer lasers had been mainly used as research devices since their development in the 1970s. From a broader scientific perspective, the invention of excimer laser lithography has been highlighted as one of the major milestones in the 50-year history of the laser.

- The interconnect innovations of the late 1990s, including chemical-mechanical polishing or chemical mechanical planarization (CMP), trench isolation, and copper interconnects—although not directly a factor in creating smaller transistors—have enabled improved wafer yield, additional layers of metal wires, closer spacing of devices, and lower electrical resistance.

Computer industry technology road maps predicted in 2001 that Moore's law would continue for several generations of semiconductor chips. Depending on the doubling time used in the calculations, this could mean up to a hundredfold increase in transistor count per chip within a decade. The semiconductor industry technology roadmap used a three-year doubling time for microprocessors, leading to a tenfold increase in a decade. Intel was reported in 2005 as stating that the downsizing of silicon chips with good economics could continue during the following decade, and in 2008 as predicting the trend through 2029.

Recent Trends

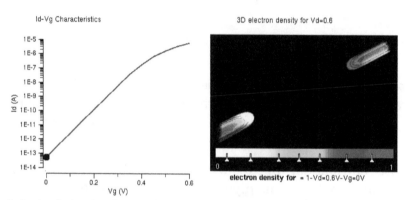

An atomistic simulation for electron density as gate voltage (Vg) varies in a nanowire MOSFET

The threshold voltage is around 0.45 V. Nanowire MOSFETs lie toward the end of the ITRS road map for scaling devices below 10 nm gate lengths. A FinFET has three sides of the channel covered by gate, while some nanowire transistors have gate-all-around structure, providing better gate control

One of the key challenges of engineering future nanoscale transistors is the design of gates. As device dimension shrinks, controlling the current flow in the thin channel becomes more difficult. Compared to FinFETs, which have gate dielectric on three sides of the channel, gate-all-around structure has ever better gate control.

- In 2010, researchers at the Tyndall National Institute in Cork, Ireland announced a junctionless transistor. A control gate wrapped around a silicon nanowire can control the passage of electrons without the use of junctions or doping. They claim these may be produced at 10-nanometer scale using existing fabrication techniques.

- In 2011, researchers at the University of Pittsburgh announced the development of a single-electron transistor, 1.5 nanometers in diameter, made out of oxide based materials. Three "wires" converge on a central "island" that can house one or two electrons. Electrons tunnel from one wire to another through the island. Conditions on the third wire result in distinct conductive properties including the ability of the transistor to act as a solid state memory. Nanowire transistors could spur the creation of microscopic computers.

- In 2012, a research team at the University of New South Wales announced the development of the first working transistor consisting of a single atom placed precisely in a silicon crystal (not just picked from a large sample of random transistors). Moore's law predicted this milestone to be reached for ICs in the lab by 2020.

- In 2015, IBM demonstrated 7 nm node chips with silicon-germanium transistors produced using EUVL. The company believes this transistor density would be four times that of current 14 nm chips.

- Revolutionary technology advances may help sustain Moore's law through improved performance with or without reduced feature size.

- In 2008, researchers at HP Labs announced a working memristor, a fourth basic passive circuit element whose existence only had been theorized previously. The memristor's unique properties permit the creation of smaller and better-performing electronic devices.

- In 2014, bioengineers at Stanford University developed a circuit modeled on the human brain. Sixteen "Neurocore" chips simulate one million neurons and billions of synaptic connections, claimed to be 9,000 times faster as well as more energy efficient than a typical PC.

- In 2015, Intel and Micron announced 3D XPoint, a non-volatile memory claimed to be significantly faster with similar density compared to NAND. Production scheduled to begin in 2016 was delayed until the second half of 2017.

While physical limits to transistor scaling such as source-to-drain leakage, limited gate metals, and limited options for channel material have been reached, new avenues for continued scaling are open. The most promising of these approaches rely on using the spin state of electron spintronics, tunnel junctions, and advanced confinement of channel materials via nano-wire geometry. A comprehensive list of available device choices shows that a wide range of device options is open for continuing Moore's law into the next few decades. Spin-based logic and memory options are being developed actively in industrial labs, as well as academic labs.

Alternative Materials Research

The vast majority of current transistors on ICs are composed principally of doped silicon and its alloys. As silicon is fabricated into single nanometer transistors, short-channel effectsadversely change desired material properties of silicon as a functional transistor. Below are several non-silicon substitutes in the fabrication of small nanometer transistors.

One proposed material is indium gallium arsenide, or InGaAs. Compared to their silicon and germanium counterparts, InGaAs transistors are more promising for future high-speed, low-power logic applications. Because of intrinsic characteristics of III-V compound semiconductors, quantum well and tunnel effect transistors based on InGaAs have been proposed as alternatives to more traditional MOSFET designs.

- In 2009, Intel announced the development of 80-nanometer InGaAs quantum well transistors. Quantum well devices contain a material sandwiched between two layers of material with a wider band gap. Despite being double the size of leading pure silicon transistors at the time, the company reported that they performed equally as well while consuming less power.

- In 2011, researchers at Intel demonstrated 3-D tri-gate InGaAs transistors with improved leakage characteristics compared to traditional planar designs. The company claims that their design achieved the best electrostatics of any III-V compound semiconductor transistor. At the 2015 International Solid-State Circuits Conference, Intel mentioned the use of III-V compounds based on such an architecture for their 7 nanometer node.

- In 2011, researchers at the University of Texas at Austin developed an InGaAs tunneling field-effect transistors capable of higher operating currents than previous designs. The first III-V TFET designs were demonstrated in 2009 by a joint team from Cornell University and Pennsylvania State University.

- In 2012, a team in MIT's Microsystems Technology Laboratories developed a 22 nm transistor based on InGaAs which, at the time, was the smallest non-silicon transistor ever built. The team used techniques currently used in silicon device fabrication and aims for better electrical performance and a reduction to 10-nanometer scale.

- Research is also showing how biological micro-cells are capable of impressive computational power while being energy efficient.

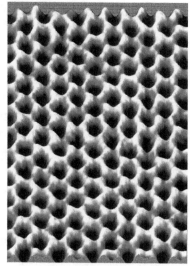

Scanning probe microscopy image of graphene in its hexagonal lattice structure

Alternatively, carbon-based compounds like graphene have also been proposed. First identified in the nineteenth century, an easy method of producing graphene was not available until 2004. Being a particular form of carbon, graphene typically exists in its stable form of graphite, a widely used material in many applications – the "lead" in a mechanical pencil being an example. When a single monolayer of carbon atoms is extracted from nonconductive bulk graphite, electrical properties are observed contributing to semiconductor behavior, making it a viable substitute for silicon. More research will need to be performed, however, on sub 50 nm graphene layers, as its resistivity value increases and thus electron mobility decreases.

Graphene nanoribbon transistors have shown great promise since its appearance in publications in 2008. Bulk graphene has a band gap of zero and thus cannot be used in transistors because of its constant conductivity, an inability to turn off. The zigzag edges of the nanoribbons introduce localized energy states in the conduction and valence bands and thus a bandgap that enables switching when fabricated as a transistor. As an example, a typical GNR of width of 10 nm has a desirable bandgap energy of 0.4eV.

Driving the Future via an Application Focus

Most semiconductor industry forecasters, including Gordon Moore, expect Moore's law will end by around 2025.

In April 2005, Gordon Moore stated in an interview that the projection cannot be sustained indefinitely: "It can't continue forever. The nature of exponentials is that you push them out and eventually disaster happens." He also noted that transistors eventually would reach the limits of miniaturization at atomic levels:

> "In terms of size [of transistors] you can see that we're approaching the size of atoms which is a fundamental barrier, but it'll be two or three generations before we get that far—but that's as far out as we've ever been able to see. We have another 10 to 20 years before we reach a fundamental limit. By then they'll be able to make bigger chips and have transistor budgets in the billions."

In 2016 the International Technology Roadmap for Semiconductors, after using Moore's law to drive the industry since 1998, produced its final roadmap. It no longer centered its research and development plan on Moore's law. Instead, it outlined what might be called the More than Moore strategy in which the needs of applications drive chip development, rather than a focus on semiconductor scaling. Application drivers range from smartphones to AI to data centers.

A new initiative for a more generalized roadmapping was started through IEEE's initiative Rebooting Computing, named the International Roadmap for Devices and Systems (IRDS).

Consequences

Technological change is a combination of more and of better technology. A 2011 study in the journal *Science* showed that the peak of the rate of change of the world's capacity to compute information was in 1998, when the world's technological capacity to compute information on general-purpose computers grew at 88% per year. Since then, technological change clearly has slowed. In recent times, every new year allowed humans to carry out roughly 60% more computation than possibly could have been executed by all existing general-purpose computers in the year before. This still is exponential, but shows the varying nature of technological change.

The primary driving force of economic growth is the growth of productivity, and Moore's law factors into productivity. Moore (1995) expected that "the rate of technological progress is going to be controlled from financial realities". The reverse could and did occur around the late-1990s, however, with economists reporting that "Productivity growth is the key economic indicator of innovation."

An acceleration in the rate of semiconductor progress contributed to a surge in U.S. productivity growth, which reached 3.4% per year in 1997–2004, outpacing the 1.6% per year during both 1972–1996 and 2005–2013. As economist Richard G. Anderson notes, "Numerous studies have traced the cause of the productivity acceleration to technological innovations in the production of semiconductors that sharply reduced the prices of such components and of the products that contain them (as well as expanding the capabilities of such products)."

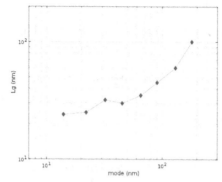

Intel transistor gate length trend– transistor scaling has slowed down significantly at advanced (smaller) nodes

An alternative source of improved performance is in microarchitecture techniques exploiting the growth of available transistor count. Out-of-order execution and on-chip caching and prefetching reduce the memory latency bottleneck at the expense of using more transistors and increasing the processor complexity. These increases are described empirically by Pollack's Rule, which states that performance increases due to microarchitecture techniques are square root of the number of transistors or the area of a processor.

For years, processor makers delivered increases in clock rates and instruction-level parallelism, so that single-threaded code executed faster on newer processors with no modification. Now, to manage CPU power dissipation, processor makers favor multi-core chip designs, and software has to be written in a multi-threaded manner to take full advantage of the hardware. Many multi-threaded development paradigms introduce overhead, and will not see a linear increase in speed vs number of processors. This is particularly true while accessing shared or dependent resources, due to lock contention. This effect becomes more noticeable as the number of processors increases. There are cases where a roughly 45% increase in processor transistors has translated to roughly 10–20% increase in processing power.

On the other hand, processor manufacturers are taking advantage of the 'extra space' that the transistor shrinkage provides to add specialized processing units to deal with features such as graphics, video, and cryptography. For one example, Intel's Parallel JavaScript extension not only adds support for multiple cores, but also for the other non-general processing features of their chips, as part of the migration in client side scripting toward HTML5.

A negative implication of Moore's law is obsolescence, that is, as technologies continue to rapidly "improve", these improvements may be significant enough to render predecessor technologies obsolete rapidly. In situations in which security and survivability of hardware or data are paramount, or in which resources are limited, rapid obsolescence may pose obstacles to smooth or continued operations.

Because of the toxic materials used in the production of modern computers, obsolescence, if not properly managed, may lead to harmful environmental impacts. On the other hand, obsolescence may sometimes be desirable to a company which can profit immensely from the regular purchase of what is often expensive new equipment instead of retaining one device for a longer period of time. Those in the industry are well aware of this, and may utilize planned obsolescence as a method of increasing profits.

Moore's law has affected the performance of other technologies significantly: Michael S. Malone wrote of a Moore's War following the apparent success of shock and awe in the early days of the Iraq War. Progress in the development of guided weapons depends on electronic technology. Improvements in circuit density and low-power operation associated with Moore's law also have contributed to the development of technologies including mobile telephones and 3-D printing.

Other Formulations and Similar Observations

Several measures of digital technology are improving at exponential rates related to Moore's law, including the size, cost, density, and speed of components. Moore wrote only about the density of components, "a component being a transistor, resistor, diode or capacitor", at minimum cost.

Transistors per integrated circuit: The most popular formulation is of the doubling of the number of transistors on integrated circuits every two years. At the end of the 1970s, Moore's law became known as the limit for the number of transistors on the most complex chips. The graph at the top shows this trend holds true today.

As of 2017, the commercially available processor possessing the highest number of transistors is the 48 core Centriq with over 18 billion transistors.

Density at minimum cost per transistor: This is the formulation given in Moore's 1965 paper. It is not just about the density of transistors that can be achieved, but about the density of transistors at which the cost per transistor is the lowest. As more transistors are put on a chip, the cost to make each transistor decreases, but the chance that the chip will not work due to a defect increases. In 1965, Moore examined the density of transistors at which cost is minimized, and observed that, as transistors were made smaller through advances in photolithography, this number would increase at "a rate of roughly a factor of two per year".

Dennard scaling: This suggests that power requirements are proportional to area (both voltage and current being proportional to length) for transistors. Combined with Moore's law, performance per watt would grow at roughly the same rate as transistor density, doubling every 1–2 years. According to Dennard scaling transistor dimensions are scaled by 30% (0.7x) every technology generation, thus reducing their area by 50%. This reduces the delay by 30% (0.7x) and therefore increases operating frequency by about 40% (1.4x). Finally, to keep electric field constant, voltage is reduced by 30%, reducing energy by 65% and power (at 1.4x frequency) by 50%. Therefore, in every technology generation transistor density doubles, circuit becomes 40% faster, while power consumption (with twice the number of transistors) stays the same.

The exponential processor transistor growth predicted by Moore does not always translate into exponentially greater practical CPU performance. Since around 2005–2007, Dennard scaling appears to have broken down, so even though Moore's law continued for several years after that, it has not yielded dividends in improved performance. The primary reason cited for the breakdown is that at small sizes, current leakage poses greater challenges, and also causes the chip to heat up, which creates a threat of thermal runaway and therefore, further increases energy costs.

The breakdown of Dennard scaling prompted a switch among some chip manufacturers to a greater focus on multicore processors, but the gains offered by switching to more cores are lower than the gains that would be achieved had Dennard scaling continued. In another departure from Dennard scaling, Intel microprocessors adopted a non-planar tri-gate FinFET at 22 nm in 2012 that is faster and consumes less power than a conventional planar transistor.

Quality adjusted price of IT equipment: The price of information technology (IT), computers and peripheral equipment, adjusted for quality and inflation, declined 16% per year on average over the five decades from 1959 to 2009. The pace accelerated, however, to 23% per year in 1995–1999 triggered by faster IT innovation, and later, slowed to 2% per year in 2010–2013.

The rate of quality-adjusted microprocessor price improvement likewise varies, and is not linear on a log scale. Microprocessor price improvement accelerated during the late 1990s, reaching 60% per year (halving every nine months) versus the typical 30% improvement rate (halving every two years) during the years earlier and later. Laptop microprocessors in particular improved 25–35% per year in 2004–2010, and slowed to 15–25% per year in 2010–2013.

The number of transistors per chip cannot explain quality-adjusted microprocessor prices fully. Moore's 1995 paper does not limit Moore's law to strict linearity or to transistor count, "The definition of ‹Moore's Law' has come to refer to almost anything related to the semiconductor industry that when plotted on semi-log paper approximates a straight line. I hesitate to review its origins and by doing so restrict its definition".

Hard disk drive areal density: A similar observation (sometimes called Kryder's law) was made in 2005 for hard disk drive areal density. Several decades of rapid progress in areal density advancement slowed significantly around 2010, because of noise related to smaller grain size of the disk media, thermal stability, and writ ability using available magnetic fields.

Fiber-optic capacity: The number of bits per second that can be sent down an optical fiber increases exponentially, faster than Moore's law. Keck's law, in honor of Donald Keck.

Network capacity: According to Gerry/Gerald Butters, the former head of Lucent's Optical Networking Group at Bell Labs, there is another version, called Butters' Law of Photonics, a formulation that deliberately parallels Moore's law. Butters' law says that the amount of data coming out of an optical fiber is doubling every nine months. Thus, the cost of transmitting a bit over an optical network decreases by half every nine months. The availability of wavelength-division multiplexing (sometimes called WDM) increased the capacity that could be placed on a single fiber by as much as a factor of 100. Optical networking and dense wavelength-division multiplexing (DWDM) is rapidly bringing down the cost of networking, and further progress seems assured. As a result, the wholesale price of data traffic collapsed in the dot-com bubble. Nielsen's Law says that the bandwidth available to users increases by 50% annually.

Pixels per dollar: Similarly, Barry Hendy of Kodak Australia has plotted pixels per dollar as a basic measure of value for a digital camera, demonstrating the historical linearity (on a log scale) of this market and the opportunity to predict the future trend of digital camera price, LCD and LED screens, and resolution.

The great Moore's law compensator (TGMLC), also known as Wirth's law – generally is referred to as software bloat and is the principle that successive generations of computer software increase in size and complexity, thereby offsetting the performance gains predicted by Moore's law. In a 2008 article in InfoWorld, Randall C. Kennedy, formerly of Intel, introduces this term using successive versions of Microsoft Office between the year 2000 and 2007 as his premise. Despite the gains in computational performance during this time period according to Moore's law, Office 2007 performed the same task at half the speed on a prototypical year 2007 computer as compared to Office 2000 on a year 2000 computer.

Library expansion: was calculated in 1945 by Fremont Rider to double in capacity every 16 years, if sufficient space were made available. He advocated replacing bulky, decaying printed works with miniaturized microform analog photographs, which could be duplicated on-demand for library patrons or other institutions. He did not foresee the digital technology that would follow decades later to replace analog microform with digital imaging, storage, and transmission media. Automated, potentially lossless digital technologies allowed vast increases in the rapidity of information growth in an era that now sometimes is called the Information Age.

Carlson Curve: is a term coined by *The Economist* to describe the biotechnological equivalent of Moore's law, and is named after author Rob Carlson. Carlson accurately predicted that the doubling time of DNA sequencing technologies (measured by cost and performance) would be at least as fast as Moore's law. Carlson Curves illustrate the rapid (in some cases hyper exponential) decreases in cost, and increases in performance, of a variety of technologies, including DNA sequencing, DNA synthesis, and a range of physical and computational tools used in protein expression and in determining protein structures.

Eroom's Law: is a pharmaceutical drug development observation which was deliberately written as Moore's Law spelled backwards in order to contrast it with the exponential advancements of other forms of technology (such as transistors) over time. It states that the cost of developing a new drug roughly doubles every nine years.

Experience curve effects says that each doubling of the cumulative production of virtually any product or service is accompanied by an approximate constant percentage reduction in the unit cost. The acknowledged first documented qualitative description of this dates from 1885. A power curve was used to describe this phenomenon in a 1936 discussion of the cost of airplanes.

Grosch's Law

Grosch's law states that a computer's hardware should exhibit an "economy of scale" which means the difference in performance between two computers is generally the difference in their price, squared. It comes from a quote by computer scientist Herbert Grosch in 1965, in which he said:

> "There is a fundamental rule, which I modestly call Grosch's law, giving added economy only as the square root of the increase in speed — that is, to do a calculation 10 times as cheaply you must do it 100 times as fast".

Seymour Cray made a similar observation:

> "Computers should obey a square law — when the price doubles, you should get at least four times as much speed".

The best known of many attempts to provide a measure of computer performance in terms of price, originally formulated by H. R. J. Grosch as: performance = constant $\times$ price^2.

Reliance on this law, which was approximately true at the time, led to the concept of "economy of scale", i.e. that large computers were less expensive per operation than small computers. Since that time other values of the exponent have been suggested: a good case can be made for the value 1 rather than 2. Current (LSI) technology has almost completely invalidated Grosch's law.

References

- McCool, Michael D.; Robison, Arch D.; Reinders, James (2012). "2.5 Performance Theory". Structured Parallel Programming: Patterns for Efficient Computation. Elsevier. pp. 61–62. ISBN 978-0-12-415993-8

- Computer-organization-amdahls-law-and-its-proof: geeksforgeeks.org, Retrieved 25 June 2018

- Snyder, Lawrence (June 1986). "Type Architectures, Shared Memory, and The Corollary of Modest Potential" (PDF). Annu. Rev. Comput. Sci. 1: 289–317. doi:10.1146/annurev.cs.01.060186.001445

- Keyes, Robert W. (September 2006). "The Impact of Moore's Law". Solid State Circuits Newsletter. Retrieved November 28, 2008

- What-is-the-sun-ni-law: wisegeek.com, Retrieved 16 June 2018

- Ito, Hiroshi (2000). "Chemical amplification resists: History and development within IBM" (PDF). IBM Journal of Research and Development. Retrieved 2014-05-20

- Disco, Cornelius; van der Meulen, Barend (1998). Getting new technologies together. New York: Walter de Gruyter. pp. 206–207. ISBN 3-11-015630-X. OCLC 39391108. Retrieved August 23, 2008

- Kerckhoffs-principle: whatis.techtarget.com, Retrieved 25 April 2018

- Hill, Mark D.; Marty, Michael R. (July 2008). "Amdahl's Law in the Multicore Era". IEEE Computer. 41 (7): 33–38. doi:10.1109/MC.2008.209. UW CS-TR-2007-1593

- Liddle, David E. (September 2006). "The Wider Impact of Moore's Law". Solid State Circuits Newsletter. Retrieved November 28, 2008

- Groschs-law, dictionaries-thesauruses-pictures-and-press-releases, computing: encyclopedia.com, Retrieved 14 July 2018

- Jorgenson, Dale W.; Ho, Mun S.; Stiroh, Kevin J. (2008). "A Retrospective Look at the U.S. Productivity Growth Resurgence". Journal of Economic Perspectives. Retrieved 2014-05-15

Permissions

Index

9 781682 857281